Therapy
Across Culture

Perspectives on Psychotherapy

editor: Colin Feltham
Sheffield Hallam University

Each book in this challenging and incisive series takes a particular perspective on psychotherapy to place it in its intellectual and cultural context. Disciplines which will be brought to bear in this series will include sociology, anthropology, philosophy, psychology, science and feminism.

Therapy
Across Culture

INGA-BRITT KRAUSE

SAGE Publications
London • Thousand Oaks • New Delhi

First published 1998

SAGE Publications Ltd
6 Bonhill Street
London EC2A 4PU

SAGE Publications Inc
2455 Teller Road
Thousand Oaks, California 91320

SAGE Publications India Pvt Ltd
32, M-Block Market
Greater Kailash – I
New Delhi 110 048

British Library Cataloguing in Publication data

A catalogue record for this book is available
from the British Library.

ISBN 0 8039 7526 0
ISBN 0 8039 7527 9 (pbk)

Library of Congress catalog card number 97-062540

Typeset by Mayhew Typesetting, Rhayader, Powys
Printed in Great Britain by Redwood Books, Trowbridge, Wiltshire

For Geoffrey, Jakob, Luise and Siri

Contents

Acknowledgements

Writing a book is both a social and an individual project. The influences are wide and derive from social trends as well as from biographical and private events and processes. I came to systemic psychotherapy at a time when medical anthropology was in the making and at a time when it was not quite respectable for the academic anthropologist to find an interest in 'applied' matters. It was, however, this tension between objective conditions and subjective experience, which then was beginning to be written about and which has been a preoccupation in both anthropology and therapy since, which precipitated a personal and professional crisis and which led me to stray from the more familiar path in and through anthropology.

I had concluded an interdisciplinary research project based in the Department of Psychiatry at one of London's teaching hospitals. The project examined ideas of mental illness expressed by Punjabi patients and I remember my growing unease when in the context of multicultural London and health service politics I frequently would be asked to address audiences of psychiatrists on this subject. Why should it be me rather than a Punjabi patient or a Punjabi professional with personal experience of the subject? It was not so much that I doubted the quality of my own work, but rather that it seemed impossible to ignore the importance of the political context. The research could not be non-political, it could not in that context take priority over other more subjective and more involved voices and yet I knew that the data and the knowledge I had accumulated was not useless. Becoming a systemic psychotherapist, or a family therapist as it was called before the advent of the United Kingdom Council for Psychotherapy, was thus my personal answer to a search for a professional area of work in which social context and subjectivity come together and where both must be addressed.

I cannot pretend that this professional move was straightforward. It was, however, fortunate for me that I was part of a trend. As the bibliography to this book testifies, many anthropologists are now thinking along the same lines and I have been greatly helped in both my theoretical and clinical work by these authors. I have also received wonderful professional and personal support from many people. In particular I thank Roland Littlewood for many years of encouragement and stimulating conversation and for reading this manuscript as well as many others. I also thank Arturo Varchevker, my first clinical tutor, for sharing with me his knowledge and his skill. He will recognise some of the material presented here. And I thank Alan Cooklin for his imagination and his courage in bringing anthropology to a clinical setting.

Many others have made a contribution to this book by advice, by encouragement, by argument, by example, through dialogue and by their concern for me. In particular Geoff Brown, David Campbell, Elsa Jones and Archie Smith all read different chapers at various stages of completion and offered their comments, and Rabia Malik helped with compiling the bibliography. Archie Smith also allowed me to refer to his own clinical work. I thank them all and I am also grateful to Jeff Faris for his permission to use an extract from a personal account. I owe a debt to my colleagues at the Marlborough Family Service for putting up with my preoccupation and for some of the time my absence. I hope that they will find in the book some compensation for this sacrifice. However, most importantly, I am deeply grateful to my clients and particularly to those who gave their consent to having details about themselves and our work together recorded. I have changed personal details wherever possible, but I am mindful that in writing about their lives I may expose them to consequences which neither I nor they can foresee.

Finally I must acknowledge the patience of my husband and my three children who in the midst of family life have not only tolerated, but also encouraged what sometimes seemed a very difficult undertaking.

London, July 1997

1

Introduction

In the mid-1990s the interest in culture is ubiquitous. We find it talked about everywhere. People say 'we do this in my culture' or 'in my culture we do not do that'. Everywhere we turn, culture is the basis of some sort of classification, of whether people receive or are denied resources, of whether specific policies operate or not. Health and public services record the cultural background of those who use them and culture, or its near equivalent, ethnicity, appears as a category to be ticked on population census forms. In schools and on training programmes we worry about being culturally sensitive and about cultural representation; we worry about taking due account of culture. In Britain and several other European countries as well as in America, this is not simply the result of a multicultural society, for these societies have been multicultural for a very long time. It is a colonial legacy.

The issue is complex. Why, for example, is it difficult for white British, or white Germans or Danes for that matter, to give an account of their own culture? Bring a group of health service professionals together and you will find that the white members from the dominant cultural sections of society either have difficulty acknowledging their cultural origins or that the very topic of origin and belonging raises notions of nationalism, inequality and discrimination. Yet there is a fascination throughout these societies with culture and cultural difference. How can this be? And what is this 'culture' and this difference which fascinates?

For some years I have worked as a systemic or family therapist in a busy London National Health Service setting where amongst other treatments families and individuals are offered systemic psychotherapy. Although clients can refer themselves, they tend to be referred by various agencies and professionals such as schools, social services, general practitioners, psychiatric services and community services. On the whole, therefore, clients are not self-selected in quite the same way as are clients who seek out some type of psychotherapy or psychoanalysis themselves and who agree to pay for it privately. Consequently our clients tend to represent a very broad cross-section of the communities living in London, and many of the clients with whom I meet are from cultural backgrounds different from my own. They come to seek help with complaints relating to somatic symptoms, to mental illness, to emotional suffering, to housing and immigration, to difficulties in relationships and to the general quality of their lives. Often they have some ideas themselves about what is wrong and what needs to be done and mostly these ideas, on the surface at least, appear to be very different from those which I myself would articulate were it me or one of my relatives who were suffering.

When working cross-culturally in this setting I have been struck by two somewhat contradictory observations. On the one hand it is not difficult to make personal contact, to strike up a conversation or to make some kind of connection. If I do not have the necessary linguistic skills, I can invite an interpreter to help, and I can gesticulate or grimace or use some sort of body language. A connection may be greatly facilitated by an interpreter but it does not depend on it. On the other hand if clients come back and if therapy progresses it is not unusual that a gulf appears. There seems to be no understanding, I feel at sea not knowing where to anchor the experiences which are being communicated to me. There seems to be no common ground. How do I know that which is normative from that which is idiosyncratic? How do I identify pathology? One possibility is to ignore this discovery of uncertainty and proceed as if everything is as usual. Professionally this is dangerous, for it precludes developing an understanding of what is going on and may lead to self-indulgence. It is also the colonial path. The other possibility is to stay with the uncertainty and to adopt different strategies in order to find out more.

To me this contradiction is familiar from anthropology, or rather from that aspect of anthropology which is referred to as ethnography and which involves asking real people questions and making sense of their answers. There has always been a tension in anthropology between rejecting the inequality espoused by colonialism and exploiting it. There is a similar tension currently in Euro-American societies focused on anti-racist awareness and equal opportunities. As a discipline anthropology has been preoccupied with what is generally human and what is culturally specific, but it is a mark of contemporary anthropology that the question of how we might access this whole subject matter is receiving more attention. This means that grand theory can no longer be considered apart from methodology or from an understanding of how it is that persons talk across culture.

The question is far from trivial. Persons from different cultural backgrounds talk to each other in the course of their everyday lives. In such ordinary encounters most persons are content to leave the question of understanding to an unspoken assessment about their communication which they each make and which may never be discussed. If the communication is more or less successful those who have struck up a conversation may go on talking or they may develop a more long-term relationship. Eventually they may even talk about why it is they feel they can communicate. If the communication is not successful they may never meet again or if they do they may avoid each other or they may communicate just what is necessary. Such cross-cultural encounters may not be different from any other encounters between people, although there may be and usually are subtle ideological orientations or discriminations about cultural difference which enter into the private and intimate lives of persons.

The ethnographic or the therapeutic cross-cultural encounter is a somewhat different case. Of course informants may refuse to talk or they may tell the ethnographer to go away. Although there are not many accounts of this in the ethnographic literature, this does happen and in fact it happened to me when I first set out to collect ethnographic data in North Western Nepal. I imagine that all psychotherapists have experienced something similar. Sometimes clients do not come back after the initial meeting and neither letters nor telephone calls yield an explanation. It may be tempting to attribute this to denial, reluctance or to clients not being ready for therapy. However, secretly the therapist may also acknowledge that perhaps if she had said something different, perhaps if she had spoken in a different tone, to a different member of the family, a different set of events might have unfolded. After all as much as we are puzzled by culture, different cultures also attract our attention. We are attracted to different mores and traditions, to outlandish ideas and stories as much as to foreign goods which we can consume and devour and eventually appropriate either positively or negatively as our own. How can psychotherapists be disciplined about this attraction for the 'cultural other'?

Broadly, this is what this book is about and I came to write it not only because I was struck by the similarity in the process of asking questions and talking across culture in ethnography and cross-cultural therapy, but also because it seems to me that from this practical point of view the two disciplines have something to offer each other. As I see it at this stage the exchange is mostly one-way from anthropology to psychotherapy, but were psychotherapists to take the anthropological critique seriously this could be the beginning of the development of a different kind of ethnography, an ethnography which can take proper account of inner worlds.

Surprisingly perhaps, cross-cultural psychiatry is a few steps ahead of psychotherapy in this respect. Thus for some time now psychiatric researchers have been conscious of the limitations of their research instruments, particularly when applying these to populations for whom they have not been anthropologically validated (Kleinman 1987; Krause et al. 1990). A question about individual autonomy for example cannot be assumed to be valid, unless it can be shown that the respondents have notions of agency similar to those held by the person who designed the question in the first place or at least informed by similar principles to those found in the cultural tradition from which the questionnaire is derived. This has meant a welcome and often fruitful collaboration between psychiatry and anthropology, and many psychiatric research projects which aim to include cross-cultural samples now incorporate periods of ethnographic fieldwork in order to assess the validity of questions and in order to design new ones.

In actual fact it can be argued that it is easier to do this in research than in psychotherapy or psychoanalysis because these latter disciplines not only do not ask isolated questions, they also explicitly emphasise the process of communication. In psychotherapy and psychoanalysis it is the person as a whole who is of interest, not just his or her symptoms. Indeed some cross-cultural psychiatric and psychological researchers have highlighted this. Even though questionnaires may be adjusted so that the questions are more culturally valid, this still does not address the central question of how one may translate from one cultural paradigm to another, since such a translation entails not just comparing parts, but also comparing social, cultural and philosophical contexts (Malik 1997). It is after all against the background of such wholes and not in compartmentalised parts that individuals live their lives. So although cross-cultural psychiatry has made a start by raising the question of anthropological or rather ethnographic validity, few psychiatrists have gone far enough. It is part of the argument of this book that in order to understand how others live their lives, an understanding of how one's own life leads to participation in social, cultural, public and intimate relationships is a crucial first step. A few cross-cultural psychiatrists and medical anthropologists have turned the attention on to their own cultural contexts (Taussig 1993; Young 1995; Jadhav 1996; Littlewood 1996a) but generally there has been little examination in detail of how psychiatrists communicate with their patients across culture. Psychotherapy, which incorporates forms of self-assessment and self-description as a central part of the training process, is perhaps better poised to take these issues forward.

THE CONTENT

This is a book for psychotherapists, psychoanalysts and counsellors who work cross-culturally. It is written from a systemic point of view because I believe that in order to understand and address culture and cultural connections a systemic framework is necessary. Culture is a social construction and is therefore maintained, reconstituted and changed through social relationships both public and private, general and intimate. Culture, therefore, cannot be accessed sufficiently through the narrow personal relationship between the psychotherapist and the individual client or between psychoanalyst and analysand, especially not if the cultural backgrounds of therapist and client are markedly different. In such a case the therapist cannot assume that intimate relationships, personhood, etiquette and norms are as she expects and one way of checking this out is to acquire some understanding of the context and relational processes which constitute the background to the lives of clients. Culture necessitates some understanding of social, economic, political and familial patterns of behaviour and ideas and the way these enter into the internal lives of individual persons. Although this perhaps fits more comfortably with the approach of the systemic or family therapist, and all the clinical material described here derives from my own practice as a family therapist, this framework, which draws a fuzzy line between internal and external worlds, can also inform the practice of the psychotherapist and the psychoanalyst who works with individual clients. There may be something of interest for the anthropologist here too, for just as I believe that systemic psychotherapy can make a significant contribution to cross-cultural practice, so it is also clear that anthropology has much to offer psychotherapy. The first step to which I hope this book is a contribution is to find a way for the two to engage with each other, not just about theory but also about the practical task of how to communicate cross-culturally.

In the chapters which follow it has been my aim to cover the ground between practice, theory and involvement, a ground shared by the ethnographer and the psychotherapist. I do not primarily write about theory. My focus is on the practical and immediate issues which arise during communication in cross-cultural therapy. However, this focus implicates theory (Bourdieu 1977 [1972], 1990). It is influenced by, but not derived from, my professional context of Euro-American postmodern social science. Nor is it that I particularly share the view of some contemporary anthropologists and systemic thinkers that there can be no difference between theory and method. I prefer to think about theory as the hypothetical, a legacy from family therapy (Selvini Palazzoli et al. 1980), and method as something we do which involves grappling with reality. There are then many realities, each with its own continuity and its own practice, its own knowledge and its own partiality. This is a legacy from anthropology (Hastrup 1995). I do not believe that we need to shy away from generalising. First, because generalisations themselves are partial, but second because there are some common aspects of humanity and cross-cultural work that provide a powerful leverage on theorising about this.

Chapters 2 to 6 can be read in different ways. They may be read as a general introduction to anthropology. Thus Chapter 2 gives a summary of the ethnographic method from the beginning of the development of ethnography to more contemporary ideas about ethnographic research. Chapter 3 provides a summary of different kinship structures and practices and Chapter 4 addresses the social construction of emotions and provides a summary of the Oedipus debate in anthropology. Chapter 5 examines ritual and Chapter 6 discusses taboo and classification. Alternatively these chapters may be read as an introduction to cross-cultural practice in (systemic) psychotherapy. Each chapter discusses clinical examples from my own work and relates this to the general topic under discussion. Thus in Chapter 3 my own examples demonstrate how kinship enters into therapy sessions if therapists know how to recognise it. In Chapter 4 I elaborate on Bateson's notion of ethos in relation to the difficulties which were brought to therapy by two different families. Chapter 5 is somewhat controversial as far as ritual and family therapy is concerned, because I am critical of the way some systemic psychotherapists have worked with

ritual and their approach to meaning in general. In Chapter 6 the difference between secrets and taboo is discussed again with reference to some
clinical examples and I address the thorny issue of how material which
cannot be spoken about may nevertheless be accessed by the psychotherapist. In cross-cultural therapy this presents some difficult challenges.

Finally the chapters may be read more conceptually as a journey from
the outside to the inside and back again following themes which straddle
this divide. Kinship is crucial because not only does kinship organise
families and households into groups of people who are especially connected to each other and who may act together more often than they do
with outsiders. Kinship also regulates the recursive interaction to which
infants are exposed from birth and is therefore instrumental in the construction of personhood, gender and the very activity of relating. In this
sense kinship must always appear as the 'natural way of things' but this is
doubly so in Anglo-American societies where biology rather than social
connections receives ideological emphasis. Emotion, feeling or affect are
similar types of processes, communicating to the world at the same time as
expressing and reconstituting intimate relationships. However, neither
kinship nor emotions are exclusively or completely tied up with language
as a representation of meaning. I argue in Chapters 5, 6 and 7 from
different points of view that a preoccupation with language as meaning and
symbols does not at all help the cross-culturally practising psychotherapist
to begin to understand her clients. I argue that ritual is best approached in
terms of ritual action rather than symbolism. I show that some aspects of
culture are not accessible to actors themselves and therefore cannot be
approached in terms of what they mean to them. Increasing clients'
awareness of the processes in which they participate is an aim of all types of
psychotherapy and psychoanalysis. But this implies that therapists can
understand things which clients themselves cannot access and in cross-
cultural therapy this is problematic. Therefore I argue that cross-cultural
therapy must begin by therapists being curious about what clients do as
well as about the meaning of the words they use. Similarly if therapists shift
the emphasis from 'what' to 'how' clients communicate in the beginning
phases of therapy, they are more likely to ask questions which take account
of context, style, etiquette and ethos. They are therefore also more likely
to ask questions which are meaningful and which can be answered. In
Chapter 8 I draw all this together arguing that responsible cross-cultural
therapy must start with the therapist reflecting about herself. Such reflection ought to include not only an assessment of past and present intimate
relationships but also an understanding of the wider socially constructed
relationships and practices in which she participates.

A note on definitions is necessary. I use psychotherapy or therapy
throughout as generic terms referring either to individual, family or systemic psychotherapy. I am myself a family or systemic psychotherapist and
I do not claim to have exhaustive knowledge about any other type of
therapy.

I have avoided using the term Western because of its imprecision and its stereotyping overtones. References to anthropology are references to social anthropology developed in Britain or to ideas currently expressed in Britain, some of which are influenced by work undertaken elsewhere. There was previously in anthropology a distinction between American and British anthropology which could be glossed as a distinction between cultural and social anthropology, but this distinction is much less clear now than it was a few decades ago. I myself trained as an anthropologist in Britain and this accounts for my emphasis on British anthropology, but it was also in Britain that social anthropology came to be identified with a particular technique of ethnographic field research known as participant observation, which I describe in greater detail in Chapter 2. I also use the designations British, American and European or a combination of these to refer to philosophical traditions which have originated in these geo-graphical areas. I use the more local terms English and American to refer to kinship and ethnographic material from these societies.

Throughout I use the terms culture and society, cultural and social and although these are also terms which we use in everyday language, these are difficult concepts. There is no clear agreement amongst anthro-pologists on the precise distinction between them and the reason for this will, I hope, become clear. Culture implicates society and society impli-cates culture, but this hardly makes things easier. I like to follow Tim Ingold and say that 'culture is a vehicle for the conduct of social life' (Ingold 1986: 257), but for the general reader this too may be difficult. As a guide one might say that I use the term 'society' to refer to action and behaviour and the patterns thereof also including patterns of interaction and social relationships, while I use the term 'culture' to loosely refer to the ideas which people have about all this. Culture then is about meaning, both in individual instances and in patterns. But this, as we shall see, is also where we run into difficulties.

2

The Making of Ethnography

Training analysis, transference and countertransference are central methods for training and practice in psychoanalysis. In a parallel manner field research has been and still is a crucial part of learning how to be an anthropologist and of the continuing practice of social anthropology. Field research is to anthropology, one seasoned British anthropologist has remarked, 'as the blood of the martyrs is to the Church' (Lewis 1976: 27). As a method of accumulating and constructing anthropological knowledge fieldwork has been hugely popular amongst anthropologists in Britain and in America throughout this century, except perhaps for a period during the 1970s and early 1980s when interest in French philosophy and structural anthropology was on the increase. Although there are differences between the history of anthropology in America, Britain and France echoing some of the differences found in philosophy and in the development of psychoanalysis in these countries, I do not want to elaborate on these differences since these are not important for my purposes.

Before the First World War British anthropologists were preoccupied with grand theories about human diversity which were largely speculative and marked by an evolutionary perspective in which non-western 'primitive people' were considered on a path of development to better and more enlightened circumstances. In the 1920s this began to change. In 1922 two books were published, one by Bronislav Malinowski *Argonauts of the Western Pacific* (Malinowski 1961 [1922]), a study of exchange on the Trobriand Islands, the other by A.R. Radcliffe-Brown, *The Andaman Islanders* (Radcliffe-Brown 1922), a study of ritual as well as of other things. The work of these two men had a profound and long-lasting influence on British social anthropology.

By coincidence Malinowski, who was an Austro-Polish citizen, had been at a conference in Australia when the First World War broke out. Instead of interning him the Australian authorities allowed him to carry out field research on the Trobriand Islands close to New Guinea and it is this research which subsequently came to set the standard for modern anthropological research. Most previous anthropologists had worked through interpreters and had obtained information either by transcribing texts or by working through carefully selected informants. Malinowski's style was different. He learnt to speak the Trobriand language well, observed directly and over a long period of time many aspects of Trobriand life and participated personally in many activities. At the time this was equivalent to a methodological revolution.

The new techniques led to new theories and also to new styles of presentation. The present rather than the past came to be considered interesting and this had several spin-offs. Other societies and cultures could now be seen as living concerns rather than as museum pieces or exotic malfunctioning survivals of the past. Whereas previously anthropologists had been interested in large-scale conjecture about customs and curious modes of thought and had compared these across the world independently of their contexts, the context now became all important and anthropologists began to become expert in one society defined in a particular space and time. Perhaps most importantly customs, ideas and ways of living which had before seemed irrational and exceptional now came to be understood as well functioning and sensible alternatives, at least by the anthropologists who had studied them. This is not to say that the public at large or even other disciplines saw it the same way. A story goes about one of Malinowski's best known books, *The Sexual Life of Savages* (Malinowski 1929), being banned from a well-known girls' school because of the subversive effect it had on the sexual innocence and moral character of the young women there. In a very real way then, not recognised by the anthropological profession until recently and several decades after Malinowski's death, the development of participant observation as a fieldwork technique had a profound effect on the people studied, on the fieldworker, on the discipline and a less obvious but nevertheless moulding influence on issues and themes of both public and private morality in the ethnographers' own countries. For those involved, this type of fieldwork can thus be compared to first encounters in psychoanalysis where 'the emotional upheaval . . . changes the two participants who will never be the same people again' (Symington 1986: 30).

Unlike most of the social anthropologists who followed in the tradition of participant observation Malinowski was interested in human nature and in individuals. His approach was 'functionalist' in the sense that he assumed that social institutions serve the needs of individuals and that if one studied individuals in one social context one could learn something fundamental about human nature everywhere. He became famous not just within social anthropology but also in psychoanalysis where his debate with Ernest Jones about the universality of the Oedipus complex is well known if somewhat discredited. This debate has been revived recently and I shall return to it in Chapter 4.

A COMPARATIVE SCIENCE

Radcliffe-Brown, who became as influential as Malinowski, had a different temperament. He had carried out fieldwork in several places but was not passionately committed to 'the complex problems of translation and interpretation that fieldwork necessarily entails' (Leach 1982: 30) in the way so characteristic of Malinowski. Radcliffe-Brown was a theorist rather than an empiricist and had been deeply influenced by the French sociologist Emile Durkheim. He took up the idea that societies were contemporary concerns which the new techniques of fieldwork emphasised, but he did not pay much attention to individuals. Instead he considered a society to be like an organism, that is to say a whole made of interconnected parts and which to some extent, although how far was not clear, has a life of its own. A society was seen to be something individuals are born into and which constrains and socialises them through the operation of rules and sanctions. The task of the fieldworker therefore was not just to understand the diversity and complexity of surface phenomena in the field but also to uncover the logical consistencies or structural principles which can help make sense of customs, behaviour and ideas which otherwise seem confusing and dysfunctional (Radcliffe-Brown and Forde 1950). The function of a custom, a belief or a particular behaviour pattern was seen to be the part it played in the maintenance of the structural principle on which social life is based.

In anthropology this approach is referred to as structural-functionalism and it shares a great deal with the better known functionalism of Talcott Parsons. Both these approaches came to be thought of as scientific paradigms for social anthropology and the social sciences generally and were based on the model of the natural sciences from which key terms and references were also derived. Once it was felt acceptable to consider societies as whole organisms structured by different principles the next step was to compare these wholes and structures and then construct typologies of societies. This was referred to as the comparative method (Radcliffe-Brown and Forde 1950) and eventually came to be thought of as the corner-stone of British anthropology. Now history was not considered important and society was seen as a laboratory. The observer was thought of as an 'objective scientist' rather than as a living human being who like those he was observing, learnt through experience and personal relationships. Over a period of two decades or so what had begun as a realisation of the need for the anthropologist to access the knowledge and experiences of real living persons (informants) became a body of theory and practice in which individuals, persons and psychological processes were minimally acknowledged. Indeed it was openly declared that anthropologists should opt for descriptions and theories which excluded psychological and psychic processes altogether (Evans-Pritchard 1951).

For the most part this attitude or theoretical orientation caused a covert tension and a sort of discomfort for anthropology whenever the subject of the production of anthropological knowledge came up. One of the most important achievements in anthropology since then is therefore that this discomfort has become explicit. Consequently, anthropology has much more to say to the therapy professions now than was the case when Malinowski boldly criticised Ernest Jones and the Freudian paradigm in the 1920s (Parsons 1969). But it is not only anthropology which has changed. The therapy professions themselves, partly under the influence of prevailing postmodern philosophical themes have also shown a greater interest in social and cultural processes and the way these affect internal worlds. As there are parallels between what therapists do in their consulting rooms and what anthropologists do in the fieldwork situation, a more detailed discussion of the problems and challenges which have been given expression in the current anthropological preoccupation with method and practice will be illuminating, and it is to this I now turn.

ETHNOGRAPHY

What I have referred to as fieldwork or field research in anthropology may also be referred to as ethnography. When the anthropologist is in the field of study, observing and participating, surveying, interviewing and chatting she or he is an ethnographer. In this sense ethnography is a research process. The term may, however, be used in a more inclusive way to refer to the written text or the audio or visual recordings in which the findings or experiences of the anthropologist about the daily life in another culture are presented. In either case this use of the term tends to imply that the reader can expect to learn some 'facts' about people or a way of life and will not only be presented with a theoretical discussion about anthropological theory. In reality the relationship between empirical findings and the theoretical persuasions of the author were rarely clearly delineated or even made explicit in traditional anthropology. Thus, for example, in keeping with the tradition in structural-functionalist anthropology, ethnographies also tended to be written to mirror organic conceptions of society with a chapter on economics followed by chapters on politics, kinship, religion and so on. The personal observations of the ethnographer and the strains and stresses which influenced her were rarely discussed or referred to except perhaps in a preface or in footnotes.

So what is the scientific status of ethnography? Is it to be considered an objective research tool or a subjective process in which the ethnographer focuses on material which for reasons, which may or may not be conscious or explicable, takes her fancy? At the time of Malinowski and Radcliffe-Brown, ethnography was considered a science and the experiences of the anthropologist in some way remote from what it was he or she was observing. However, nowadays few anthropologists would regard it as a straightforward process to engage, observe and record what one observes, let alone claim that this process has the kind of objective status similar to the claims made by research in the physical sciences. What is new in recent thinking about ethnography is not just that ethnography refers to the whole process involved in the production of anthropological knowledge including observation, recording, living, engaging as well as writing and presenting but that the ethnographer has a duty to make her personal and theoretical reflections accessible to her readership (Marcus and Fischer 1986). Because culture and society are seen as heterogeneous and because the 'ability of the fieldworker to inhabit indigenous minds is always in doubt' (Clifford 1988: 47) there is now much less confidence about the scientific status of ethnography as a research process.

This leaves the anthropologist with a conundrum. This is the puzzle of how it can be possible to add to a framework of comparative knowledge about the diversity of human social life, the reference point of which cannot lie in any one individual or any one group of individuals, by using techniques which rely almost exclusively on intersubjective communication and interaction (Carrithers 1992; Hastrup and Hervik 1994). This position is not of course unique to the anthropologist. It is also shared to some extent by psychoanalysts and psychotherapists of all descriptions insofar as they too lay claim to some sort of objectivity while using techniques which cannot easily be described as such. It is, however, important to emphasise that the 'to some extent' for anthropology has been and still is specifically aiming to address human diversity on a more extensive scale than are the various types of traditionally western therapies and it is precisely this wider cross-cultural scope of anthropology which attracts the interest of other disciplines.

As I suggested above few anthropologists would nowadays openly adhere to an absolutely rigid realist position at least as far as theory is concerned. With respect to the practicalities of research, however, it has been difficult to find and use alternatives which adequately reflect the complexity of these issues. This is perhaps why one very popular way out of the conundrum for modern anthropologists has been to place an emphasis on ethnography as a kind of writing or a text, that is to say to critically examine the authority of the authorship rather than the content of the text and to prioritise language as an articulation of the personal experience of the ethnographer rather than as a way of describing 'reality' (Clifford and Marcus 1986; Geertz 1988).

As a rough guide to the different positions one may consider the different way the terms 'fieldwork, ethnography and anthropology' tend to be used. Generally speaking those who see fieldwork, ethnography and anthropology as separate although overlapping domains of activity also tend to be optimistic about the production of knowledge apart from the self-scrutiny of the anthropologist (Carrithers 1992; Hastrup 1992; Hastrup and Hervik 1994; Jenkins 1994; Lindquist 1995). For them fieldwork tends to refer to the physical position of the researcher in a place of study, ethnography to a research method and a research process which culminates in the presentation of a text or a film, and to anthropology as a body of theory. Those who tend to conflate the three terms and who tend to give more weight to ethnography also tend to consider this as a 'general method for writing and thinking about culture from the standpoint of participant observation' (Clifford 1988: 9). As such the method is not particularly identified with anthropology, but tends to encompass an approach in which theory and practice are not distinguished and are assumed not to be distinguishable (Clifford 1988; Geertz 1988, 1993 [1973]). The advocates of this approach tend to align ethnography with the fields of literature, art and poetry rather than with social science.

Despite the sense of excitement and the tremendous boost which participant observation gave to anthropology, it has been argued that the development of participant observation was much less radical than has often been claimed and that the method corresponds well with an objectivist view of the world, in which 'man has distanced himself from nature and the universe of which he was part, and has asserted his capacity to remodel things according to his will' (Dumont 1982: 233, quoted in Herzfeld 1987).

Accordingly, insofar as anthropologists continue to practise participant observation and to claim its uniqueness as a research method they also necessarily envelop themselves in a stance in which there is no final and absolute escape from some form of objectivism. In fact despite the attractiveness of approaches which abdicate responsibility for an objectivist position, fieldwork and participant observation continue to play a key role in the private and professional lives of anthropologists. Students of anthropology as well as fully trained anthropologists continue to live for extended periods, sometimes years, in places other than home and in particular they continue to learn foreign languages and local vernaculars well enough to be able to communicate with informants. Indeed no self-respecting anthropologist would nowadays be content to rely on interpreters and secondary sources for major chunks of ethnography. This emphasis on language is perhaps Malinowski's most unchallenged legacy: even those whose interests focus on reality as a domain of contested meaning and the nature of authorship do not dispute it. Yet this emphasis implicates more than a linguistic competence; it also entails a general ability to communicate with different kinds of people – old, young, men, women, chiefs, commoners and so on – and to communicate in situations where people do not use words at all (Basso 1970; Ingold 1992). The anthropologist cannot get away from having to use her self in this process. Again there are clear parallels with the practice of the psychotherapist.

The process of conducting fieldwork and using participant observation also has direct pragmatic significance to the anthropologist. In the various institutions of learning it is regarded almost as a heroic act (Shweder 1984), as a rite of passage without which it is not possible to become a bona fide anthropologist. It is seen as the first step towards the launching of a career of working and writing and some sort of relevant employment often within a specialism defined as an ethnographic area. These circumstances and institutional arrangements place restrictions on the self-reflective possibilities in the process. It is not necessarily a result of more or less conscious omnipotence or self aggrandisement that anthropologists talk about 'my people', it also reflects a sometimes romantic and perhaps sincere attachment to human processes and relationships which for various reasons, some of them no doubt personal, are less accessible at home. In every budding anthropologist there is a possible escapist, but unlike psychotherapy or psychoanalysis it is not a training requirement that anthropologists should be frank about these very personal processes which guide their choice of profession and they are very rarely encouraged to think about it. Instead the institutionalised mechanisms which maintain a polarity between 'them' and 'us' are subtle and covert. One such mechanism has been the insistence traditionally that fieldwork should be conducted in far away exotic places with enough difference between ethnographer and informants for confusion between the one and the other to be minimal. Fieldwork in one's own society used to be actively discouraged and European ethnography, which by definition must reject exoticism and yet pursue the study of cultural otherness, has been more romanticised, more archaic and less historically comprehensive than the study of other ethnographic areas (Herzfeld 1987).

All this adds up to a position which is as ambivalent and difficult personally for the anthropologist as it is professionally. My own experiences of fieldwork, particularly during the initial months, embarrassed, perplexed, annoyed, astonished and pleased me. Although in reality these emotions and sensations differed little from what I might feel in social interaction anywhere, the context of the field situation and the enormous trouble I had taken to get there, sometimes provoked particular feelings with particular intensity. One incident early on shocked me and then became a source of valuable insight into the life of women and untouchables in a high caste Himalayan village in Nepal (Krause 1982, 1988).

My husband and I existed in the field mostly on food which we bought from farmers or local shops. This meant that our diet was monotonous and uninteresting for a large part of the year, as the most available food included only staples such as second rate rice, wheat or barley flour, salt, peppers and very rarely spinach. We were not of course knowledgeable about particular delicacies which could be gathered from the jungle as the year progressed. I was extremely pleased therefore, one day to be passing a neighbour's terrace and to be offered a lapful of new fernshoots by the woman of the house. This happened to be the first day of my period and I was observing the same rules as other women, that is to say I was staying outside the kitchen area and spending my time in parts of the house which would not be affected by my polluted state. By doing this I was showing that I was willing to adhere to local rules for behaviour and that I was not pregnant. I did not realise the extent to which this was observed and recognised until on the terrace after the offer of fernshoots was made, when without thinking I stepped forward to take the vegetables, my neighbour immediately took two steps back and asked 'was I not unclean?' She then asked me to step back so that she could throw me the ferns. I was shocked and outraged, wondering how any social system could tolerate such outrageous discrimination. It was only much later that I realised that what I had in part reacted to was my own definition of self and that unlike the villagers this stayed self-centred and static no matter what the natural or social circumstances. I also later learnt that being excluded from the kitchen for a few days every month gave me an opportunity to join exclusively with other women in the same polluted state and those occasions not only served as a respite from hard work, it was also great fun. As an immediate reaction I had interpreted this event as a personal attack since it had implicated my identity as a western woman and my bodily processes, which in my frame of reference I take to be natural. The discord within me which the event provoked highlighted a contextuality which I could not have accessed either through a description of it or through having observed it happening to someone else. It was crucial for my understanding that I had been there (Geertz 1988).

Fieldwork is of course full of such events, but some stand out more than others. Thus, for example processes involving general human conditions such as bodily processes and life events such as births and deaths tend to provoke personal and emotional awareness of diversity in the ethnographer. During my own fieldwork I received news of the death of my maternal grandmother, with whom I had been very much engaged during my childhood and whom I loved dearly. I experienced great comfort when my Hindu friends encouraged me to observe their rules and practices for mourning including accepting that I was in a polluted state, abstaining from certain foods and keeping myself separate from others for a period. Yet at the same time I also experienced bewilderment and anger at the excluding nature of these rules which again kept me outside the cooking area and separated me from my husband and at a comment which was made to me by a well meaning neighbour that at least it was not my paternal grandmother who had died.

Other anthropologists have written about the effect of such general events on the ethnographic process. Most notably perhaps is the account by Renate Rosaldo of how he came to understand the intensity of the rage felt by Ilongot men after bereavement when he lost his own wife, who also was an anthropologist, in a tragic accident in the field (Rosaldo 1984). It is because of the information conveyed by these routine and extraordinary examples of human events and the impact of them on the ethnographer's body and person during fieldwork that we can consider participant observation as 'engaged learning' (Carrithers 1992) or as 'experiencing participation' (Csordas 1994). By the same token we must accept that these activities do not set the ethnographer apart from her informants, that on the contrary they are by definition the processes involved in gaining and maintaining social knowledge generally (Herzfeld 1987). Again there are parallels here between the relationship between the ethnographer and her informants and the therapist and her clients.

LANGUAGE AND ETHNOGRAPHY

The discussion of ethnography so far points to several problems with the view that considers language to be identical to or the essence of culture and ethnography analogous to the presentation of a text. Sometimes this approach is referred to as literary anthropology and one of the main advocates of this approach, Clifford Geertz, has received an unusual amount of attention from family therapy. Geertz is perhaps most famous for considering anthropology as an interpretive science. By this he does not mean interpretation in the sense used by the psychoanalyst or the psychotherapist, that is to say interpreting material presented during sessions according to a particular body of theory. Geertz's view is more relativist and he is not concerned with the a priori existence of a theoretical framework, rather ethnography in his view is at the same time description and theory. Geertz's view is that there simply are shared meanings out there in the world and that 'societies, like lives, contain their own interpretations. One has only to learn how to gain access to them' (Geertz 1993: 453). The method to be learnt is ethnography, but an ethnography which studies meaning rather than behaviour and seeks understanding rather than laws of causes and effects. Culture is for Geertz a web of meaning rather than a series of patterns of behaviour and the anthropologist can study this web as she studies a collection of texts by straining 'to read over the shoulders of those to whom they properly belong'(Geertz 1993: 452). In doing this ethnography becomes 'thick description', a notion which Geertz borrowed from Gilbert Ryle.

'Thin description' is a description of what someone is doing in terms of physical movement (Ryle used the example of a wink, i.e. rapidly contracting an eyelid) and 'thick description' is a description of what someone is doing in terms of the meaning and all the possible meanings which could be given to that physical movement in the context in which it took place (i.e. a parody, a twitch, a fake-wink, a wink, a rehearsal etc.). The aim of ethnography is to describe how the physical movement comes to have meaning in these different ways and how this relates to salient cultural themes and structures (Geertz 1993: 7). By analysing symbols and meaning in the terms of which people actually present them to themselves and to one another Geertz argued, ethnography deals in experience-near concepts rather than the experience-far concepts of philosophy, science and theoretical debate (Geertz 1974).

Few anthropologists would disagree with this and some have even argued that this was nothing new, that 'thick description' always has been what ethnography was all about (Howe 1984). In particular what has been unique about anthropological field research has been the exposure both to behaviour and to meaning. Informants might tell you many things but being present in the same locality for a prolonged period of time also allows for observation of what happens when people interact and communicate with each other. Geertz did not opt for keeping this dual emphasis. Instead he took this emphasis on the experience-near in the direction of language and meaning and did not place much emphasis on those other aspects of Ryle's notion of thick description which may be so experience-near that they are expressed in unconscious patterns and therefore not open to reflection. These complexities are central to what has been referred to as the anthropological project (Hastrup 1992). They are also ubiquitous in any kind of cross-cultural understanding, and I shall return to them below, particularly in Chapters 6, 7 and 8.

In family therapy, as in other branches of psychotherapy, Geertz's solution to the anthropological conundrum has become popular in connection with the emerging emphasis on construction, languaging and the narratives with which patients present their lives and their problems (Anderson and Goolishan 1988, 1992; White and Epston 1990; Andersen 1992; Gergen and Kaye 1992; Lax 1992; DiNicola 1993; Pare 1995) and generally of course the approach is a well-known postmodern phenomenon which has had an influence on all the social sciences. As there are similarities between the way this position is articulated in ethnography and in psychotherapy the critique of the literary approach in anthropology can also be read as a critique of the use of the analogy in a broader sense.

As I noted above, literary anthropology arose as a response to the recognition that the way ethnographic material used to be represented was highly problematic. The idea that different disciplines could be organised by (objective) abstract and generalising frameworks and that these frameworks could adequately reflect the material they were meant to interpret and elucidate was considered at best dubious and possibly erroneous (Giddens 1976; Bourdieu 1977 [1972]; Clifford and Marcus 1986; Clifford 1988). Furthermore, as suggested above problems of description have tended to be conflated with problems of presentation and this has given rise to a spurt of experimental ethnographic writing (Feld 1982; Shore 1982; Marcus and Fischer 1986) in which ethnographers attempt to capture and communicate the experience of living in the field 'in the way it really was for them'. In some cases such accounts go as far as focusing exclusively on the ethnographer and convey very little about the ethnographic context except in the way it impinges on the author. In the words of Moore when commenting on the work of Crapanzano (1980) this approach to ethnography 'is much more than the comprehension of the self by the "detour of the other", this is the imaginary constitution of the self, the desire to make sense of self through assigning value and meaning to experience' (Moore 1994: 119).

So what started out as an effort and a desire to represent the world of informants as it really is, in some cases ends up as representations in which the anthropological self is more in evidence than ever before and furthermore as Moore points out this 'I' of the ethnographer is also seen to be unproblematic (Moore 1994: 116). Crapanzano for example refers extensively to the work of Jean-Paul Sartre and finds parallels between the predicament of Jean Genet (Sartre 1964) and that of his chief informant, an illiterate Arab Moroccan tilemaker with the name of Tuhami. But the parallel is drawn loosely and impressionistically as an aid for Crapanzano himself and does not, and is not meant to, suggest that Tuhami sees it this way (Crapanzano 1980). What began as doubt about a positivistic method thus culminates in a stance of self-representation in which the actual social and moral context of that self has all but disappeared. One can find similar developments in those branches of theory in systemic and individual psychotherapy which emphasise co-construction (see Chapter 7) and discourse analysis (Stancombe and White 1997).

The preoccupation with language and with representation, implicitly and sometimes even explicitly, conveys the idea that the problems involved in understanding or comprehending something are the same as those involved in putting something into words and writing these down. This assumes a close correspondence between thoughts and words and also suggests that words restrict or limit what we think. Once something is down on paper or once something is put into words it takes on a life of its own and becomes a fixed reference point for other (also verbal) communication. Although we may all be familiar with experiencing this kind of restriction of words written or spoken, for analytic purposes, that is to say for the purpose of seeking a framework in which we can communicate about our endeavours as ethnographers, anthropologists or therapists, this view is imprecise and is, it can be argued, a fallacy. It is a fallacy because it confuses the name for something with the thing itself. 'The word "cat" cannot scratch you' Korzybski famously remarked (quoted in Bateson 1973: 153) and as all family therapists know this distinction between 'name' and 'thing' or in the expression preferred by Bateson between 'map' and 'territory' is one of the basic principles for systemic therapy. A map or a representation cannot consist of those objects which it denotes because it is in the very nature of messages and representations that they are abstract from real time and space (Bourdieu 1977; Taylor 1993). If we ignore this distinction we predispose ourselves and our disciplines to convey timeless, general and non-specific contexts and relationships. Real life is experienced in terms of bodily sensation, emotion, motivation and choice in the context of specific relationships and to portray these uncertain and dynamic aspects of existence we need to address all forms of communication. It may not be possible to represent, categorise or reflect on sensory experiences until well after the event and even so words may serve as a gloss rather than as an accurate description of such experiences. In this way experiencing and comprehending is not like creating a text or even like speaking a language and the ethnographer may have access to certain themes of meaning precisely because she has participated in the events rather than as a result of her linguistic skills (Lindquist 1995). Despite Geertz and despite the difficulties, behaviour and the meaning of behaviour are not so easily separated, a theme which I shall return to several times in the chapters which follow.

Along these lines it has also been argued that the cognitive processes which take place in everyday thought do not involve linking propositions in a single linear sequence in the way language represents reasoning. Instead cognitive processes are arranged in multi-stranded chunks of signification which allow for the storing of vast amounts of information and also for quick switching between different chunks so that complex information can be accessed quickly enough to be implicated in practical everyday activities (Nadel et al. 1989). As Bloch points out this means that people are not easily able to describe their own thought processes through words and it implies of course that anthropologists have the same difficulties when they attempt to present their own findings through a text (Bloch 1992). Bloch suggests a different and for therapists interesting solution to the conundrum.

Bloch, too, must of course rely on what people say as information, but as an ethnographer he focuses on a different process than conversation and dialogue as a necessary source for his own understanding. In line with classic anthropology he refers to this as intimate participant observation over long periods of time. This kind of process, he says, bears a much closer resemblance to the mental and neural processes of storage and retrieval which people use in everyday life and because of this it is more likely to produce significant and useful data. For the Zafimaniry, a group of shifting cultivators in Madagascar, with whom Bloch has worked over many years, there appear to be a number of lived-in models which guide everyday activities. Examples of these models are Zafimaniry notions of what people are like and how they mature, of differences and similarities between men and women, of what a good marriage is like, of what trees and wood are like and of what houses are like. As far as Bloch is concerned one of the advantages of starting ethnographic enquiry in this way is that

> the anchoring of conceptualization in the material – the body, houses, wood, styles of speaking and in practices – cooking, cultivating, eating together – means that the cultural process cannot be separated from the wider processes of ecological, biological and geographical transformation of which human society is a small part. Culture is not merely an interpretation superimposed on these material facts but integrated with them. (Bloch 1992: 144)

The important characteristic of the Zafimaniry models is that they refer to aspects of life which for the Zafimaniry go without saying. That is to say they refer to the obvious, but they have, nevertheless been learnt. They have been learnt as a baby learns to approach her mother's body or learns to negotiate the material aspect of the house (Bloch 1992), or as a child learns to share food or the socially appropriate response to sound (Feld 1982). This means that the ethnographer, if she pays sufficient attention and is exposed for long enough, may be able to interpret material about which her informants may not be able to explain very much because it is obvious or 'natural' to them. But there is more to it, for the ethnographer, too, learns in this manner. For her too not only is language implicated, but so also are much wider and perhaps hazier conceptualisations of society and relationships as this anecdote from fieldwork with the Ilongot, who live in the Phillipines, told by the late Michelle Rosaldo demonstrates

> One day, early in fieldwork, my Ilongot 'sister' Wagat asked a child to bring her betel pouch from across the room. Wanting to please and be helpful, I jumped to the task. Wagat laughed when I handed the pouch to her, and told me I was like an unmarried maiden, who fetches objects when told. But when I looked hurt, she went on to assure me that I, like a child, would learn to speak by being commanded – and by fetching what she had asked for, I had demonstrated that I 'knew' its name. (Rosaldo 1980: 73)

Learning experience-near concepts does thus not only implicate language but also other types of non-verbal communication. We can then reconfirm the importance of fieldwork and participant observation for ethnography and for anthropology. It is precisely because the ethnographer participates in practical events which implicate all our senses, our bodies as well as our minds, that anthropological knowledge is possible. What then are the implications of this for cross-cultural therapy?

In a recent seminar an eminent social anthropologist who had been examining the effect of the violence following the assassination of Indira Ghandi in 1984 on the lives of Punjabi Sikh women (Das 1990) was asked whether she had had any therapeutic effect on the individuals whose case histories she collected. She denied that she had, explaining that she had not conducted interviews but had pieced together her account from disjointed bits of conversation more often than not initiated by the women themselves. She did not see this as being like therapy in any way. Clearly for this anthropologist the context of the conversation and who it was initiated by was important for an interpretation of what it achieved. She would not presumably see conversations which take place between therapists and clients mostly on the territory of the therapist, mostly within the frame of help seeking and a relatively clear goal of improving the quality of life and mostly starting from the conceptual framework of the therapist, on a par with the conversations which the ethnographer has with her informants. The ethnographer may know more and at the same time less about her informants. She ought to know more about the cultural and social frameworks which form the background to her informants' lives, but she may have less access to the intimate attachments and aversions which shape and motivate a person's actions and feelings. In this domain the therapist has an advantage, because it is these, whichever expression they may be given, which by definition form the focus for therapeutic conversations.

Still the question from the floor was not misconceived, because the questioner, himself an anthropologist, knew that, like therapists, anthropologists gain their knowledge through personal contact: participation and conversation can only be achieved through direct interaction with other human beings. Therapy and ethnography are both grounded in social relationships, both are constituted through a type of social interaction. This point of view places the similarity between informants and ethnographers, therapists and clients in the foreground. As Herzfeld puts it 'Participant observation is only a fiction in as much as we treat it as an activity significantly different from that of the people under observation' (Herzfeld 1987: 90). Or, as noted by Jenkins when commenting on his work on the practices of French cattle farmers in a market place in south-west France,

> The knowledge gained by an anthropologist is close to that gained by a good operator in the market place: it has to do with apprenticeships undertaken, habits acquired, negotiations achieved, failures of comprehension coped with, all within shifting interacting contexts. (Jenkins 1994: 452)

If this is the case with the knowledge of the anthropologist, it is also reasonable to insist that this is the nature of the knowledge needed and used by a therapist. Therapeutic activity like anthropological activity is a form of normal social interaction. We may ask our patients whether they have anybody else to talk to and in this way implicitly acknowledge the encounter between therapist and client itself as an instance of social life. Whatever else might be hoped to be achieved, talking with other persons is a form of life. Conversations can concentrate on different things and as Bloch and others have pointed out certain phenomena constitute points for transhuman and cross-cultural connections better than others. Thus Bloch wrote about material aspects of existence: body, houses, wood; Carrithers has written in a similar vein about disapproval (Carrithers 1992: 171) and Hastrup about hunger (Hastrup 1993).

The point about these phenomena is that they have been experienced (at least to some extent) by ourselves, by ethnographers and therapists alike and that it is because of this experience which we ourselves have had that we can go some way to begin to understand the experience of others. It is an understanding of others built on our own ability to imagine, empathise and conceptualise (Obeyesekere 1990; Carrithers 1992; Hastrup 1992). While this kind of approach to the understanding of others is well known in psychotherapy and psychoanalysis, the scope for imagining difference and variety has been limited in these disciplines. In anthropology it has been the other way around: the scope for imagining and understanding human differences has been at the centre of the discipline while the potential for using this in personal encounters has remained undeveloped. I shall argue that cross-cultural therapeutic practice requires a bit of both and that a self-reflective approach is crucial. However, before I can present this argument it will be necessary to address some of the areas and issues which are particularly poignant when a therapist attempts to understand and communicate across cultural differences.

3

Kinship and Social Life

Family or systemic therapists write about families, not about kinship and not very often about kin. In fact it is rare for family therapists to make clear what they mean by the term 'family'. In a recent book Jones shows remarkable awareness of variation on this subject and poses sensitive questions, but the solutions offered by her are nevertheless limited if assessed from a cross-cultural perspective:

> What do we mean by family? This may seem an obvious question, but it is one that has received different answers over the course of time. Is a family a household, in which case does it include non-related individuals who live in the household and participate in daily interactions, while excluding bio-logically related individuals who live elsewhere? Or does it mean only those who are biologically related or in some long-term relationship (heterosexual or homosexual) which society would recognise as a partnership? The answer to such questions would partly depend on culture. . . . I shall assume that a family consists of at least two generations. This may include parental figures who are of the same or different genders, step-parents, divorced parents who live apart but participate in the therapy . . .; it will also include a child generation, whether these children are adult or under age, genetically linked to one or both parents, or adopted or fostered. (Jones 1993: 55)

Jones is of course partially right. At one level the question about what a family is seems obvious to us. It consists of at least two generations and includes a parental generation and a child generation. Reading between the lines we find the notion of a family as a place where children grow up, where children are socialised to be the focus. Accordingly, when children grow up and have their own children there is likely to be a break in the practical and emotional links with the previous generation. This is, as I shall discuss below, not partly dependent on culture. Rather, Jones's definition *is* a cultural one, and it probably belongs to contemporary Anglo-American society. This, then is the reason why the meaning of 'family' appears obvious to us: because family therapists (and anthropologists as I shall discuss) have used their own cultural definition of this unit as if it is 'objective' and 'scientific' (Fisek 1991). Apart from making her assumptions explicit, Jones does not discuss this coincidence. Neither do most white family therapists practising in Britain today.

Jones's uncertainty is also revealing. Families are either households, that is to say residential units with the interaction and dependence which that implies, or they are biological units with the inclusion of sexual relationships. It seems that family therapists cannot imagine other variations on principles for recruitment of families than those which happen to be the basis for the organisation of their own families and their own attachments. In this chapter I want to address why this should be the case and in giving an answer I examine English and North American kinship in some detail as well as some examples of different types of thinking and different types of models from other cultural contexts. I also sample some of the knowledge produced by traditional anthropological approaches and outline some of the implications of the challenges outlined in Chapter 2 for these issues. Finally I present some clinical examples where these sorts of issues present themselves and where awareness about them can be useful to the therapist.

THE NATURALNESS OF FAMILY RELATIONSHIPS

The way we think and feel about families and family attachments appears to us inevitable and in some respects as the only way it could be. This is hardly surprising since from infancy these very relationships have been the vehicle for the mediation of our experience for us (Trevarthen 1987). Of course our experiences of early relationships are located in particular historical contexts (Toren 1993), but this is unlikely to be obvious to us, since much of this material lies towards the limits and maybe even beyond everyday consciousness.

It is easy to justify this notion that the way our families are organised and the shape of our attachments is the 'natural way' by referring to evolution or general human nature. After all we know that of all mammals human children require the longest period of learning and maturation and that this means that human infants depend on their carers for a long period of time. Add to this the argument that the universal tendency to enforce similar incest prohibitions (Fox 1983 [1980]) has given humans significant social evolutionary advantage and the increasing body of genetic research which focuses on characteristics shared between parents and their biological offspring and there can be hardly a doubt that the way we behave and think today can be amply and scientifically justified on the basis of general human biological requirements. We can project this argument backwards or forwards and while we may leave some room for the existence of organisational and behavioural variation, basically what we observe in our own families is the direct articulation of a pan-human condition, regardless of historical or cultural context. The effect of this sort of conflation is that what *we* do and the way *we* think appears to be natural.

But if this is the way it works for us, if these are the circumstances of our certainty, the same may be the case for other people in different cultural contexts and with different ideas about the way things were (and with different blueprints for values and behaviour). Consider for example a myth told to the ethnographer Steven Feld by the Kaluli people who live on the Great Papuan Plateau in the Southern Highlands Province of Papua New Guinea. This myth is about a boy and his elder sister fishing for crayfish. This sibling relationship is known as *ade*. Three times the older girl catches a crayfish and refuses to give it to her younger brother, claiming instead that she will give it first to her mother, then to her father and finally to her older brother. In the end the boy feels very sad and catches a shrimp. He pulls the meat out of the shell of the shrimp and places it on his nose. His nose turns red and at the same time his hands become his wings. He is now transformed into a *muni* bird (fruit dove) and flies away. His sister regrets not having offered him the crayfish and begs him to come back, but in vain. The boy has become a *muni* bird and he cries out the *muni* cry again and again in a minor key and with descending pitch:

Your crayfish
You did not give it to me
I have no *ade*
I'm hungry
(Feld 1982: 21)

There are several aspects of the myth and the song which convey themes which are central to Kaluli experience. *Ade* is a reciprocal term for the relationship between an elder sister and a younger brother and it implies a greatly valued cultural expectation that a brother will be looked after and provided for by his elder sister. While therapists may consider this as a pattern of inappropriately parentifying a young girl, for Kaluli the relationship between an elder sister and her younger brother is a culturally valued and deeply significant relationship.

The *muni* song features centrally in the *gisaro* ceremony. In this ceremony which takes place at night, visiting guests perform a dance in the longhouse for their hosts. It is performed by men who are dressed as *muni* birds and the object of the ceremony is for the dancers to move the hosts to tears. The content of the songs is evocative, naming familiar places in the countryside and recalling the places where the relatives of the listeners lived and died. The response to such memories being evoked is often great grief followed by anger towards the dancers which may be expressed by men who are particularly touched by the song, grabbing burning torches and jamming them into the bare shoulders of the dancers. A central theme in the song is thus the connections between relatives and the places they inhabited and this is also expressed in Kaluli society by the sharing of food. The elder sister in the myth is expected to share with her younger brother and to have been denied food is a source of despair and desolation (Schieffelin 1976). The *ade* relationship takes on a symbolism and a psychic significance almost akin to that of the Oedipus complex in other cultures.

It is not difficult to understand that for the Kaluli these particular principles appear as inevitable ones without which social intercourse could not take place. Indeed this is suggested by the experience of Schieffelin, another anthropologist who has worked extensively with the Kaluli. Schieffelin recounts his first entry to a long house:

> I sat down wearily on the edge of the men's sleeping platforms and was pulling the leeches out of my socks when a man approached with a blackened, loaf-shaped looking substance covered with greyish rubbery skin. There was a pause while the people of the longhouse watched to see what I would do. Reluctantly, I took a bite. The flavour was strongly reminiscent of plaster of paris. '*Nafa*?' ('Good?') asked one of my hosts hopefully, using one of the few Kaluli words I knew at the time. '*Nafa*' I answered when I could get some saliva back in my mouth. 'Ah' said my host, looking around to the others. They relaxed. Having eaten sago, I was established as a fellow creature. (1976: 47)

It is not just that the anthropologist here can appreciate the local produce, it is also that the acts of giving and sharing food in themselves convey a special connection. While we can understand and recognise this in our own thinking and feeling of kinship and relatedness we do not share the same emphasis. What appears as the natural family to us, that is a two-generation group of people, one being categorised as the offspring of the other living under the same roof, may not appear like that to others and what to us appears as the natural and inevitable basis for connectedness may receive a different emphasis or be interpreted in a different way by others from different cultural backgrounds.

This means that we cannot simply assume that our own (or anyone else's) family organisation and conceptions of kinship reflect the way 'it really is'. Rather, the question which arises is about the cultural and symbolic dimensions of our own thinking. Only after we have asked this question will we be equipped to ask questions about these dimensions as far as other peoples and cultures are concerned. Family therapists have been slow to confront these questions. More surprisingly perhaps, traditional anthropology has also not been interested in exposing the assumptions of its own practitioners about this. I shall move on to address the cultural content in English kinship but first I wish to examine the issues which preoccupied traditional anthropology and this will serve two purposes. Firstly, it will give me an opportunity to summarise some of the principles and variations with regard to kinship which preoccupied anthropologists in the period up to 1960. Although not true and omnipresent in the way these anthropologists thought, this material nevertheless continues to have informative value. Since most psychotherapists and family therapists receive no training in kinship theory these sections will also serve as an introduction to this subject. Second, it will enable me to critique this material and to focus on that which anthropologists left out. As we shall see what had been left out is just as important in shaping thinking about kinship as that which was extensively described. And I suggest that a similar sifting process took place for similar reasons amongst practitioners of family or systemic psychotherapy.

KINSHIP AND GENEALOGIES

Until the mid-1960s kinship was the anthropological domain par excellence. Kinship did not and does not only refer to the family or the household in the sense outlined by Jones and quoted at the beginning of this chapter. Rather, kinship refers to the ideas which lie behind the way people trace relationships and connections to each other. In this way it may of course include the relationships between people who live together but depending on the society and the cultural context in question kinship may also refer to other more general relationships between people.

Malinowski and Radcliffe-Brown were both preoccupied with studying families and both were much influenced by W.H.R. Rivers, the first anthropologist to make extensive use of what has been called the genealogical method. Rivers was a psychiatrist who is now best known for his work with traumatised soldiers from the First World War, but who also worked on colour and space perception. He joined the Cambridge Anthropological Expedition to the Torres Straits in Melanesia in 1898–9 where the genealogical method, considered to be a major British contribution to scientific ethnography, was developed. Rivers was the main protagonist of this method which was thought to be both a way of collecting data systematically with precision and a way of reconstructing family and social structure (Kuper 1988). The method consisted of asking informants to name their 'real' mother and father, to check for previous or other marriages, then to list the children in order of age, their marriages and their offspring: 'Thus was obtained the small group consisting of the descendants of [one set of] parents' wrote Rivers (quoted in Bouquet 1993: 34). The same could then be repeated for any other individual. Family therapists and systemic psychotherapists will find this way of collecting information familiar for this is also a sketchy outline of the method used when they construct family genograms (McGoldrick and Gerson 1989).

The development of the genealogical method was greatly influenced by Linnean taxonomy on the one hand and the English idea of pedigree on the other. The participants of the Torres Strait expedition were physical scientists interested in zoology, biology and genetics. There was therefore an assumption that a description of family or social organisation is also a description of genetic or biological links. The assumption that these two domains overlap was also central to the idea of the pedigree in upper and middle class England. Rivers knew that his readership was familiar with the idea of a pedigree and he explicitly conflated this idea with the genealogical method in his own explanations. Indeed Bouquet argues that the genealogical method enjoyed such great success then as well as subsequently precisely because the assumptions behind it were implicitly shared by those who were drawn into the field of anthropology. At that time these scholars and students tended to come from upper and middle class English backgrounds (Bouquet 1993: 38). Again since family therapy has been influenced by the physical sciences, in particular medicine, rather than by the social sciences and practitioners have tended to affirm rather than challenge dominant western values, there are here parallels with the way genograms have been conceptualised in family therapy.

The problems with the genealogical method which have been discussed in anthropology subsequently show that the method tends to encourage a particular point of view which may or may not be the one which informants themselves hold. For example, it was clear from the beginning that some relationships are considered less problematic than others: 'father', 'mother', 'child', 'husband' and 'wife' were relatively straightforward, but 'brother', 'sister', 'cousin', 'uncle' and 'aunt' were more difficult to fit in and in fact the use of these terms was outright discouraged by Rivers himself (Rivers 1968 [1910]). This meant that the genealogical method had a built-in bias for lineal relationships (relationships of descent i.e. mother/child, father/child, grandmother/grandchild etc.) and against collateral relationships (relationships between people in parallel lines i.e. children of two siblings (cousins), father's sibling/child (aunt, uncle/nephew, niece), mother's sibling/child etc.) and affinal relationships (relationships through marriage). Consequently ideas about kinship connections which emphasised collaterals and affines could not easily be detected by the method (see Figure 3.1).

Another problem with the genealogical method and the pedigree thinking which it discloses is its emphasis on legitimisation. Pedigrees and genealogies were written records employed by persons to make claims to titles, property or fame rather than a method of disclosing the nature or essence of English kinship connections. As Bouquet notes 'The connotations of English pedigree – snobbishness, animal breeding, "breeding" in the noble sense – were intrinsic to the original rationale for recording genealogies' (1993: 189). The English were not of course unique in finding genealogies and pedigrees useful tools for contemporary political and economic relationships. Where I worked in Nepal with the inhabitants of a former small feudal kingdom, people of high status used similar methods to claim descent from royalty and to legitimate claims to certain plots of high yielding land (Krause 1982). The point is rather that in the study of English social organisation the cultural content of the genealogical method was not or could not be realised. Instead the method became regarded as a scientific way of studying the social systems of other people and could not be seen for what it was: a particular cultural explanation. As a consequence kinship in other societies came to be seen

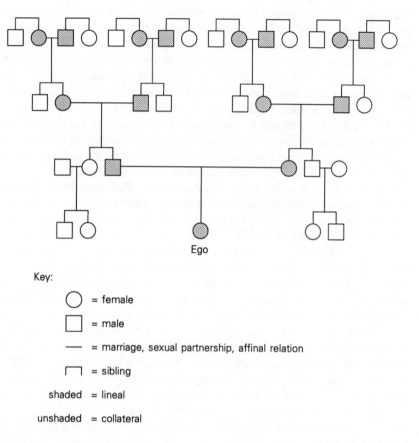

Figure 3.1   *Lineal and collateral relations from the point of view of ego*

to be based too neatly on principles of order and organisation and kinship in English and other fairly similar western cultures was considered to have vanished or to have disappeared into class or some other social phenomenon (Strathern 1984). In any case anthropologists did not find their own system worthy of study. Their own ideas and frameworks for explanation were simply seen to portray things as they really were.

MATRILINEAL DESCENT

How then did these early modern anthropologists conceptualise the world of family and kinship relationships? We can now return to Malinowski and Radcliffe-Brown and their use of Rivers's genealogical method. Both were anthropologists in the generation following that of Rivers and each developed his own ideas in a particular direction. Malinowski regarded the genealogy to be a kind of summary:

A genealogy is nothing else but a synoptic chart of a number of connected relations of kinship. Its value as an instrument of research is that it allows the investigator to put questions which he formulates to himself *in abstracto*, but can put concretely to the informant. (1961 [1922]: 15)

In fact along with this distinction between abstract and concrete Malinowski was, unlike Rivers, concerned to understand the 'flesh and blood' of kinship, which he argued is impossible to access through the skeleton of survey work (Malinowski 1961: 17). It may be the case, as Bouquet suggests, that Malinowski's approach reflected the fact that he himself was not British English, and had personal first-hand experience of at least two cultures before he came to London (Bouquet 1993: 55). Equally, however, Malinowski's style of fieldwork, known as participant observation and the context in which this fieldwork took place, predisposed him to become tuned into the day-to-day activities of family life.

Malinowski's fieldwork in the Trobriand Islands has become a famous example of matrilineal kinship. This refers to the tracing of descent from an ancestress through her daughter, her daughter's daughter and so on, that is to say in the female line. In the Trobriands this connection was important for membership of a loosely organised group of people most often referred to as a clan (*kumila*) and also important for the inheritance of property and titles and generally rights in produce from the land. This way of reckoning descent resulted in an unusual, although by no means unknown type of family organisation. The fact that relationships were traced through women did not mean that women were in control or held power, rather a Trobriand man had control of his sisters and their children and the property which they had. The situation in which women hold political power is normally called matriarchy and is different from matrilineal descent. From the point of view of inheritance of property the significant relationship was thus not that between a man and his son, but between a man and his sister's son. It was this boy who was a man's heir. Married women moved to live with their husbands, but if their sons would be likely to hold positions of managers of their estates, which according to matrilineal principles they would inherit from their maternal uncles, then these young men would be expected to move to live with their uncles once they reached puberty. This meant that a boy did not live with his father except while he was a small child, whereas girls lived with their fathers until they moved to live with their husbands and his matrilineal kinsmen and their unmarried women (see Figure 3.2). These ideas were not simply academic to Trobriand Islanders, they were symbolised and continually reconstituted through a series of complicated economic exchanges between households. Thus a man living on and cultivating his ancestral land was obliged to make regular gifts of yams (the chief crop grown by the Trobriand Islanders) to the household in which his sister was living with her husband and their children. This was a kind of symbolic acknowledgement of his sister's stake in his land, and

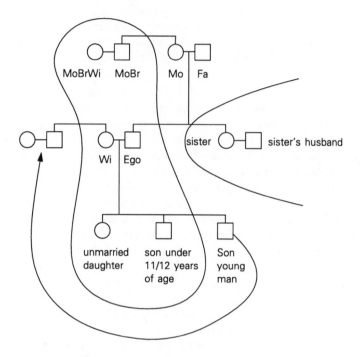

Figure 3.2 *High status Trobriand household*

it was also an affirmation of the affinal relations (relationships through marriage) between the two brothers-in-law and their kin-groups. It was also a welcome addition to the income of the sister's household.

As a result of the pattern of residence and of the principle of matrilineal descent a cross-section of Trobriand households included several different types reflecting different stages of the Trobriand life cycle. There would for example be households which contained a boy, his small sister, his mother, his father and his father's sister's son, this man's wife and possibly his children if he had any. Or there would be households which contained a husband and a wife, their sons and daughters and the husband's maternal uncle and his wife. Or there were households, particularly of low status, which contained a man and his wife, his parents and his children. This was because boys might choose to stay with their fathers if they did not have much property or any title to inherit from their maternal uncle. There might even be households which looked exactly like the nuclear ones we are so used to and which family therapists frequently meet in the consulting room (Powell 1960; Weiner 1976).

The existence of this matrilineal kinship principle did not mean that Trobrianders did not recognise relationships which were not matrilineal. Malinowski was well aware of the deep emotional conflict which exists in

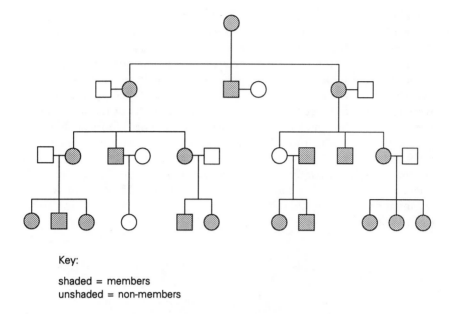

Key:

shaded = members
unshaded = non-members

Figure 3.3   *A hypothetical matrilineage or a Trobriand subclan*

matrilineal societies between a man's emotional attachment to his children and the rules of inheritance which prevent a son from inheriting property and status from his father (Malinowski 1929). This awareness led to his preoccupation with the Oedipus complex, but it was also expressed through his interest in the emotions and sentiments of family life. Family life was thus at the centre of his investigation and principles for wider kinship groups and social structure were seen to originate in close family relationships. These same principles were seen to structure and organise the subclan or *dala* (see Figure 3.3). Among the Triobriands the subclan was much more important for local organisation than was the clan. A subclan consisted of men related through their mothers, their mother's mothers, their mother's mother's mothers and so on, the sisters of these men and the children of these sisters. This group was identified with a sacred place in a territory which is the spot were the ancestress is supposed to have emerged and it included both living and dead members. Each *dala* had a territory which was managed by one of the men of the subclan and subclans were also ranked as aristocrats and commoners. Because of this corporate ownership of land the exchanges of yams between households connected by marriage described above were in fact exchanges between subclans. In this way and through many other presentations and reciprocal exchanges households, families and larger kin-groups were tied together in continuing obligations, reciprocal exchanges and dependence.

The Trobrianders have been studied by several ethnographers since Malinowski and each have contributed valuable insight, in particular into

the complexity and dynamics of Trobriand kinship and social organisation. Malinowski's portrayal of a society in which tensions and conflicts
between individuals at the level of households and families were cancelled
out by the operation of clear principles of order at more inclusive levels
is, however, a good example of anthropology as it was practised in the
decades after Rivers. Different types of social and kinship organisation
were seen to be different although equally valid ways of fulfilling human
needs in an orderly and non-conflictual fashion. The Trobriand Islands is
probably one of the most famous of matrilineal cases, and while they
often seem to have become an example of anthropological exotica, there
are many other societies where relationships traced through women
operate to varying degrees, and the issues which this type of kinship
organisation raise for thinking about family relationships cannot be so
easily dismissed.

SOCIETY AS AN ORGANISM AND THE MOTHER'S BROTHER

Radcliffe-Brown too accepted the existence of the family group as a
departure for kinship studies, but his approach developed in a different
direction and had a pervasive influence on the development of social
anthropological theory in Britain. Radcliffe-Browns's fieldwork was not
extensive and by his own admission he did not make much use of
genealogies (Radcliffe-Brown 1922). His interests in this area lay rather in
his personal wish to create an impression that he was 'by lineage and
upbringing, an English country gentleman' as Leach, one of his pupils, has
observed (quoted in Bouquet 1993: 57). It is, for example, well known
that this ambition influenced him to change his name from Brown to
Radcliffe-Brown. He emphasised order and a systematic view of kinship
even more than Malinowski. In this his methodology was influenced by
French sociologists, such as Durkheim and Mauss. He saw a tendency in
primitive societies, which did not exist in his own contemporary England,
to merge the individual with the group to which he or she belongs and
assumed that behaviour and attitudes which could be observed between
certain individuals could be extended towards all members of the group.
In Radcliffe-Brown's anthropology there was a great deal of talk about
groups, their stability, continuity and their social organisation (Kuper
1982) and little talk about individuals. There was much discussion of
roles, rights and duties and little about the self, identity, motivation and
meaning. It was a kind of 'natural science of society' (Radcliffe-Brown
1950) with societies likened to organisms in which institutions served the
function of keeping the whole thing operating in a coherent and orderly
fashion without conflict. Social structure was the arrangement of persons
in a system of social positions and social organisation was considered to be
a system of roles and activities. Emotions and inclinations, which it was
acknowledged individuals feel from time to time, were considered to be

brought into line and checked by social institutions and traditions which constrained not only what individuals could do but also the way they felt and behaved. Institutions and traditions in turn were thought to express the order in society.

Let us look at a concrete example. Like Malinowski, Radcliffe-Brown was interested in the mother's brother. He noticed that the way the mother's brother is treated by his nephew (the sister's son) varies in different societies but also that there seems to be a pattern. When as amongst the Trobrianders the mother's brother represents authority, he tends to be obeyed and feared by his nephew and he has of course certain rights over him. This contrasts with the way the Trobriand boy is treated by his own father, who indulges and spoils him and will do what he can to slip him a bit of property or other goodies which legally belong to his own sister's son. Where, on the other hand, the father is the source of authority and the relationship between the father and the son is distant and formal, as was the case among the Bathonga about whom Radcliffe-Brown (1924) wrote, and as is also the case among the Hindus I worked with in Nepal (Krause 1980) and in many other North Indian societies, then the relationship between the mother's brother and his nephew and indeed his niece is characterised by softness, indulgence and even sometimes by jokes and pranks. Indeed, sometimes the mother's brother may be the only person of an older generation with whom a person can indulge familiarity and not be restricted by the need to show respect. In other words the two sets of attitudes are inversely correlated. Radcliffe-Brown's explanation was that the choice of oppositions depended on the principle of descent which operated in a given society. The avunculate, as the relationship between the mother's brother and the sister's son was called, was in this way seen to be an institution which had two functions: it channelled and moulded individual sentiments and emotions and it reinforced positions occupied by persons in the social structure.

PATRILINEAL KINSHIP

There is no doubt about the recognition of the mother's brother in the way different people in different societies the world over think about kinship. Equally important is another relative in a similar although mirror opposite position, namely the father's sister. These two relatives are collaterals and we have already seen how they are not easily accommodated by the genealogical method, by the pedigree or indeed by the family therapist's genogram. Before we return to this in more detail we need to look at another kinship principle which is more common than matrilineal kinship, but which is not quite the mirror opposite of the Trobriand situation.

This is patrilineal kinship and it refers to the principle that relationships are traced through the father to the father's father and the father's father's father and so on (see Figure 3.4). While patrilineal relationships refer to

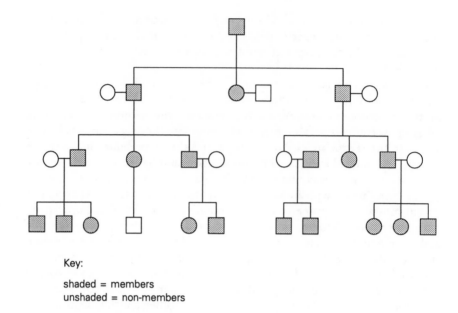

Key:

shaded = members
unshaded = non-members

Figure 3.4   *A hypothetical patrilineage*

relationships traced in this way, a patrilineage is a group of people who all can trace descent through their fathers and father's fathers to a common ancestor. This may be enough to define all these people as a group, but they may also take part in other activities together and be more or less corporate.

At lake Rara in the far west of Nepal where I worked as an ethnographer, people who could trace patrilineal descent to a common ancestor called themselves *hamata* (relations of the bone). This group of people, including mothers, widows, unmarried sisters and daughters, all sacrificed to and worshipped the same goddess together and they were all expected to avoid certain foods and physical contact with certain relatives after the birth and death of lineage members. The senior men performed rituals for their fathers and patrilineal ancestors together (*shraddh*) in order to ensure the status of these as ancestors and the status of themselves as descendants, and each smaller family unit had inherited and could trace the ownership of the land they worked back to a common ancestor. Patrilineal relationships thus were not only reckoned for the tracing of descent. They also determined the inheritance of property, titles, political positions and, as we shall see, the physical make up of the child. In patrilineal societies the rights of women in these matters may vary. Among the Thakuris and Chetris who lived at Rara, land and movable property was inherited patrilineally giving all sons an equal share while mothers and unmarried daughters and sisters had rights to produce from the land, that is, maintenance. Widows could always claim such rights from the *hamata* but when daughters and sisters married they would be given a dowry as their share of the inheritance and henceforth they were considered to be members of their husband's *hamata*. At this point they also moved away to live with their husband and his patrilineal kin. Some households in the Rara area were what might be referred to as an extended household including a husband and a wife, their married son and his wife and small children and perhaps an unmarried daughter. A few households consisted of married brothers, their wives and children, although in these it was generally expected that the household would break up and partition the property shortly. However, the majority of households were nuclear, but as was the case in the matrilineal example this did not mean that the principles of organisation and the way household members conceptualised their relationships were identical to the way these would be conceptualised by an English nuclear family.

It may be difficult for us to imagine what it feels like to live in a small-scale society where kinship and descent define where you live and how you should relate and behave towards your neighbours or the people in your social world. We seem to have a great deal of choice in who we interact with and connect up with and in comparison may find it difficult to comprehend the sorts of tensions which may arise out of other situations. In contrast with the matrilineal situation where the structural tensions revolve around the father/son/mother's brother relationship and perhaps indirectly involves the mother, one area of tension in a patrilineal situation concerns women. If women become members of their husband's kin-groups upon marriage and are expected to renounce membership in their natal families one can expect relationships between parents and their daughters and between brothers and sisters to reflect this strain (see Figure 3.5). On the other hand, if women retain membership in their families and kin-groups of origin then one can expect that members of kin-groups and lineages develop conflicting loyalties. Of course some recognition of non-unilineal relationships are not necessarily disruptive. At Rara, for example, where women became members of their husbands' kin-groups after marriage, some residual links to non-lineal kin were still highly valued. Thus the father's sister was singled out for special treatment, special gifts and special attention even though she did not perform any of the activities which defined the patrilineal kin-group. Similarly I also knew many examples of sisters-in-law (a woman and her brother's wife) who got on really well and were best friends despite the structural tension inherent in these relationships.

VISIBLE KINSHIP

The general points which emerged from the work of Malinowski and Radcliffe-Brown were immensely influential on subsequent anthropological work, in particular in Britain. Earlier writers with anthropological

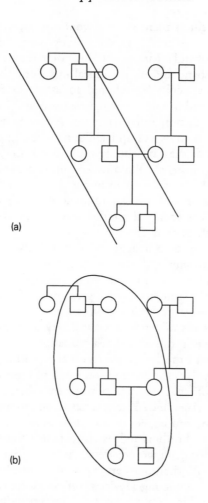

(a)

(b)

Figure 3.5   *Tension in patriliny: (a) married or cohabiting women stay*
members of their own kin-group; (b) married or cohabiting women become
members of their husband's kin-group

interests such as Maine, McLennan and Morgan (the latter had had a great
influence on Engels's views (Engels 1972 [1884])) had known about
patrilineal and matrilineal organisation but they had largely considered
these in an evolutionary perspective and sometimes as left overs from
earlier historical periods. With the development of ethnographic fieldwork came the notion that all parts of a society 'hang together' or 'fit'
and serve a function, even if this function was a general one, namely to
further integration and stability. At the same time those aspects of other
societies and cultures which were most different from the society of the
ethnographer received the most attention. Thus the unilineal principles of
descent (matrilineal or patrilineal) came to be seen as great discoveries and

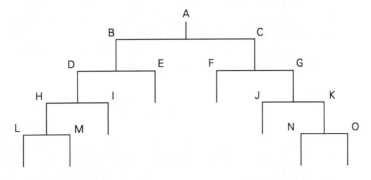

Figure 3.6 *A patrilineal Nuer clan. Evans-Pritchard's depiction of a Nuer clan as a genealogical structure, in which the letters in the diagram represent persons from whom the clan and its segments trace their descent and from whom they often take their name (Evans-Pritchard 1940: 193). (Reproduced here by permission of Oxford University Press)*

kinship came to be seen to lie at the root of social structure. Add to this Radcliffe-Brown's insistence on the necessity of stability, continuity and definite group membership (Radcliffe-Brown 1940) and it is not difficult to understand how kin-groups came to be considered corporations which transcended the lives and motivations of individual persons. Relationships between such groups, for example between lineages, subclans and clans as shown in Figure 3.6 came to be represented as if they were genealogies. As Bouquet aptly remarks: '"Pedigree" seems to have made way for "paradigm"' (Bouquet 1993: 75).

Students of Radcliffe-Brown and Malinowski pursued these ideas in different ways and many brought home ethnographic data which sat uneasily with the orthodox interpretation of this model. For example Firth (1936) and Fortes (1949) were both concerned with people who were related not unilineally but bilaterally through both their parents as consanguines (common blood) and Fortes distinguished between filiation which referred to the relationship between a parent and a child and descent which he defined as the connection between the domestic and the socio-political domain. Perhaps the most spectacular example of how what came to be labelled 'descent theory' survived in the face of empirical data which suggested otherwise was Evans-Pritchard's work among the Nuer of Sudan. Evans-Pritchard's own ethnography suggested that the way people considered themselves related to other members of a group (a lineage or a clan) was based both on relations of descent and on relationships based on neighbourly and friendly feelings and connections (Evans-Pritchard 1940). Yet Evans-Pritchard's portrayal of the Nuer became famous in anthropology as an example of a segmentary lineage system, in which groups of people whose membership was considered to be defined strictly on the basis of unilineal descent (usually patrilineal descent) unite against each other in political struggles often to the point of deadly fighting. The idea of corporate kinship groups clearly appealed both to the anthropologist and his audience (Bouquet 1993: 74) and despite much criticism (Barnes 1967; Kuper 1982; Scheffler 1985) lineage theory has continued to be influential.

WHAT WAS LEFT OUT

There were, however, societies such as the Yakö (Forde 1950) where people reckoned descent both through their father's line and through their mother's line and although posing a challenge to the image of enduring, exclusive membership of a corporation this was accommodated by naming the principle of organisation cognatic descent. In other words the descent model with its key idiom of unilineal descent was again placed in the foreground. In societies where relationships between cognates were either not highlighted or were not brought to the attention of the ethnographer these relationships were largely ignored. Just as the genealogical method could not easily detect collaterals the unilineal descent model could not accommodate children and descendants of brothers and sisters (mother's brother and father's sister) except as a residual category. Similarly, in those societies where kinship connections were traced bilaterally, that is to say through both fathers and mothers including of course most European societies, kinship did not seem to have any significance beyond the level of the elementary or the nuclear family.

Nor could the descent model accommodate relationships which arise through marriage. Radcliffe-Brown saw marriage as a disruptive process full of stresses and strains and as something which had to be kept under control by the strength of unilineal kinship principles. As a result, again echoing the genealogical method and the genogram, affines or in-laws could not easily be included in the model. Immediate affines became kin for the next generation and eventually were subsumed by and merged with full members of the kin-group and in any case they were considered to be structurally unimportant. This view was challenged spectacularly by French anthropologists, notably C. Lévi-Strauss and L. Dumont who in what has become known as alliance theory, began to develop ideas about how repeated marriages may link kin-groups into permanent relationships which may be of political and social significance. Alliance theory thus contained a dynamic which lineage theory lacked. In the latter, time was hardly considered as long as the social order was reproduced while in the former there was a recognition that over time certain practices generated wider patterns, some of which were more stable than others. Perhaps most importantly for my purpose here, because of its emphasis on marriage choices and preferences, alliance theory opened up the possibility of separating strategies for kinship practice from official blueprints about how things ought to be. In other words alliance theory began to make it possible for kinship theorists to examine how rules might be broken and new rules incorporated.

While descent theory thus left out of view a whole range of familial and social relationships as if they did not exist, the anthropologists of the day also did not realise the effect which their own backgrounds and explanations had on the theories generated to explain kinship in societies, which in every way appeared to be very different from their own. The influence of the pedigree on the genealogical method has already been mentioned and the emphasis on the need for continuity and stability in social organisation in face of the chaos and the confusion which reigned during the pre- and inter-war years in Europe is another example. Anthropology was considered a science modelled on the natural sciences in the sense that the analytical concepts used were believed to be inherent in the data. In this respect there was just one voice of dissent and this belonged to someone familiar to family therapists, namely Gregory Bateson. Bateson recognised that analytical concepts were merely one way of organising ideas about the material and so in his analysis of the *naven* ceremony amongst the Iatmul of New Guinea he used three different explanatory perspectives: the sociological, the ethological and the eidiological (Bateson 1958 [1932]). Unfortunately, at the time his method was largely ignored by his fellow anthropologists.

ENGLISH KINSHIP

I have noted how anthropologists of the pre-, middle and post-war periods were surprisingly uninterested in their own kinship. In part this was because kinship in western societies, in contrast to kinship in the societies which anthropologists studied at the time, was considered a non-political phenomenon internal to the (mainly nuclear) family. What was seen to be kinship in other societies was in the western setting considered to be social and lie '"beyond" kinship, impinging as a different order of phenomena' (Strathern 1992b: 92). Further, since English kinship is cognatic or bilateral, that is, gives equal weight to tracing connections through two biological parents, both mother and father, it appeared to consist of a naturally undifferentiated set of relatives and as the way things really were in the natural world. There was therefore no need to use social theory to understand it (Strathern 1992a, 1992b: 89). Consequently English kinship had vanished and 'disappeared' into class or some other social phenomenon (Strathern 1984). These conclusions were strongly supported by the first major study of middle-class English kinship by Firth, Hubert and Forge (1969). This was regardless of the fact that cognatic and bilateral kinship was found elsewhere in the world, and as we have seen, that much effort was put into understanding the social significance of this in the context of descent theory. Bouquet considers this a puzzle,

I have suggested that the British social anthropologist's voice was decidedly middle-class, and that the enormous interest in the kinship of others fits uncomfortably with an image of middle-class 'kinshiplessness'. (1993: 82)

Both she and Marilyn Strathern have pointed to principles which are embedded in the English view of kinship and which have been influential in organising the development of kinship theory and since family as well as individual psychotherapy theory also originates from largely Anglo-Saxon middle-class roots we need to take a look at this cultural account.

The idea of pedigree is in English associated with selective breeding as one might undertake with horses or dogs and suggests a genetic model of relationships. Bouquet has examined Beatrice Potter's Peter Rabbit stories and suggests that these reveal a model for animality, personhood and distinction in English kinship deeply informed by ideas about genetics (Bouquet 1993: 185ff.). On the same point Strathern has argued that what is a preoccupation with biological as opposed to fictive or step-relationships in English kinship has recently been expressed through the debate concerning the new reproductive technologies in which priority is given to the genetic or the birthing mother (Strathern 1992a). She suggests that unlike the view in many other societies, for the English what is natural is also seen as real. Natural parents are seen as real parents even when they have not contributed to the upbringing of the children. Strathern further suggests an important theme expressed through the English view. In English society marriage is seen to be a relationship between two individuals whereas the relationship between two families which arise at marriage is generally played down. The marital union is a way to start a family, that is to say marriage is about reproduction. However, contrary to the Trobriand and the Rara babies who each in their own way encompass old persons, English babies are seen as new persons, new individuals with their own unique genetic make up and their own unique potential. In England kinship is about reproduction and not so much about connection (Strathern 1992a: 119) and what is being reproduced are unique individuals rather than social relationships. This is well reflected in the English system of kinship terminology (Figure 3.7) which shows the extensive use of personal names, a characteristic which is quite absent from the kinship terms of reference which I collected during my work with Hindus in the Himalayas (Figure 3.8).

In Strathern's view this theme is further refined in the English idea of the individual in the 1990s. She points to the inherent opposition between individual and society in English kinship thinking:

What I have called modernist or pluralist in this kinship thinking produced the figure of the person as an individual, made up of the physical materials that made up other individuals but recombining them in a unique way. In this sense, the person was a whole individual. But what made the person a whole individual was not what made him or her part of a any wider identity. In

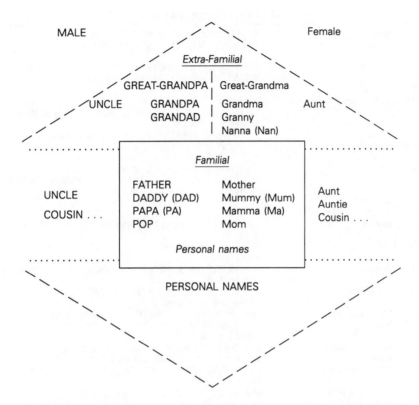

Note: The figure is arranged in generation levels. For cousins and other kin of own generation and below personal names are used.

Figure 3.7 *Terms of address to consanguine kin in 1960s middle-class London. (Reproduced by permission of Routledge from* Families and Their Relatives: Kinship in a Middle-Class Sector of London, *by R. Firth, J. Hubert and A. Forge, 1969)*

relation to society, the individual was incomplete – to be completed by socialization, relationships and convention. (Strathern 1992b: 92)

In many other societies individuals are persons *because* of the part they play in a wider collective. In England, however, individuals are parts of numerous different systems – part of the kinship system, part of the naming system and part of society – but are not seen to replicate wholly any one of these systems. Individuals are at the same time part of nature and part of society (Strathern 1992a). It is this plurality which is characteristic of 1990s English kinship for it allows for a model of kinship which at the same time places a positive value on diversity and personal choice and is able to get away with ignoring the social dimension altogether such as was expressed by Margaret Thatcher a decade ago: 'There is no such

RĀRĀ KINSHIP TERMINOLOGY[1]

1	bāje[2]	FF, MF, FFB, FMB, MMB, MFB, H of any bajai
1A	bajai	FM, MM, FMZ, MMZ, MFZ, FFZ, W of any baje
2	buwā	F
2A	jetho buwā/kāncho buwā	FeB/FyB, MZH, FFBS, FFZS, MMZS, FMBS, MZHB, WBWF, WZHF, H of hethi/kancho muwa
3	muwā	M
3A	jethi muwā/kāncho muwā	MeZ/MyZ, FeBW/FyBW, MFBD, MMBD, MFZD, MMZD, FZHZ, FBWZ, WZHM, WBWM, HBWM, HZHM, W of jetho/kāncho buwā
4	māmā, māuli	MB, MFBS, MFZS, MMZS, FBWB, MZHBWB
4A	māijyu	MBW, W of any māmā, Z of any māijyu
5	phuphu	FZ, FFZD, FFBD, FMBD, FMZD, MZHZ, FZHBW
5A	phuwājyu	ƎZH, H of any phuphu, B of any phuwājyu
6	sāsu	HM, WM, HMZe and y, WMZe and y, HMBW, WMBW, HFBW, WFBW, BWM, ZHM
6A	buhri sāsu	HFM, WFM, HMM, WMM
6B	phuphu sāsu	HFZ, WFZ
7	sasurā	HF, WF, HFBe and y, HFZH, WFZH, HMZH, WMZH, BWF, ZHF
7A	buhro sasurā	HFF, WFF, HMF, WMF
7B	māuli sasurā	HMB, WMB
8	dhāi/bhāi[3]	B, FBS, FZS, MBS, MZS, ZHZH, WBWB, WZH, HZH, H of bhāujyu/buāri
9	didi/bahini	Z, FBD, FZD, MBD, MZD, BWBW, WBW, HZHZ, HBW, W of any bhinajyu/juwain
10	bhāujyu/buāri	BW, BWZ, BWBWBW, ZHZ, (ms), W of dhāi/bhāi
10A	buāri	SW, SWZ, BSW, ZSW, DHZ, ZSWZ, SSWM, WBSW, DDHM, DSWM
11	bhinājyu/juwāin	ZH, ZHB, ZHZHZH, WBWZH, H of didi/bahini
11A	juwāin	DH, SWB, BDH, ZSWB, DDHF, SSWF, SDHƎ
12	jethan/sāla (ms)	WB, WFBS, WMBS, WFZS, WMZS, BWB, any B of own W, any B of BW
12A	jethali/sāli (ms)	WZ, WFZD, WFBD, WMZD, any Z of W
12B	jethan (fs)	HeB, any eB of H
12C	Jethi (fs)	HeZ, any eZ of H
13	devar (fs)	HyB, any yB of H
14	nanda (fs)	HyZ, ZHZ, any yZ of H
15	srimān (fs)	H
15A	srimāti (ms)	W
16	choro	S, BS (ms), FBSS (ms), MZSS (ms), ZS (fs), MBDS (fs), MZDS (fs), HBS, WZS, SWZH, DHZH
16A	chori	D, BD (ms), FBSD (ms), FZSD (ms), MZSD (ms), ZD (fs), MBDD (fs), MZDD (fs), HBD, WZD, SWBW, DHBW
17	bhatija	BS (ms), HBS (fs)
17A	bhatiji	BD (ms), HBD (fs)
18	bhānja	ZS (ms), HZS (fs)
18A	bhānji	ZH (ms), HZD (fs)
19	bhadau	BS (fs), ZS (fs)
19A	bhadai	BD (fs), ZH (fs)
19B	bhadau sāla	WBS (ms), WZS (ms)
19C	bhadai sāli	WBD (ms), WZD (ms)
20	nāti	S of choro/chori, bhatija/bhatiji, bhanja/bhanji, bhaudau/bhadai
20A	nātini	D of choro/chori, bhatija/bhatiji, bhanja/bhanji, bhadau/bhadai

1 Only terms of reference are included here. Generally terms of address are the same as those for reference except that in the former the honorific – *jyu* is added when a senior is addressed.
2 With minor variations all the terms presented in this table are used by both Chetris and Thakuris.
3 The former term denotes elder than ego, the latter younger than ego.

Figure 3.8 *Kinship terms of reference used by Hindus in North West Nepal in the 1970s*

thing as society. There are individual men and women and there are families' (Margaret Thatcher, 1987, quoted in Strathern 1992a: 144, 211). According to Strathern's analysis this is clearly expressed in contemporary morality. If society has disappeared and family life has been reduced to a life-style and the individual has been reinstated, morality must be seen to come from within. The individual is seen to know naturally what to do and attention to one's own interests is now a virtue. Accordingly context as an idea of any importance has also gone (Strathern 1992a).

KINSHIP IN FAMILY THERAPY

For family therapists and for therapists generally all this ought to be food for thought. On the one hand, 1990s English kinship poses a challenge to systemic ideas and to the notion of relationships which generally informs systemic family therapy practice. On the other, family therapy itself has also been profoundly influenced by the ideology of its practitioners, who if not exclusively English have tended to be upper or middle class and significantly influenced by Anglo-American traditions. We can now for example see the definition of a family quoted in the beginning of this chapter in a new light. We can also find many similarities between the genealogical method as outlined by Rivers and practised by several generations of anthropologists and the genogram used by family therapists. Finally we can now understand the reluctance in family therapy to study general principles of kinship more clearly.

In many ways Malinowski and Radcliffe-Brown and many of their students did exactly what Bateson later warned against. They confused the name of a thing with the thing itself. Indeed, as we have seen, their refusal to consider kinship theory as a way of conceptualising the material rather than as inherent in the data itself meant that they could not easily make a distinction between the way people organised themselves on the ground and became motivated to action and the schema the anthropologists used to understand social and cultural practices and institutions. This blind spot was further aggravated by the unrecognised influence of their own (unstudied and unquestioned) ideas about kinship relationships which despite influence from abroad remained dominated by English ideology. This is how it came about that the societal aspect of English kinship, that which was seen to socialise, mould and influence, but which was not seen to completely submerge or constitute an individual person, received the most emphasis. Since the English idea implied a sphere which imposed order and continuity on what was otherwise seen as diverse and unique individuals, it was this which became a defining characteristic of social organisation everywhere. One of the main assumptions of twentieth-century English kinship thus also became an assumption of anthropology. Descent was thought to be a natural fact and a unilineal version (matrilineal or patrilineal) the most efficient way of generating orderly and enduring societies. Such order was in English ideas reflected in the cultural institution of the pedigree, but this was also conflated with the scientific principles seen to operate in the natural world. As far as English society was concerned such order was seen to be generated in a different way and kinship to be a vanishing or at least a residual institution. Since anthropologists had to go abroad to find what they called kinship this area of enquiry also escaped family therapy and psychotherapy generally because practitioners in these disciplines rarely had reason to look beyond their own cultural limits. Consequently for them kinship simply did not exist.

The same assumptions as those made by anthropologists can also be seen to operate in the standard use of the genogram in family therapy. McGoldrick and Gerson describe the genogram in the following terms:

> Genograms are graphic pictures of the family history and patterns, showing the basic structure, family demographics, functioning and relationships. They are a shorthand used to depict the family patterns at a glance. (1989: 164)

They give an example of how genograms can be used by describing the life history of Sigmund Freud and they start and proceed in exactly the way outlined by Rivers: that is to say with the marriage of Freud's parents and then on to the children from this marriage. Freud's father had been married twice before and the offspring of these marriages are duly noted. On the whole the genograms have a lineal rather than collateral emphasis and affines or in-laws (notably the relatives of Freud's own wife) are presented as their own lineal group of relatives rather than as collaterals for the next generation. Freud's family relationships included two important affinal ones: that between himself and his wife's sister and the marriage between his own sister and his wife's brother. However despite the importance to Freud of both his youngest daughter, Anna, and his wife's sister, Minna, McGoldrick and Gerson do not comment on the relationship between the aunt and the niece. In Freud's case this may be justified by the material, but as we have seen in other societies collateral relatives, such as those originating from brother/sister relationships may be of great significance. Amongst the matrilineal Trobrianders and the patrilineal Chetris and Thakuris at Rara and the Kaluli of New Guinea the relationship between a brother and a sister is important structurally as well as recognised in personal lives. It is doubtful whether the genogram automatically can pick up the significance of these relationships, and therefore obvious how this procedure may lead to important oversights in intra-cultural and particularly in cross-cultural work.

This brings me to another point which concerns the extraordinary choice of example made by McGoldrick and Gerson. One can readily understand the attraction of trying elegantly to provide insight into the background and family relationships of a public personality such as Freud. However, what the authors do not highlight in their account is that the bulk of the material to which they refer derives from previously published biographical accounts by authors, some of whom knew Freud better than others, and also from Freud's edited letters. They do not seem to be aware of the public nature of this account: the material they use is official and has already been legitimised. It has been published previously and although the authors do not point this out, must have been subject to permission from Freud's estate as well as other legal restrictions. It is not therefore a record depicting a live process of how Freud himself saw his family relationships, of how these relationships operated during his life and impeded on his own sense of kinship and family, however much the authors would like to describe it in this way and however much they assume that they can understand the motivations behind the events. As Bourdieu has suggested legitimate and practical relationships may serve different functions: 'practical kin make marriages, offical kin celebrate them' (1990: 168).

Genealogical relationships, or rather those relationships which are marked in the genealogy, may conceal practical relationships, that is to say the relationships of blood, sweat and tears and of everyday life, so that these do not become accessible in public and legitimate accounts. As McGoldrick and Gerson show through their choice of example and as has been shown in anthropology again and again, unless it is used with great care, sensitivity and imagination, the genogram and the genealogical method produce material which is no more than the legitimate account. And the critique may be taken even further for to accept such an account as the real thing is to repeat the mistake of the early anthropologists and to skew the material in the direction of regularity and order.

Bourdieu makes two additional points about practical relationships. Firstly, practical relationships are relationships which are maintained because their maintenance has an immediate practical (economic, political or symbolic) function to those who engage in them. This is not, however, simply a matter of individual preference and choice as if persons existed in a vacuum. Rather, and this is his second point, practical relationships are also a product of the history of the economic and symbolic changes which have taken place through previous generations (Bourdieu 1977 [1972]). One may term this tradition and it means that practical relationships today are influenced or generated by the legitimate relationships of the past. In the context of this chapter this means that the ideology of kinship relationships as these are seen to have functioned over years is also important for our understanding of the present. It also means that despite the over-simplification the work on patrilineal and matrilineal descent cannot be dismissed altogether.

KINSHIP AS A CULTURAL CONSTRUCTION

What then is the significance of this for psychotherapy? Firstly, it should assist us to recognise that our own notions of kinship are culturally constructed. As we have seen the English kinship system is characterised by an idea that biological relationships traced bilaterally and equally through both parents provide a conceptualisation of family relationships as a sort of background of 'real' or 'natural' relationships against which an individual person can choose and generate his or her own unique trajectory. We (and here I include the notions which I myself hold and which are derived from Scandinavia and Northern Europe) may talk about blood relationships as being a necessary condition for this recruitment. But for us this notion of 'blood' is a bilateral one. In other places such a notion of 'blood', if it exists, may be defined differently, for example only the blood which flows through the father or only blood through the mother. In yet other places again it is not blood but some different substance which is significant as was the case for the Thakuris and Chetris of Nepal, who refer to connections of the bone, and in yet other places it may not be a bodily substance which is emphasised but a social act or a ritual which define relations between kin. Similarly in many societies kinship affiliation may be acquired not only by birth but also by marriage, initiation, adoption or indeed through some other sustained pattern of interaction. The differences are subtle enough to be easily overlooked, yet significant enough to seriously question our own notions of family connections and relatedness.

Any therapist working cross-culturally will meet these issues regularly. I met with the following Bangladeshi family over a fairly long period of time. In this family it was the mother and wife who had alerted the concern of professionals. Mrs Ullah was referred to the service in which I work by her GP because her family and in particular her husband was complaining about her slowness and her tendency to check things over and over. She lived with her three children and her husband. Her eldest son was 18, her daughter 14 and her youngest son 10. Mrs Ullah herself was 34 and one of nine siblings, three brothers and six sisters, the children of a high ranking army officer. The family was well respected, but had also met misfortune. Mrs Ullah's youngest brother had died as a child, her father had died when she was 13 and soon after that her eldest brother who was also an army officer was killed in action. At the time she was referred she had one brother left but he had become bankrupt and lived in a different part of Bangladesh from the family home and neither Mrs Ullah nor her mother had much contact with him. Mrs Ullah's mother had succeeded in marrying her to the son of another army officer, although of lower rank than her father and brother. She was 15 at the time of the marriage and at 16 she had her first child. Mrs Ullah's mother and sisters lived in Bangladesh. Mr Ullah was the eldest son of five siblings, three brothers and two sisters. Both his younger brothers and his mother lived in England whereas his sisters lived in Bangladesh with their husbands and children. I met with the family and began to try to understand the situation with the help of an interpreter.

In the first session Mrs Ullah complained of being unhappy and that no one in the family would listen to her. Her husband complained that she was ill in the head in some way and he demanded an X-ray and other physical investigations. An argument broke out in this session in which Mrs Ullah spoke about sorcery and her husband dismissed such ideas as old fashioned and without relevance in England.

In a subsequent session in which her husband was not present Mrs Ullah was more forthcoming about the way she considered her own predicament. From the time of her marriage her affines, her husband's brothers and mother, had been against her. They had voiced their opposition to the marriage itself but her husband had been in love and had wanted to go ahead and her own mother had also been keen to get her married into a good family. From the very beginning of the marriage she had lived with her affines and they had physically abused her. Her husband had sometimes stood up for her, but later on when he came to England on his own the abuse had been completely unchecked. Not long after she had joined her husband in England he had also started to be violent and verbally abusive to her. At the time of referral she considered that her in-laws had practised some sort of sorcery by putting something into her food and that this was why life for her was so unhappy and useless and why her husband beat her.

In order to begin to understand the way Mrs Ullah saw her own situation and therefore the possible ways out of it, it was important to remember that the kinship structure in the part of Bangladesh where she came from was patrilineal and that when women marry they are considered to become full members of their husband's kin-group (Fruzetti 1990 [1982]; Gardner 1995). From the point of view of Mrs Ullah her husband's kin were her nearest relatives and she did not, in the way an English woman might, have rights and expectations of redress from her own family. Thus, for example, when I commented on her bruises and she told me about a particularly savage beating she had received from her husband I explained to her that it is illegal in England for husbands to treat their wives in this manner and asked her why she had not telephoned the police, since she knew of other wives who had done just that. In response Mrs Ullah's eyes filled with tears and she said that all this time she had not said because she came from such a good *bangsa* and if only her father had been alive she might have had some way out. *Bangsa* means family but in the widest sense. More precisely it refers to the patrilineally related group of persons who all can trace relationships to a certain male ancestor and whose standing and status is affected by the conduct of female members particularly in relation to shameful deeds or *sharom* (shame) (Gardner 1995).

Apart from pointing to the importance of a kinship principle Mrs Ullah was also pointing to the particular context of her own case. Her position in relation to her husband's kin was further weakened by the composition and context of her own patrilineal kin. Her father had died before she became of marriageable age and she had no effective brothers. This particular situation had no doubt pushed Mrs Ullah's mother to make practical decisions for her daughter. Without her husband and eldest son and without close male representatives of the patrilineal kin Mrs Ullah's mother must have been worried about financial hardship and also about keeping the reputation and the status of the family. The decision to marry off her eldest daughter quickly to a respectable man in Mr Ullah's position would have seemed a good solution. If Mrs Ullah's own father had been alive his superior position also might have prevented her affines from maltreating her. As it had turned out Mrs Ullah's position in her marriage was difficult to maintain: she had to do it on her own and could not confide in her mother because this would imply criticism of her mother's choice and hence disrespect. Further since Mrs Ullah, despite being considered a member of her husband's kin-group, still represented a foreign element in that family (Fruzetti 1990) she was an obvious target for sorcery (Gardner 1991). It seemed to me that it was not difficult to understand the sorcery allegations. Mr Ullah's relatives had indeed been poisoning his wife's life right from the beginning and the reason for this may be understood to have been connected not so much with anything Mrs Ullah herself had or had not done, but rather to have been a result of her structural position in relation to these relatives and the fact that her presence had prevented a better and more lucrative affinal connection. I understood Mrs Ullah's symptoms both as an expression of her extreme unhappiness, but also as a result of a long-lasting abusive situation she had to endure both now but also during the years when she herself was developing as a young adult.

Our response to the situation was to use a combination of under-standing based on the principles outlined above for Mr Ullah's and the family's predicament and showing a strong commitment to the law which makes it illegal to beat your wife. I always showed respect for Mr Ullah, asking him whether I could speak to his children or his wife in his presence, but I also spent 90 minutes in a home visit repeating over and over again that however much reason he would have to be angry with his wife because she is slow and does not do the housework satisfactorily, in Britain today it is illegal to beat your wife for any reason whatsoever. I had notified the Domestic Violence Unit in the area and I had also let him know that I had a duty to let them know if I thought that he had hit Mrs Ullah. Eventually I and my interpreter were able to help Mr Ullah recover some self-control and the violence ceased. This then opened up a space where we could begin to address with them the history and dynamic of their relationship. I shall return to this case in Chapter 4 but for the moment I want to note the importance of understanding the predicament of Mrs Ullah and the kinship sentiments both she and her husband had expressed for work with this family.

EGO FOCUS OR ANCESTOR FOCUS

The second point which examining the kinship of other cultures high-lights for therapists concerns the focus. In Anglo-American societies we tend to think of descendants before we think of ancestors. This is clearly conveyed in the genogram, which invariably encourages an ego-focus. This focus tends to convey two corresponding notions, namely that identity is passed from parents to children, and that it is equally a matter of individual choice and ability. However, where babies are not seen to be new persons, but rather to share substances with their parents or their ancestors or where what is being reproduced is a relationship rather than a unique individual, the primary focus for the individual person in terms of how he or she traces relationships may be either relationships with ancestors or with a collectivity as a whole. In these cases identity may move up through the generations, that is to say the actions of individuals may reflect on the status or position of the ancestors instead of on to subsequent generations. An enquiry which concentrates on movement down from a marriage to the descendants of that marriage may therefore miss important and meaningful connections and therefore also misunderstand individual intentions and motivations.

A few years ago I saw a family where differences in ideas about kinship and about 'being a person' and the expectations of the children in this respect created great anguish. This family consisted of a man of Norwegian descent and a Gujerati woman and their three daughters. The marriage had been difficult for years but the crisis heightened when the mother and the eldest daughter, who was 15, began to fight physically. This was when the family came for therapy. Mr Olsson's mother was English whereas his father was Norwegian. His mother had died when he was 11 and his father had gone back to Norway as soon as he and his elder sister had been able to manage on their own. Nowadays Mr.Olsson visited his father in Norway at least once a year. Mrs Olsson was the eldest of many siblings. As a young woman she had eloped with a lover to a large Indian city. The relationship did not last and she had come to London where she had worked hard as a secretary. Her father had recently died and she had received her share of the inheritance from her brothers, who had partitioned the ancestral estate.

The fights between Mrs Olsson and her eldest daughter focused on age-appropriate behaviour and sexual modesty in public places. During the therapy Mrs Olsson recognised that she was now seeing the position which her own mother had been in when she herself as a young girl had wanted more freedom and had eventually eloped. She recognised that now she was addressing the same issues.

Mr Olsson strongly took the side of his daughter in these matters emphasising her need to be the same as her peer-group so that she could have the same possibilities and the same potential in her own development. For Mrs Olsson it was not so much that her daughter challenged a bashful attitude to heterosexual intimacy. In fact both she and her husband agreed that their sexlife had been brilliant and she had been very active in this. They spoke openly about this in my presence during the therapy. What really pained Mrs Olsson and what she found impossible to accept was that her daughter refused her authority and ridiculed her cultural view. She described this as a blow to her self-esteem and to the respect that she currently received from her Indian friends and could expect to receive if she was to return home. At the time I made a note to myself that whatever the difficulties which Mrs Olsson had experienced in her own childhood with her own parents, the problem for her now was also that the daughter's attitude and behaviour seriously challenged the authority of the group which Mrs Olsson used for internal reference.

This aspect of Mrs Olsson's cultural background was also exactly what seriously threatened Mr Olsson's view of kinship relationships between parents and their children, since this would mean that his daughter (and by extension he himself) would have to accept to be different and perhaps not compete equally with others. The battle with notions of sameness and difference in this family took on such intensity that the husband used racist language towards his wife and she reported him to the police for racial abuse and the marriage ended with a long protracted divorce.

The power inequality in this marriage meant that the husband set the agenda. Indeed the husband felt so completely undermined by his wife's more collective view that any effort on my part for the family to take seriously this minority view led to the husband sabotaging my interventions. My input probably meant that the divorce came sooner and quicker than it would have done had the couple not been in therapy, but the main point is that the power inequality also facilitated the suppression of differences in the operation of kinship connections and that this became an issue of racism. In this way kinship can be seen to strike close to the bone.

HOUSEHOLD, FAMILY AND KINSHIP PRINCIPLES

In order to understand the motivation and actions of persons, therapists need to have some idea of the structure and organisation of social and family relationships which serve as a backdrop for individual activity and practice. Therapists also need to be sensitive to the possibility that attachments and connections between relatives may operate in a different way from the ways with which they are themselves familiar or from the way these are depicted in Anglo-American kinship. Even in Anglo-American kinship the ideological emphasis on the nuclear family is not sustained in practice, where divorce and separation is becoming increasingly common giving rise to many different household forms and to fluidity in definitions of kinship relationships according to access, contact and economic contributions in reconstituted families (Strathern 1992a; Simpson 1994; Gorell Barnes et al. 1997). In English kinship this takes place against a background and an ideology of bilateral connections in which a person is herself the focus, but other people in other societies with different cultural ideas may emphasise some relationships rather than others, one side rather than the other or one side for some purposes and the other side for other purposes. Which relationship is emphasised may also vary according to context. In this way connections between people who consider themselves kin may not only be significant to family relationships but may also be of crucial economic and political significance for the wider organisation of society. Households, families, subclans and clans may all be based on similar principles and who is and is not significant to each other in day-to-day activities is something which needs to be decided practically, that is to say who does what with whom, who shares what with whom, who helps, who cooks, who does what work, who builds the house and so on. While this kind of enquiry reveals material interesting and relevant to therapists it is also likely to expose salient principles about intimate relationships.

These last points are not, however, easily recognised by family or individual psychotherapists and part of the reason for this is the focus on 'the family' rather than on kinship. As we have seen the insistence that kinship in Anglo-American societies is relegated to the internal relations of the nuclear family is a cultural construction. This *is* the English view of kinship and its acceptance as natural fact obscures the emphasis on the incompleteness of the unsocialised individual which lies at the heart of English kinship thinking and ideology.

It is probably always going to be a dubious undertaking to aim to define 'the family' and 'the household' in any absolute way. The relationship between family and household will always require detailed social and historical analysis and any general definition is therefore likely to restrict rather than illuminate understanding of specific local situations. The term 'nuclear' family obscures more than it reveals (Moore 1988). It is impossible to tell from the composition of an elementary family what the wider kinship principles which influence organisation, relationships and sentiments might be. Nuclear households may exist in societies where kinship is traced bilaterally as well as in societies where a unilineal principle receives emphasis. As kinship refers to a variety of relationships, some of which may be crucial for the understanding of the wider context of families, it seems high time that psychotherapists recognise the limitations of classification and the limitations of the conflation of families with households. Instead we need to be curious both about the official and about the practical aspects of other ways of organising family relationships. Only then will we be able to access the external and internal worlds of our clients.

4

Families, Attachments and Emotions

In the previous chapter I showed that there has been a tendency in anthropology and in systemic psychotherapy for certain types of accounts, mainly those which are based on a priori assumptions of objectivity and scientificity, to gloss over real life processes and to present a distorted picture. If those who engage in this practice also occupy a dominant position, such as the structural functionalists did in British anthropology, this distorted picture is also likely to become dominant theory. The mainstream structural functionalists failed to distinguish the 'thing from its name' and at the same time ignored how models were practically applied. This blind spot was not detectable partly because English kinship was thought to have vanished and to be concerned only with relationships inside the elementary family. As kinship stood for social principles of organisation, elementary family relationships came to be seen to be psychological and emotional, but not social, and on the whole they were not of great interest to British anthropologists. True to fashion, however the internal family relationships, together with the attachments, emotions and motivations with which they were seen to be implicated, came to be considered as universals. In this respect structural functional anthropology and traditional family therapy made similar assumptions (Maranhao 1984; Krause 1993).

I have repeatedly referred to Bateson because he occupied a unique position in both anthropology and family therapy. In fact Bateson was influenced by Radcliffe-Brown (Bouquet 1993; Nuckolls 1995). His cybernetic model, inspired by an innovative, but nevertheless functionalist study of the Naven ceremony among the Iatmul, was clearly in tune with the idea that the function of parts is to maintain the whole in order (as Radcliffe-Brown might have stated it) or in homeostasis (as the systemic psychotherapist might prefer to put it). Systemic or family therapy was of course also deeply influenced by the general intellectual climate in mid-century America and Britain which was dominated by a Parsonian structural-functional view of family functioning (Goldner 1985; Leupnitz 1988). As this view made much of the observed and little of the observer it had a totalising and formalising effect (Bourdieu 1977 [1972]) and did not leave much room for the understanding of variations in family organisation or process, except in terms of pathology (Fisek 1991). While traditional or modernist family therapy (Hoffman 1993) made assumptions about the universality of the structure and organisation of the family, at the same time it also articulated an assumption, also present in psychotherapy generally, that intimate and familial relationships universally adhere more or less to the same (as it happened) western model.

Emotions, feelings and motivations of individuals did not attract the attention of family therapists. Cybernetics and systems theory was aimed precisely at getting away from pinning individuals down and at understanding persons in terms of their position in a system of relationships instead (Haley 1978). So family therapists did not write or talk a great deal about individual internal or external experiences or representations and these did not feature highly in clinical practice, except in a few exceptional cases (see for example Satir 1964; Minuchin et al. 1967; Whitaker 1989). Despite this emphasis, however, assumptions about emotions and motivations were implicit. It would be impossible to imagine an approach to therapy which did not have some theory about these issues and in systemic psychotherapy as in most modernist anthropology, the theory was covert rather than overt. It implied the assumption that emotions, motivations and feelings occurred and were generated inside the bodies of individual persons as an aspect of physical and biological processes and that they were universal (Krause 1993). There was some recognition of cultural variation (Minuchin et al. 1967) but this was largely seen as the icing on the cake covering up recognisable and sustained human similarities.

Since then much has changed in systemic psychotherapy and in anthropology. It has become apparent that these earlier models lacked sensitivity to variations in practice, that there were serious problems about long-term change and that these models were themselves social constructions which frequently did not allow other voices to be heard. This in turn has also highlighted the balance of power in therapy and helped therapists realise that their practice can be (sometimes inadvertently) prejudicial and discriminatory. It means that yet another dimension of doubt and self-scrutiny must be added to empathy and respect in the therapeutic encounter and how therapists understand emotions, motivations and intentions of others, and especially of those others who appear on the face of it to be very different from themselves, is crucial to all these issues.

In this chapter I examine internal family relationships, that is to say the relationships which exist between persons of ascending and descending generations who are connected through begetting and being born, through parenting, through sexual partnerships and through belonging in some way to the same group of people. These are people who are intimately connected and who tend to invest in each other emotionally in an ongoing way. In Chapter 3 I discussed kinship and the family from a sociological point of view, and in this chapter I move inside family relationships to a more psychological view. This has wider implications not only for family relationships but also for any type of relationships and communication between humans because it reveals the need for us to take a more measured view about human differences and similarities than has hitherto been possible. It must therefore be the starting point for any kind of contemporary thinking about cross-cultural therapeutic practice.

I begin by examining Bateson's work on ethos (the relationship between the emotional content of individual behaviour and the emotional emphasis of the culture as a whole) amongst the Iatmul and I discuss the idea that emotions are culturally and socially constructed. I then discuss material from the Kaluli and some cases from my own clinical practice. I outline the arguments against relying heavily on language as an explanatory paradigm and finally I move on to describe and summarise the debate about the universality of the Oedipus complex which has taken place in anthropology, but which has been strangely neglected by psychotherapists. As the idea that emotions are culturally constructed is becoming widespread and popular I think that this debate is of interest because it gives some indication about the way different patterns of social interaction, particularly between parents and children, contribute to the cultural emphases and value of crucial emotional themes.

BATESON, ETHOS AND SCHISMOGENESIS

I have already mentioned that Bateson was a remarkable anthropologist, some have even called him a maverick (Ingold 1986). A student of Radcliffe-Brown, he worked well within the structural-functionalist approach of this style. Indeed, his analysis of the Naven ceremony amongst the matrilineal Iatmul picked up Radcliffe-Brown's own interest in the mother's brother/sister's son complex and the term 'ethos' is said to have been suggested to Bateson by Radcliffe-Brown as a way of providing a formalised approach to patterned sentiments (Nuckolls 1995: 367). The complexity of Bateson's approach has not been lost on family therapists. Thus Hoffman, a prominent theorist in family therapy, links Bateson both to the established cybernetic view of which she now disapproves and to a relational view of communal and intertwining stories which she now glosses as co-construction (Hoffman 1993: 112). It is perhaps more accurate to connect Bateson with both a mechanical and a sociological view of systems in which much of our current preoccupation with interpersonal and cross-cultural communication was anticipated but not developed. But as Bateson's approach is complicated and spans different fields as well as a wide timescale a closer look at his anthropological work will clarify some issues.

Amongst the Iatmul of New Guinea the Naven ceremony was a developmental step in the life of a boy. The Iatmul were matrilineal and we would expect to find some marker or elaboration of the relationship between a sister's son, referred to as *laua*, and a mother's brother, referred to as *wau*. When a boy achieved something which showed that he was becoming a competent young man, such as having built a canoe or having killed a man, his mother's brother, his *wau*, would have special reason to be proud of him and he would show this by dressing up as a woman (a mother) and strut about in a degrading manner looking for his *laua*. If he found the young man he would run up to him and rub his buttocks up and down the *laua*'s leg in what was considered an obscene sexual gesture. If we remember that the mother's brother was a figure of authority for the boy, this behaviour can be understood to be outrageous and an inversion of what would normally be expected. It was known as *naven* behaviour and a large ceremony could involve many other people taking part in a type of inverted display, for example the *naven* behaviour of an elder brother's wife was to beat her husband's younger brother.

Instead of finding the explanation for the ceremony in the matrilineal kinship principles of Iatmul social organisation as Radcliffe-Brown might have done, Bateson thought that the *naven* ceremony raised a crucial question, namely

> . . . although the structural position of the *wau* is such that his actions in the *naven* ceremony can be described as its logical development, we still do not know why the culture should have followed up this line of logic. (Bateson 1958 [1932]: 82)

The kinship principles which guided the Iatmul had laid down the existence of lines of possible behaviour, but this did not explain why individual persons should be motivated to follow these lines. The answer, according to Bateson was to be found in the general ethos or rather in two connected emotional orientations which were present in Iatmul society and culture. By ethos Bateson meant deeply embedded motivational experiences which people share by virtue of their common childhood experiences (Bateson 1958: 33) and he described a man's ethos and a woman's ethos.

The men's ethos was characterised by an aggressive, competitive and individualistic pride displayed by men in their ceremonial houses, particularly during heated debates about the ownership of totems but also on other occasions when they put on great displays for the entertainment of women. The women's ethos was characterised by a sense of quiet joy and selfless cooperation without any similar ostentatious display. The two went together as two sides of the same coin, neither aspect making sense by itself but rather being defined in opposition to the other. In conflict each side would push the other towards greater accentuation thus mutually reinforcing opposites and differentiation. But for each there were also elements of the opposite emotional experience. These latent aspects were expressed when for other reasons such as in the Naven ceremony, the dominant ethos was challenged. In that ceremony the *laua*'s boasting of his own newly achieved accomplishment would be countered not by symmetrical behaviour from his *wau* as would normally be expected amongst grown men, but by the inversion and complementary behaviour.

This is schismogenesis as family therapists know it and the idea was used by Bateson and his colleagues to describe and explain the dynamic processes which take place between populations, between family members in western families and in the battle an alcoholic has with 'the bottle' (Bateson 1973). In fact Bateson did not hit upon the idea of schismogenesis until the 1958 second edition of *Naven* where he discussed cybernetic theory in the epilogue and for him this insight solved the awkward problem of functionalism to which I referred in the previous chapter. In traditional structural-functionalist theory the purpose of a process (integration and stability) could not be understood except as the explanation for the process itself and thus nothing could be seen to exist which does not contribute to its own existence. The cybernetic system substituted the idea of purpose with the idea of self-correction. It therefore allowed for a separation of origin from continued existence and promised a functionalism free of teleology. This is the functionalism which later became central in systems thinking in family therapy and the development perhaps explains why *Naven* never became an ethnographic or theoretical text for family therapists. Bateson's attempt to specify pathways for self-correcting behaviour in the complementary schismogenesis between the *wau* and the *laua* (Bateson 1958: 289) was not convincing and he merely called for further study, which he himself never carried out. It is, however, worth remembering that the idea, which later was used to describe the systemic and interconnected aspects of human behaviour in many different contexts, derived from cross-cultural investigation and ethnographic fieldwork.

Bateson's ethological method considered emotions to have a motivational force derived not from the emotions themselves, that is to say from internal qualities present inside individuals, but from the dynamic in the relationships in which they participate and this anticipated much anthropological work in the area of the social construction of emotions as well as some questions which are just beginning to be asked in systemic psychotherapy. In Bateson's anthropological work we can therefore glimpse a preview to the struggle to understand not only kinship relationships and behaviour but also how these might be internalised through dynamic processes and represented in cultural ideas and cognitive and motivational schemas. Though to use this terminology is to anticipate much more recent work to which I shall return below.

SOCIAL CONSTRUCTIONISM

Bateson had been a prominent member of the Culture and Personality School which developed in the 1930s at Columbia University in the

United States. Other famous members were Margaret Mead and Ruth Benedict and they were concerned with the connections between the sentiments of individuals and the internal workings of culture. The idea, which was publicised by Benedict in her *Patterns of Culture* (1934) was that culture has a standardising effect on individuals. Standardised thoughts and standardised emotions were seen to be common and general to everyone from a particular culture and to impose a pressure to conform. As Bateson himself later explained it, the hypothesis is circular, because the general and pervading characteristics of a culture are supposed to both express and promote the standardisation of individuals (Bateson 1973: 83). This circularity came to be understood as a kind of statement about the extent to which different aspects of a world or a system hang together. Political and economic institutions, ideas, individual behaviour, emotional orientations, inclinations and experiences could be seen to comprise a perfect fit and express similar, or at least compatible, points of view. Thus Benedict described the cultures she examined 'as a clinical psychologist might describe the personality structure of a patient' (Bock 1988: 49).

Here there are again echoes of systemic approaches in psychotherapy in which a connection between feelings and symptoms and wider systems of relationships is assumed and problems are considered to result from the experience of 'a bad fit' between behaviour and beliefs (Cronen and Pearce 1985; Campbell et al. 1991). In both views it is the nature of the connection, the fit or the hanging together, which is at issue. A strong correlation means that culture becomes blurred with personality and behaviour becomes blurred with belief. As a consequence cultural differences become personified and stereotyped and ideas reduced to behaviour. This is misleading for we have no grounds to expect that the ways individuals differ from one another within any or all cultures have anything to do with the ways cultures differ from one another (Shweder 1973). Any theory which postulates a connection between culture or beliefs and behaviour cannot avoid also being a theory about individuals and about how cognition is related to action (D'Andrade 1990). In other words, it is neither empirically accurate nor theoretically defensible to conflate individual and social levels of existence.

For the most part these problems have not appeared to be acute for psychotherapy because until recently most systemic and individual psychotherapy was construed as intra-cultural. That is to say in a fundamental way therapists have assumed that their own understanding of a situation is pretty close to what their clients themselves understand. When client and therapist come from similar cultural backgrounds such an assumption can to some extent be justified. However, it is a different matter when therapy involves cross-cultural communication and therefore explicitly or implicitly must be based on cross-cultural comparison. Work in anthropology on emotions has pointed to ways in which we might begin to address such issues of ethnocentricity.

The Kaluli again

I have already referred to the importance of the sharing of food for social life and connectedness amongst the Kaluli of New Guniea studied by Schieffelin (1976) and Feld (1982), and I now want to present Schieffelin's view of the most important Kaluli emotional themes (Schieffelin 1985). The Kaluli do not themselves express an articulate theory of feelings and emotions. Rather, their views are embedded in their understanding of emotional themes and in what these themes reveal about the Kaluli view of human personality and behaviour. Three such themes are of particular importance insofar as they are recognised as such by the Kaluli themselves and play a central role in ceremonies. These are the emotions which we might gloss as 'anger', 'grief' and 'shame'. Our gloss can only be an approximation, for the terms used by the Kaluli themselves do not coincide with any term or concept which we can identify in English. For a start the Kaluli do not talk about anger as a noun. Instead they refer to a type of feeling or the state of an individual, to the state of being angry, sad or ashamed.

In Kaluli anger may be referred to in different ways. There are different terms depending on the intensity of the feeling and for how long it has been felt and there is also a special term for talking angrily to one's spouse. Grief is distinguished according to its severity such as a special term for grief experienced as a result of misfortune or death. There are also two terms for shame depending on the intensity of that feeling. Schieffelin warns against placing too much emphasis on an analysis of lexical terms and points instead to the importance of an examination of the way Kaluli talk about and express their feelings in various contexts and he invokes Bateson's observation that in order to understand what motivates interaction and behaviour it is first necessary to have some notion of the emotional emphasis or value of the system, that is to say of the prevailing ethos.

Schieffelin's understanding of Kaluli ethos focuses on two dimensions in Kaluli emotional life: personal dynamism and assertiveness, which mainly applies to men, and vulnerability, dependency and appeal which as we have seen was expressed in the story about the *muni* bird in Chapter 3. Anger is expressed in an explicit and declarative mode and it is almost always, whether the reason for the anger is loss, insult, injury or disappointment, interpreted in terms of a justified right to compensation. This means that the general framework which considers individuals in terms of their rights to reciprocity and sharing vis-à-vis others and which, as we have seen, operates in the assertion of relationships and belonging as expressed in food exchange (see Chapter 3, p. 25) also provides an interpretative framework for emotional states. This has two implicatons for anger. Firstly, when a person is angry it is implied that he or she has suffered a loss and second, because loss in the scheme of reciprocity and sharing means that one is entitled to a return, the angry person has a legitimate expectation of redress:

When a man has suffered wrong or loss, he may stamp furiously up and down the hall of the longhouse, or the yard outside, yelling the particulars of his injury for everyone to hear in order to arouse their sympathetic attention and inspire their backing for redress. (Schieffelin 1985: 176)

Anger may then become appeal and appeal may also be expressed in the way of the younger brother in the *muni* bird story. This was an attempt to evoke compassion and intimacy through the expression of vulnerability, sadness and grief. The song was a sad song and as the repeated appeal of the boy was not heard the mood turned to grief. Both anger and sadness may then be used by the Kaluli to assert justified claims and engage others in material or emotional reciprocity. But this may also be qualified according to the particular context of the encounter. If someone attempts to use this strategy to manipulate in an unjustified way, others may adopt shaming as a strategy for placing a break on the interaction. Shaming may take the form of a righteous speech and if effective removes the legitimate claim of the original appeal. In either case, that of successful appeal (through anger or grief) or that of unsuccessful appeal stopped by shaming, the social process of sharing and reciprocity constitutes a frame of reference. Thus Schieffelin argues that his account of Kaluli anger, grief and shame may be read as a clear case of the social construction of emotions:

> Kaluli emotions, however privately experienced are socially located and have a social aim. To this degree they are located not only in the person but also in the social situation and interaction that . . . they help to construct. (1985: 180)

By introducing the idea that the Kaluli themselves have a body of knowledge and ideas about human personhood or personality (often referred to as ethnopsychology) Schieffelin is able to give a more subtle account of the relationship between ideas and behaviour than was possible when using frameworks derived from American or European psychological theory. In Schieffelin's approach individual behaviour and ideas are mediated and shaped by the social contexts in which they are used. However, instead of giving the impression that individual persons mechanically follow social conventions or are socialised into these conventions to the extent that personal and individual variations disappear, the account of the Kaluli gives us some way of grasping the social and cultural background against which individuals live their lives and therefore of understanding at least part of the rationale for their actions, thoughts and feelings.

SOCIAL CONSTRUCTIONISM AND SYSTEMIC PSYCHOTHERAPY

It took half a century from the time when Bateson began his work on ethos for the idea that emotions may be socially or culturally constructed to catch on in anthropology. Firstly, as has already been mentioned because in the structural-functionalist version of British anthropology, psychology was thought to be out of bounds and second, because it took that long for questions which related to the way one could think about experience to begin to be articulated. Paradoxically, in systemic psychotherapy or family therapy where Bateson has had the status of a founding father and where the social and interactional aspects of emotional connections is of central interest, it is only recently that Bateson's early insights have begun to be appreciated.

The conviction that family members are emotionally tied together served in family therapy as an explanation for why individuals join, stay in relationships with or separate from each other (Bowen 1978). It did not lead to an emphasis on internal representations nor did it provide a focus for an examination of cultural diversity in the meaning of motivational and emotional processes. Such processes were generally approached in organisational and structural terms and most family therapy views on the nature of emotions attributed these to the individual internal (physiological) domain. Thus although they acknowledged affect and feeling in the treatment process and considered these as isomorphic with the behavioural domains, Minuchin and the structuralists (Minuchin 1974) also assumed motivation universally to derive from the need of humans for emotional connectedness to or confirmation from/of others. Since the meanings of these connections were not of particular interest the specific nature of these connections were not commented upon.

The approaches of Haley and the Milan School were more specific. Like Radcliffe-Brown, who was concerned with roles and the place human beings occupy in social relationships, Haley did not pay much attention to why individuals join a system or a relationship (Krause 1993). Consequently individual motivation, which he at different times understood as a quest for control (Haley 1976) and as benevolent concern (Haley 1980), was put down to universals in human nature and opposed to patterns of behaviour and interaction observed in families. A similar universality was put forward by the Milan school. For them 'psychotic' family members were caught up in a game which was characterised by *hubris*. Hubris is a Greek word and means arrogant pride which in some way invites its own downfall and for the Milan therapists this explained why members could not leave or withdraw from the game since this would mean that the game would stop (Selvini Palazzoli et al. 1978). They used *hubris* as a metaconcept, thus assuming this to be a generic human disposition and a general motivational force in families or in certain types of families. They did not justify this in cross-cultural terms and despite their interest in meaning they appear to have been unconcerned about wider meanings and beliefs when these differed significantly from those beliefs and ideas used and operated by the therapists themselves.

On the whole, traditional family therapy followed the cybernetic line of reasoning which Bateson took from 1958 onwards and very few noticed that Bateson himself did not give up striving for an integration of his earlier anthropological work with his later work in mental health. Thus, for example, although this was not spelt out, the disagreement between Haley and Bateson over power and control (Sluzki and Ransom 1976; Berger 1978; Dell 1989) was not only about the corruptibility of power and the 'epistemological lunacy' (Bateson 1978: 463) of elevating a particular (cultural) type of power relationship to an explanatory principle, but also about how the relationship between a culturally defined emotional emphasis and the actions of individual persons could be understood (Krause 1993: 47–8).

If emotions are no longer seen to belong exclusively to individual internal physiological domains but are also considered to be socially constructed appraisals, as shown both by Bateson's own material on the Iatmul and by Schieffelin's material on the Kaluli, then emotions can be addressed within a systemic framework of thought and practice and need not be relegated to the periphery or excluded altogether. This has important implications for individual and systemic psychotherapy. For one thing it means that emotions are not essences with a life, as it were, prior to or outside human interactions. For another it means that emotions are communications which must at least in part be continually reconstituted and reconfirmed through interactions and relationships. Finally, following Bateson it will not do to state that the function of a cultural detail or a sequence of behaviour is the expression of a particular emotion without also being aware of the meaning and value of that emotion generally in a particular family. This means that part of the therapist's initial task is to acquire enough understanding of the social and cultural background of her client(s), individuals or families, to be able to consider their specific individual situation against this more general context.

Over a period of 12 months I worked with an Indian family from East Africa in which the emotional emphasis was subtly different from what I have learnt to expect from white English families. This family consisted of Mr and Mrs Khan, their daughter who was 22 and their son who was 16 and at the time I met with them they had been in England for eight years. Both parents were born in East Africa where their respective families had settled from Gujerat. Both families were extremely wealthy and religious Muslims belonging to the Ismaili sect. Mr Khan was the only son and had five sisters, whereas Mrs Khan had three brothers. They had always been closely involved with the community of Ismailis and for many years Mr Khan had been a *mukhi* (an important elder and steward) in the community. The couple had met and fallen in love and had managed to marry despite extreme opposition and hostility from Mr Khan's father, who did not consider Mrs Khan's family of high enough status. However, the manner in which the marriage had finally materialised confirmed rather than denied the religious devotion and respect of Mr and Mrs Khan, for the Aga Khan himself had intervened and blessed the marriage and after this all opposition from Mr Khan's father and family had vanished. Following their marriage Mr and Mrs Khan had settled in French-speaking Africa and had like so many of their community built up a successful business there (Benedict 1968). Mrs Khan had been ill for many years with a physical illness which had not been properly diagnosed in Africa and the family had come to England for treatment. They were now living in England and had started a business here too, but this had not done well and they were facing a much reduced standard of living. They had asked for family therapy because they were seriously worried about their only son who was disrespectful to his parents, not interested in going to the Mosque, or anything else which they the parents valued, and who was not putting enough time into his studies. These difficulties had particularly surfaced between Mrs Kahn and her son.

After an initial session in which the family told their story the sessions tended to focus on the family ethos of respect and devotion. Mr and Mrs Khan came with their son on most occasions. We talked about the different upsets which both Mr and Mrs Khan had experienced during their lives together: the difficulties of their marriage through which they had nevertheless managed to reconcile respect and love for their own parents with their own wishes; the trauma of a long-lasting illness experience for Mrs Khan who had nevertheless been a devoted wife and mother; the shock of not being financially successful; the upset which they were now going through as a result of their son not being interested in the community, or in becoming a businessman and his rudeness to his mother, ignoring her requests and interrupting the activities which she enjoyed. Finally both parents, but particularly Mr Khan, felt extremely distressed at the prospect of their daughter marrying her white English boyfriend (a non-Ismaili). Both Mr and Mrs Khan talked again and again about their own parents and the importance of family and community. Mrs Khan explained how she still now had to remind her son to brush his teeth, to have a bath and to do his homework and in the sessions she frequently interrupted her son to answer the question which I had asked him. Mr Khan, on the other hand, tended to be much more unconcerned about his son, explaining that he had changed and that he had given up trying to control his son and that he often now got extremely exasperated with his wife for not being able to leave their son alone. This change had happened since his business had not worked out.

If this had been an English family a systemically minded therapist might conclude that Mrs Khan was unusually overinvolved with her son and accordingly understand the difficulties between Mrs Khan and her son as a result of the difficulties which existed in the marital relationship. At first I also took this view. I tried several times to get Mr Khan to assist his wife in being firm with their son but this did not work. Mr Khan appeared more and more slumped and ineffective, although still intellectually alert with a growing interest in psychotherapy. He did not think that he had a problem with his son and he was quite happy to leave the management to his wife and to encourage her to be strict and firm but he was also convinced that he could do nothing about this. Eventually it became clear to me that there were at least two reasons why such standard family therapy thinking did not quite fit.

Firstly, the importance of respect and devotion was highlighted in the family's own discourse which frequently took the form of an exegesis of these concepts, a process which became a kind of search for meaning of how for each respect ought to be shown and in fact was not shown. Mrs Khan demanded attention because of her illness and because of all the work she had put into the family. Mr Khan withdrew more and more and demanded less and less. However, during this the social value and emotional emphasis of these concepts also became apparent. Ismailis are a devotional sect of mostly Shi'a Muslims who trace succession back to the seventh Imam, Ismail (Shackle and Moir 1992). They are devoted to the Aga Khan who as a divine king represents the contemporary community (Morris 1968). Secular activities play a central role as does the accumulation of wealth and prestige and are, as Weber argued for North European Capitalism, an intricate part of a pious stance. The publicly acknowledged emotion of devotional love and respect which the Khan family struggled to define had authoritarian qualities associated with a male social domain, with adherence to the authority of the Aga Khan and with financial success. This is a quite different emphasis than the emotion which is evoked in other devotional sects, such as in the worship of Lord Krishna in Pushti Marg, in urban business communities in Western India which emphasise maternal tenderness, anxiety and sorrow (Bennett 1990). Of course I am not trying to say that Mr and Mrs Khan did not have such feelings for their children also, but these were not the ones which were publicly condoned. In fact the aspects of devotion which were publicly valued were those which Mr Khan felt unable to display at the moment.

Second, from this point of view Mr Khan was personally hit the hardest by the misfortunes which the family had suffered. The impeccable devotion of his family to the community, to business and to what both Mr and Mrs Khan termed 'religion' had earned him great respect. In this capacity and as a wealthy member of the community he could have looked forward to making honourable and prestigious affinal connections inside the community at the marriage of his daughter. Now with a declining financial position he could no longer hope to adhere to such ideals and although it upset him he now preferred to reject the psychological implications of the social practice and ideology of his community. The real issue then was how Mr Khan could regain his self-respect and this involved a reinterpretation of the dominant ethos. In the treatment this was not easy because in each of their own ways Mr Khan and Mrs Khan were inclined towards a break with the past rather than a development of continuity and change. Mr Khan by refusing to identify and honour any of the values to which he previously had publicly adhered, including the devotion and respect of his only son, and Mrs Khan by insisting on it being her turn to receive the emotional and practical devotion if not of her husband at least of her son. I decided to help Mrs Khan develop her own independence, but the predicament of this family could not be understood without considering the dominant cultural emotional themes. Rather than aiming at readjusting who supported whom, it was more useful to develop a general dialogue in the family during which these salient emotional themes could begin to be reinterpreted in the light of changed social and material circumstances.

Emotions are thus not simply bodily or physiological states into and out of which individuals move. It is more useful to understand emotions as processes of appraisal and communication which draw on cultural themes of meaning and which are reconstituted, experienced and changed in the course of evolving social relationships. This means that persons from different backgrounds may find common emotional themes, which unite and attract them, but which nevertheless may only partially overlap. It also means that the therapist must acquire some understanding of the meaning of the emotional themes salient for any particular interaction and of the dynamic processes involved in their divergence or convergence.

My next example involves a mixed couple and it anticipates many of the issues which I shall discuss later, particularly in Chapter 7. I want to suggest that although in this family husband and wife did not share the same cultural understandings, insofar as their cultural backgrounds were different, they were preoccupied with similar emotional themes from different points of view. Like the Iatmul this couple had a dominant ethos with two strands to it.

The couple was referred because of the husband's violent feelings and the fear that he might become violent towards his wife or himself. He was a handsome man in his late twenties of Hispanic origin. He grew up in a provincial town in a socialist state in an atmosphere of violence and was picked up several times by the police and tortured. At the time of referral he was seeking political asylum in Britain. His father had been a violent man, both towards his mother and towards his son and during his childhood he had often begged his mother to leave his father. He was intelligent but self-deprecating about his own abilities. His wife was a few years older and white English. She worked in the Civil Service and considered herself a feminist and a political activist. In fact the couple had met each other while she was on a trip to his country in connection with her work for a left-wing organisation. Her father had been an alcoholic and had left her mother who had struggled on her own with two daughters. The couple lived in a house owned by the wife and shared with two of her girlfriends.

The second session with this couple was a tumultuous one. The husband had been violent towards his wife in the street on their way to the session and she came into the therapy room saying that her husband had tried to kill her. After I had pointed out that he would have to find a way to contain his violent feelings if the therapy was going to continue

(Goldner et al. 1990) the rest of that session was spent on exploring how he could ensure that violence would not happen again. He talked about respect and explained that he had discovered his wife talking to a black man with whom she had had an affair after he had met her but before they had married. He said that his wife had brought shame to his honour, that she had become dirty like a whore, but that despite all the nasty things he himself had been involved in, he was still clean because he was sexually and morally virtuous. His wife said that she did not know how she could respect or have children with someone who talked this way. She said that she thought he was a racist and that she despised this part of him. This in turn led him to reopen a long-standing argument between them.

As a political exile he had begun to write a book critical of the human rights abuses in his own country, but because of his wife's involvement with the political organisation which was actively supporting his country, this activity was presenting problems for her. When he told this story to me she responded by disqualifying him and his experience as a victim by saying, 'He wanted to expose his country, so he started writing these things down. I said to him . . . I did not actually stop him . . . I said you can go ahead and do it, but there is nothing in this that is new. I did not stop you . . . I said you could go ahead . . . I believe in open debate, one side can put the argument against the other side.' I acknowledged this disqualification and the verbal violence which was taking place in the name of democracy and the fact that they were bringing a human rights issue right into their own marriage. This turned out to be a significant moment in the therapy.

At least one reason why this woman and this man had come together was their mutual concern for respect and the rights of persons. This was the ethos of their relationship, but for each of them the interpretation of this was coloured by their own specific cultural and personal back-grounds. She was a political activist concerned with equality in the political tradition of a radical European and at the same time the feminist in her saw women as helpless victims whose rights to respect for themselves have been curtailed by patriarchal ideologies. He saw her as a woman whose sexual conduct and especially her purity could reflect his own honour and respect in accordance with notions of virility and machismo commonly expressed in the society from which he came. His other side, however, the side which was very much a reality in his experience, was that of a helpless victim, undeserving of respect and with little honour in the eyes of others. It was this side with which his wife had initially engaged.

In all ways concern with respect was central to both of them. They could both be oppressors or they could both be victims. At one level, in their coming together, they each fiercely defended their own position as respect deserving and in this capacity they each operated as oppressor or disqualifier in relation to each other (Sluzki 1988). At another level they were each victims who could not command respect. It was as if respect became an obsession existing in a vacuum rather than located in a shifting context with reference to the content of their interaction. As soon as one of them got the upper hand in the symmetry the other would feel victimised and the dominant ethos would be reaffirmed and reconstituted. The husband found it difficult to accept his helpless position as a dependant of his wife since in his view this did not deserve respect. For her part the wife had become involved with him as a political victim who had been unjustly treated and tortured. But when he turned into a competent man through making constructive use of his victimisation he naturally did so in accordance with his own cultural background and his own gendered personhood. This involved her in some respects being a 'traditional' woman, a position she found difficult to accept since in her view such a woman did not deserve respect. For his part he admired the independent woman who could do what his beloved mother could not, but when she asserted her independence he was at a loss.

Although the emotional emphases of Hispanic culture and English culture are different, the couple shared an experience as victims and a concern for justice. This was enough of an overlap for them to construct a mutually meaningful ethos, which although malfunctioning became a central theme in their married life. This ethos was reproduced through the way each of them remained faithful to cultural constructions of gender which each brought with them into the marriage and which became central mechanisms for symmetrical escalations between them. They each almost became caricatures, she of the feminist and he of a macho male. Gender became a political issue. And at the same time this obstinate demand for respect prevented either of them from recognising their cultural differences and the extent to which these were intricately bound up with both their gender and their personhoods. Once the therapy was focused on how their emotional orientations interlinked it became possible for them to acknowledge that they were both victims and oppressors and to develop ways in which they could show respect for each other as persons.

CONSTRUCTIVISM

During the 1970s and 1980s it was no longer assumed in the social sciences that what we experience as reality is the way it really is. This raised two central questions. The first was, as we have seen, about the extent to which human behaviour, knowledge and feeling are socially and culturally constructed. The second was about how we as ethnographers or therapists can understand what goes on. This question had been asked before in many different ways, but once it became clear that much of the detail of human activity could not be understood by examining internal bodily and mental processes the question received new poignancy.

In systemic psychotherapy where the idea of socially constructed emotions has only recently been acknowledged (McNamee and Gergen 1992; Hoffman 1993; Reichelt and Sveaass 1994; Pare 1995) it was the second question which was asked first and the answer was thought to be found in the constructivist thinking of Maturana and Varela (Maturana 1980, 1988; Maturana and Varela 1980). At first there seemed to be some confusion about whether or not constructionism and constructivism amounted to the same thing (Real 1990; Speed 1991; Efran and Clarfield 1992; Hoffman 1993; Flaskas 1997). The two approaches share a philosophical tradition which can be traced from Vico, to Kant and Wittgenstein, but they have also developed along different lines. Constructivism emphasises humans as individual biological organisms while constructionism focuses on human beings as interpreting persons living in communities (Hoffman 1993; Pare 1995). Thus the shift from one to the other amounts to a significant paradigmatic shift from biology to sociology (Flaskas 1996). I have already examined constructionism as far as emotions are concerned, and I now take a look at constructivism and the implications of constructivist models for cross-cultural psychotherapeutic work.

The constructivist paradigm originally focused on individuals, the way they sense what goes on around them and the way they process information. Briefly, the idea is that any organism develops along the lines set out in its biological structure (autopoeisis). Autopoeisis has two aspects. First, nothing happens in a living system that its structure does not permit and second, the structure of an organism makes possible all that can happen to it in its individual history. Autopoeisis applies to all features of living systems, but particularly to experience and perception and this means that organisms or individuals are seen as the source of all reality and that there can be no objective knowing about other objects or realities. Objectivity must, so to speak, be put in parenthesis (Maturana 1980). Interaction between organisms takes place as consensual coordinations which organisms themselves operate according to their own perceptions of the universe around them. In this sense consensus refers to the match or the fit between individual organisms rather than to similarity or absolute agreement. In family therapy these ideas stimulated what has become known as second-order cybernetics and it shifted the attention from the observed world to the observer as a reference point for knowledge. Unfortunately they invited a certain amount of biological reductionism since the idea of autopoeisis seems to be more applicable to lower forms of organisms whose biological programming directs them to interact than for complicated ones such as humans, who are endowed with consciousness and agency, and who therefore might decide not to have anything to do with each other or who might change their minds along the way (Gellner 1985).

Nevertheless constructivism was something of a revolution. The therapist was no longer able to sustain the position of 'objective' outsider looking in. The elegant interventions which had been central to the development of the structuralist and strategic approaches now appeared located in the therapist's own position which was, knowingly or unknowingly, imbued with power and control (Hoffman 1985). Addressing this problematic several innovative approaches emerged, all struggling to find a more honourable and sustainable position for the family therapist (see for example Keeney 1983; Campbell and Draper 1985; Anderson and Goolishan 1988; Byrne and McCarthy 1988; McCarthy and Byrne 1988; Tomm 1988; Walters et al. 1988; Epston 1989; White 1989; Goldner et al. 1990; Perelberg and Miller 1990; Andersen 1991; Reichelt and Sveaass 1994). But the developments since then have also taken a path which has created different but nevertheless thorny problems for cross-cultural therapeutic thinking and practice. In the pages which follow I focus on these and try to unravel them.

POST-CONSTRUCTIVISM IN FAMILY THERAPY

The original Gordon Conference on Cybernetics in 1984 must have been an exciting event. So many eminent and interdisciplinary thinkers came together and, although many others had begun to develop along the same lines, the conference and the work of the constructivists Maturana, Varela, von Foester and von Glaserfeld came to signify the new developments. The pickings were rich and in many ways systemic psychotherapists are still digesting them. From the beginning it had been necessary for the constructivists to justify the parallel which they drew between relatively simple biological organisms and much more complex ones such as human beings. The latter were considered autonomous systems and this referred to the notion, which Bateson had also put across, of mind as both a biological and a collective entity (Bateson 1973; Bateson and Bateson 1987). Thus Varela observed:

> the act of understanding is basically *beyond our will* because the autonomy of the social and the biological systems we are in goes *beyond* our skull, because our evolution makes us part of a social aggregate and a natural aggregate which have an autonomy compatible with but *not reducible to* our autonomy as biological individuals. This is precisely why I have insisted so much on talking about an observer-community rather than an observer; the knower is not the biological individual. (1979: 276) (emphasis in original)

For Hoffman, who quoted this statement in 1985, this was the nub of the matter because it highlighted the necessity for human individuals to communicate in meaningful ways with one another. However, what Hoffman and others emphasised was not human communication as such but the conversation, or the idea of conversational domains (Hoffman 1985; McNamee and Gergen 1992). Thus Hoffman went on to explain the ideas of Anderson and colleagues (1986) relating to the 'problem-determined system as the meaning system which is created by the problem and which is contributed to by all those (including the professionals) involved with the problem'. And in 1988 she began another article with a quote from von Glaserfeld who referred to the difficulty of abandoning the egocentric notion that the Earth is the centre of the Universe and he went on to say:

> It seems that now there is yet another, even more difficult step in that direction we shall have to make, namely to give up the notion that the representations we construct from our experience should in any sense reflect the world as it might be without us. (von Glaserfeld 1987: 143, quoted in Hoffman 1988: 110)

There is an ambiguity in this quote. Is von Glaserfeld referring to us in a generic sense of all Human Beings? Or is he referring to us in the sense of a community as explained by Varela above and employed in the notion of the 'observing system', or Anderson and Goolishan's 'problem-determined system', that is to say a collection of persons who share certain meanings? For any individual human being what is 'out there' is not just the physical world including other human beings, but also the way understanding is arrived at and the extent to which it is accomplished. Those who speak the same language will have different possibilities for communication at their disposal than those who do not and in either case the interaction may have different consequences. If, in this respect, we refer to all of Human Kind as a community we also conflate the bio-logical and social domains and consequently we are in danger of under-estimating social and cultural diversity.

Yet this is precisely the way much of family therapy has interpreted the constructivist ideas and the direction in which these developed within the discipline. Paradoxically this was largely due to the excessive importance family therapists attributed to language in communication. Thus in the 1985 and 1988 articles Hoffman had articulated the development of this emphasis by highlighting the linguistic rather than the behavioural aspects of Maturana's and Varela's observing systems when applied to humans. She wrote about meaning, conversational domains, dialogue and co-construction. By 1992, constructionism was becoming more popular in family therapy and at the same time psychotherapy generally was becom-ing increasingly aware of cross-cultural diversity. However, the identification of interaction and meaning with language continued to be predominant. Hoffman referred to the influence of the work of Gergen (Gergen and Davis 1985; Gergen 1990) that all social interchange is mediated through language and in the same article she introduced readers to the literary ethnography of Clifford and Marcus (discussed in Chapter 2). In other quarters too the language analogy had been keenly expressed as an emphasis on the way clients create stories about their lives as a basis for their own identity (White and Epston 1990; Lax 1992; DiNicola 1993) and a focus on the fluidity of this process often referred to as narrative (Gergen and Kaye 1992), 'languaging' (Reichelt and Sveaass 1994), storying (White and Epston, 1990; Epston and White

1992) or text (Penn and Sheinberg 1991; Frosh et al. 1996). An emphasis on language has thus been central in recent theoretical developments in systemic psychotherapy almost to the point where culture has been equated with language and verbal communication with everything which goes on in human lives.

There is nothing *wrong* in paying attention to language or in using language as an analogy. As we saw, it was interesting and quite instructive to discover the different words the Kaluli use for anger. In my own practice I am frequently guided by the words people use during sessions and if I notice a pattern I tend to make this the starting point for conversation in the way I described for the Khan family above. As was the case for this family and as I have shown elsewhere (Krause 1995) words or terms are polyvalent which is why an exploration of them may reveal important information both about general cultural themes and about individual differences. But this also means that they are difficult to pin down and it is of course not only the terms which people use which are of interest, but also and perhaps more so the concepts behind the terms and the way people use these in different contexts and at different stages of their lives.

This means that it is experience rather than dialogue which must be the starting point for any kind of knowledge of relationships and communication between people and that language events such as 'text', 'story' or 'narrative' represent only a part of what goes on. Thus when von Foester dramatically proclaimed 'the Map *is* the Territory' (Hoffman 1985: 383) and Bateson to be wrong, he was popular, but it was surely he who was mistaken. As students of systemic psychotherapy learn in their first year of training it is an epistemological error to confuse the two and to privilege words as clues to experience, identity or culture. 'If I could tell you what it meant, there would be no point in dancing it' the dancer Isadora Duncan is quoted as saying (Bateson 1973). It is possible to make oneself understood in a language whose structure and grammar one does not know (Tyler 1978) just as it is possible to act in a socially or culturally meaningful way without knowing the underlying structures and rules of the language used. And it also works the other way around: it is impossible for any one person to know all the rules which impinge on his or her existence. As Bourdieu comments, 'It is because subjects do not, strictly speaking, know what they are doing that what they do has more meaning than they know' (1977: 79).

This points to an ontological gap between words and social processes which cannot be bridged from within language itself (Hastrup 1995). Our everyday life is full of examples which demonstrate this. At two and a half my youngest daughter was fond of cutting out pictures which she or I had drawn. On one occasion she insisted that I cut out a picture of a ball. She then took the picture of the ball and proceeded to kick it round the room. After a few attempts she gave up, clearly recognising that the 'ball' did not function as a ball at all. She had put 'the ball' to practical use and it did not live up to her expectation. It was through putting into practice what she had recently learnt in a football game with her older siblings and not through the use of words that she discovered this. The representation of the ball was only one element of the experiment. This recalls Schieffelin's observation that it is through an analysis of emotional processes rather than emotion terms that the Kaluli ethos can be grasped.

This raises another point. My daughter was reacting to 'the ball' as a synchronic event. She had been introduced to football by her elder brother as part of her finding out about the world. She was not aware of the history of the football, its development or its place in English society generally. Nevertheless as an observer I could identify her moves, the swing of the foot and the run up to 'the ball' as the beginnings of special football playing skills. These had been acquired through what she had learnt about how to respond physically to a ball, and the meaning of the event therefore had specific cultural overtones to do with how English children play ball using their feet. In other words cultural aspects of playing football were reproduced and reconstituted through her playing even though she was not aware of this. In fact it could be argued that if my daughter were to become a champion football player the earlier she starts the better so that her physical competence with the ball can become 'second nature' and in this way appear to be a non-cultural process. But if my daughter then rose to great fame sports commentators would have to refer not just to her skills in kicking a piece of paper acquired when very young but also to the history of football and the role of women in it. The point is that if the observer privileges language as a domain of consciousness, of social relations and of culture then not only is the complexity of cognitive and communication processes of individual persons ignored but so also are collective social processes, their political and economic dimensions and their history (Toren 1993; Rudie 1994).

Meaning cannot then be understood without some reference both to individual and collective histories. Actions, thoughts and feelings of persons must be set against the context of social and historical conditions which provide the background for their individual lives (Giddens 1991). The cultural dimension is partly this, that it provides individuals with themes of meaning and blueprints for practice which have been communicated to them by those who have cared for them from infancy. But persons do not simply reproduce what they have consciously or unconsciously learnt. Persons also confirm or reconstitute meaning through what they do and in their interaction with others and in this sense persons are at the same time products and producers of their own history. It is because persons are not aware of this dimension of which some aspects are ingrained as 'second nature' that it is the basis for what Bourdieu calls the 'intentionless invention of regulated improvisation' (1977: 79).

I could not arrive at an adequate understanding of what was going on in the Khan family and in the relationships of the Hispanic/English couple without some notion of the cultural and historical background.

Mr Khan's emotional experience and his response to his present predicament was linked not only to his personal history but also to the history of his social group: his origins in Gujerat, his membership of the Ismaili community and the nature of secular and religious authority in this community. Similarly an acknowledgement of the husband's cultural background and the Hispanic tradition in which he had been brought up was central to the problems the couple experienced. The terms used by my clients were important pointers and shorthand expressions to what was important but they did not by any means tell the whole story.

In family therapy the importance of questions about the future have been well documented (Penn 1985; de Shazer 1991). Therapy after all is about doing something different, about changing, in the future. What has received less attention is the way the future is related to the past and the past itself as a source of new interpretations. Thus apart from family and individual histories and genograms many family therapists pay scant attention to the continuity between the past and the present. This poses a particular challenge to the therapist working interculturally because particularly in cross-cultural therapy interventions are more likely to succeed if they are to some extent isomorphic with the dominant ideologies with which individuals and families operate (Krause 1995). Since families and individuals everywhere make choices against a background of their own expectations and cultural historical themes, therapists who are aware of these themes are more likely to be helpful in opening up new possibilities. For the therapist this entails being aware of the complexity of cognitive and emotional processes and their dynamic expression in past and present practice. Language provides for, but does not encompass these processes and frequently words do not express them adequately.

SHARED HUMAN EXPERIENCES

We still, however, have to talk to each other both intra-culturally and cross-culturally. What's more, sometimes we manage to communicate across language and cultural barriers even if we might not want to claim that our communications and observations reflect objective reality. In this sense the idea of social constructionism is at the beginning of our enquiry rather than at its conclusion (Taussig 1993: xv). If so much more can now be shown to be a product of human interactive processes and relationships rather than the direct effects of human physiology and biology, how does it work? These questions are central not just to anthropology but also to psychotherapy.

The answers to this question must relate to individual actions and feelings and to practice in the sense used by Bourdieu that what people do is as important as the ideas they have about the world and that what people do is not completely consciously organised but is also unconsciously regulated (Bourdieu 1977). The answers must also incorporate a notion of culture which has some psychological reality. We are thus searching for something which all humans have in common and which denotes a capability and a potential and which may come to be realised through the ability and indeed the necessity for human beings to form relationships with each other, also sometimes referred to as sociality (Ingold 1986; Carrithers 1989). Something along the lines of what Taussig has described as the mimetic faculty, 'the faculty to copy, imitate, make models, explore differences, yield into and become Other' (1993: xiii) or Bateson's ideas about ethos or what D'Andrade has defined as cultural goal schemas. Cultural goal schemas have motivational force and they are context dependent devices. They are thus capable of incorporating different cultural scenarios and contexts. They are learnt and developed by a person through that person's practical involvement and expertise in interaction where particular goal schemas are salient (D'Andrade 1992).

Holland has commented on this with reference to American cultural models of romance. She showed that if female college students did not clearly identify themselves with the world of romance, then romance was not very likely to be salient for them, nor were they very likely to be expert in conducting romantic relationships (Holland 1992). Learning something is thus affected by how involved a person is and how successful she is in carrying out the appropriate activities and this in turn depends on the process of how a person identifies herself as an actor at a particular developmental stage in a culturally devised system. There is a motivational link between culture and action and this recalls Bloch's point about lived-in models and the way these become learnt and integrated into cognitive schemas through repeated cultural practice (p. 19). But this process is also a dynamic one and not entirely regulated. It also relies on individual persons affirming and reaffirming through their own practice, their playing and their own ideas of what has gone on before. Insofar as this is at least partially conscious, individuals make decisions and choices, they are agents whose outlooks change and develop through their lives. Culture then can be said to be a 'complex illusion inasfar as it can never be permanent, never be finally accomplished' (Robertson 1996) and it exudes an influence on everything which human beings do.

This has important implications for both anthropology and psycho-therapy because it means that culture cannot be considered to be a homogeneous bounded entity which individuals internalise en masse. Most of the time individuals hold cultural values and ideas as general themes which may have a range of meaning and which may not matter greatly to them; it is only when such schemes become the focus of choices and decisions in particular contexts of practice that individuals begin to feel strongly about them and begin to be experts in operating them. A more accurate view of culture is thus one which on the one hand refers to the ideas handed down to us through our relationships with our carers and other people and which are integral to our func-tioning in specific cultural contexts, and on the other to the interactive and recursive processes which allow individuals to reinterpret these cultural themes in the light of the circumstances of their relationships and their own lives. It is not difficult for us to be aware of this for ourselves, but it seems harder to recognise this complexity in the case of others.

So how do we begin to talk across cultural boundaries? When Bateson observed the Iatmul behave and talk in a manner which he described as emotional or indicative of their ethos he was careful to point out that this conveyed his own impressions of their behaviour and that this was crude and probably unscientific (Bateson 1958: 124). He did not, however, develop this approach. He did not go on to describe his own emotional categories and then explain how the observation of Iatmul behaviour had triggered them (Nuckolls 1995), although this is of course exactly what had happened.

There are many instances reported by anthropologists where at some deep level events seem to trigger similar emotions in both anthropologist and informants. Rosaldo, an anthropologist who worked with the Ilongot of the Philippines, reports one such event although she also warns against overstating the similarities (Rosaldo 1980). While in the field she had returned to her house one day to find that the Ilongot children had been playing a tape of Joan Baez who in a tremolo had been singing about a soldier going to war. Afterwards her Ilongot friends surprised her when they reported that they had heard a lovely female voice singing passionately about death, love and mourning. The aptness of the interpretation of the song and the sentiment it conveyed seemed amazing. The meaning of the Baez song was different for the Ilongot than for the audience to which it had been originally addressed: for the Ilongot it was beautiful because 'it stirred their hearts with angry thoughts and invoked wild violence' whereas for western audiences mourning pointed to passivity. Despite these differences, however, the sound of the music had evoked similar themes. In this respect music and certain sounds may have particular cross-cultural appeal. Thus in writing about 'The Muni Bird Song', which I quoted in Chapter 3, and other Kaluli songs Feld points to the association between a bird of the night with minor and descending pitches and sadness in these songs and the existence of similar associations in southern American blues (Feld 1982).

THE OEDIPUS COMPLEX

Other events which trigger similar types of reactions and emotions cross-culturally are those which involve connections between parents and children. These are cross-culturally universal even if at the same time they are also bound up with the life experiences of particular people in particular social contexts. It would be a mistake however to assume that relationships between parents and children are shaped and informed by identical cultural themes everywhere. Parents and children exist in all cultures, and in all cultures the roles and functions which each play vis-à-vis the other are valued and singled out as special, but at the same time the social context, social institutions such as the principles of descent and marriage, religious orientation, ideas about personhood and about the nature of relationships influence the meaning of such relationships and the social processes which maintain them. As culture cannot simply be located outside individual persons we must look for cultural variation in internal domains too, in internal worlds, in emotional attachments and in cognitive processes. The classic debate in anthropology about the cross-cultural applicability of the Oedipus complex was an attempt to address these issues, and with a growing interest in the role of the individual person in the reproduction of culture these issues have been taken up again in recent publications. Since this debate hinged around the relationship between behaviour and interaction and emotional orientations in different cultures I think it is worthwhile to summarise it.

In a sense the detailed study of matrilineal kinship in the Trobriand Islands which Malinowski produced was the first and most persuasive case for cultural variation in the unconscious (Kurtz 1992). It will be remembered that matrilineal kinship refers to the situation where kinship connections are traced through women and where a man inherits not from his father but from his mother's brother, who also has legal and family authority over him. Amongst the Trobriand Islanders, a boy lived with his father and his mother while he was an infant and then moved to live with his mother's brother where his political and economic interests were located. A girl lived with her father and her mother until she married. Finally, it will be remembered that the Trobriand Islanders did not recognise the father as a relative because he was not responsible for conception, although he did literally open the way. Actual conception was accomplished by a spirit of the matrilineal clan entering a woman.

Armed with these ethnographic details Malinowski challenged the cross-cultural applicability of the Oedipus complex and entered into a long and heated debate with Ernest Jones, Freud's British disciple and biographer (Malinowski 1929; Jones 1964 [1924]). Malinowski argued that in the Trobriand Islands ambivalent feelings existed between a boy and his mother's brother and that the relationship between a boy and his father were close and affectionate, thus not conforming to the pattern of the Oedipus complex outlined by Freud. At the same time a man had authority over his sister and their relationship was characterised by extreme avoidance and strict incest taboos. It was therefore not the mother, but the sister who was an object of erotic desire for the Trobrianders. The emotional tone of these relationships could be observed in daily life but they were also elaborated upon in Trobriand myths and dreams. In response Jones upheld the classical psychoanalytical view claiming that the Trobriand failure to recognise the biological relationship between a son and his father and also the matrilineal principles of organisation themselves, reflected a denial covering the affects which originated in the

Oedipal situation in the first place and that this had led Malinowski to fail to take proper account of sexuality. He also pointed out that since a boy lived with his father while he was an infant the hostile feelings which boys later placed on their mother's brothers were a kind of second displacement.

For both sides the debate appeared as a point of honour upon which the credibility of their respective disciplines would stand or fall (Parsons 1969). However, since psychological explanations subsequently became unpopular with British anthropologists and only a few anthropologists, such as Roheim and Devereux in the 1980s, showed an interest in psychoanalysis, it fizzled out leaving both disciplines to carry on until recently with little reference to each other. With a revival in the interest in constructionism and the new interest in discovering how subjectivity and identity are acquired which modernity has forced upon us (Giddens 1991), psychoanalysis is again seen to be relevant to anthropology and there are now several ongoing debates between the two disciplines (Heald and Deluz 1994). The debate concerning the Oedipus complex has also been revived.

Malinowski based his argument about 'the matrilineal complex' on the location of authority in the Trobriand family, rather than on sexual relationships, whereas in the situation discussed by Freud a boy's hostility to his father may be motivated either by his rivalry with him for the love of his mother or by the father's punitive authority. Taking up the debate again in the early 1980s Spiro argued that Freud's position was sound and the Oedipus complex was universal (Spiro 1982). Spiro based his argument on Malinowski's own ethnographic description which, despite Malinowski's disclaimer of this aspect of the complex, gave plenty of evidence that there was an erotic component in the relationships between a Trobriand mother and her son. He also pointed to the rather obvious fact which Malinowski seemed to have overlooked, that in the Trobriand Islands a boy does indeed live with his father during the first five years of his life, the very time when the Oedipus complex as outlined by Freud is formed and resolved. The father thus has ample opportunity to assert his position with respect to his son. Finally, with a stinging argument Spiro noted that since Malinowski accepted that taboos on sexual relationships reflected the existence of erotic desire in the case of the father/daughter and the brother/sister relationships in the Trobriand family, how was it that he did not accept a similar explanation for the existence of the taboo on mother/son incest? Indeed Spiro conflated the Oedipus complex with human sexuality. He asked how the Oedipus complex possibly could not be universal, since in every human society mothers have sexual partners (Spiro 1987: 88).

Being an anthropologist Spiro did not expect the Oedipus complex to be cross-culturally uniform. It could, he acknowledged, take different expressions in different contexts. However, he always interpreted the processes of resolution along the lines of the western paradigm. For example, he thought that in societies where painful initiation rites were practised these were evidence of an incomplete repression of Oedipal desires and the function of such rites were to help complete the repression process (Spiro 1987). The result of Spiro's way of thinking was that the western Oedipus complex was considered the norm against which all other constellations were measured and that psychological and social levels were kept apart, leaving the latter as a sort of appearance which when you examine it is only skin deep.

Spiro placed a great deal of emphasis on the physical presence of the Trobriand father in the household while his son was an infant and a small child. While this is important, he overlooked the general context into which the child is born. Obeyesekere highlighted this and also noted that this was in fact recognised by Freud (Obeyesekere 1990: 73). That is to say, a child's sexuality is not a biological reflex, but it arises from the child's social relationship with his or her mother and in this way it also reflects her social and familial relationships. In the Trobriand Islands a woman's special relationship to her brother was characterised by his authority and by strict avoidance and sexual taboos between them. This also must have been communicated to her son even though they did not all live in the same household and in this way the physical absence of the mother's brother did not 'deny the psychic reality of his presence' (Obeyesekere 1990: 74). Furthermore, since a boy must himself become a mother's brother to his sister's children and a figure of authority he must at some stage identify with this man rather than exclusively with his father. As Obeyesekere remarks, this poses a special problem for the Trobriand resolution of the Oedipus complex and suggests that the kin which are involved in the Oedipus complex varies according to the social organisation in which it occurs and that:

> In this matrilineal complex . . . there are four crucial relationships in the son's circle of Oedipal kin: father, mother, sister and mother's brother. Within this group it might well be that the child's relation to the sister and mother's brother is the set that is significant for the formation of neuroses in Trobriand. (Obeyesekere 1990: 75)

Malinowski's original insistence that a boy's erotic desire for his mother is irrelevant for the assessment of the Oedipal complex in the Trobriand has been rejected by subsequent anthropologists. In fact all commentators accept that there are in the relationships between parents and their children tensions, partly reflected in the worldwide existence of incest taboos, which must be resolved for the children to grow up as balanced socially well-functioning adults. It is now the social-psychological context of these relationships and the way this contributes to how persons interact, communicate and resolve these tensions which are under debate. We no longer assume that principles of interaction and communication are uniform even if we do concede that certain basic needs and abilities related to caring and attachment are universal. In this respect Kurtz has made an interesting argument. Obeyesekere had observed that in Hindu Indian versions of Oedipal myths it is the father who kills the son rather than the son who destroys his father (Ramanujan 1983; Obeyesekere 1990: 75–88; Trawick 1992). The son in Hindu India is thus seen to remain submissive not just to the authority of his father but also to the erotic attachment to his mother. The son must, so the classic interpretation goes (Kakar 1978; Roland 1988; Obeyesekere 1990), repudiate his masculinity often through symbolic self-castration or homosexual tendencies and consequently for Hindu men, women remain ambiguous, loving, seductive and devouring. The dichotomy between wife and whore expressed in the Hindu imagery and myths of benevolent and malevolent goddesses can therefore never be reconciled (Obeyesekere 1990: 30–1, 75–105). The only reason why this pattern does not throw up unlimited pathology is, according to Obeyesekere, because it is culturally acceptable and elaborated and because in submitting to his father the son duplicates rather than replaces him and thus submits to the power and authority of the social group.

Kurtz is unhappy with the negative overtones of this interpretation and instead proposes a different and uniquely Hindu pattern of psychological development. This emphasises the expectation of extended patrilineal family living and the consequences of this for the mother and the child. The new bride joins her husband's family in which she is initially at least treated as an outsider. Her mother-in-law and her husband's sisters all have more authority than she. With the birth of a son her position slowly begins to change as the child is not just considered hers but also and predominantly an addition to the patrilineal line and hence belongs not just to his mother but to the other agnatically related women, who all at various times take on the functions of mothers. As the infant grows and is weaned he thus moves from his natural mother with whom he has enjoyed physical intimacy to an immersion in a larger group of for him fundamentally benevolent mothers. Kurtz calls this the ek-hi phase, *ek-hi* meaning 'just one' or 'one and the same'. Of course, from the natural mother's point of view some of these mothers (notably the mother-in-law) are not necessarily experienced as benevolent and hence the ambivalent images of the goddesses which characterise the Hindu pantheon (Kurtz 1992). Kurtz argues that while children in the West move towards an internal identification with the parent when they abandon pleasure at each stage of development, in the Hindu context where the relationship between mother and infant in any case is not powerfully personalised, the child learns that emotional satisfaction is gained through activity in and on behalf of the group. In each case the renunciation has a different meaning and is culturally distinct:

In the West, infantile desires are repudiated and forgotten for the sake of a caretaker's loving demands. In India, infantile desires are recalled and overtly sacrificed for the sake of full and honoured participation in the life of a group. (Kurtz 1992: 231)

From a child's point of view the initial social group is a group of mothers and it is the incorporation into this group which opens the way for an eventual incorporation into a group of adult men. One result of this developmental process is that the submission to rather than the overthrow of paternal authority is a sign of masculinity. Castration may in this way be seen as an attempt to regain rather than repudiate masculinity and the closeness between mature men and their mothers can be understood as an instance of group relations rather than as evidence of an unresolved libidinal attachment. In both cases there is evidence of the existence of a culturally distinctive path towards the resolution of psychic tensions.

This argument attempts to take the debate to a more subtle level because it allows an appreciation of how basic processes and principles of personal interaction by which early attachments and rivalries are transcended, are culturally variable. Kurtz is clear about his aim for psychoanalytic theory:

> I want to find a way of talking about infantile sexuality, the unconscious and the importance of childhood that nonetheless allows us to do justice to the particularities of culture. Central to my project is the thought that we must construct numerous, culturally distinctive paths of development where before we have tended to see various cultures making either tenuous or confident advances along a single, universal path to maturation. (1992: 248)

While this is an improvement on the universalist arguments, this approach also raises other questions. How many different types of complexes might there be? Are there as many as there are societies? And how do we delineate societies as bounded entities anyway given the nature of culture and cultural themes as continuous and diffuse? Kurtz argues for Hindu India but much of the pattern he outlines is also found for Indian Muslims, Sikhs and Buddhists of similar cultural traditions. What then are the defining characteristics of one pattern as opposed to another? These are complex issues to which there are not yet definite answers. To be able to discern variety and to confirm that not all non-western patterns indicate pathology is clearly an important step forward for cross-cultural therapy. But perhaps the most important lesson we can learn from the debate about the universality of the Oedipus complex is the realisation that socially and culturally constructed themes of thought, emotion and action are anchored in the ontology of human beings caring for and being attached to one another. These relationships are reproduced, reconstituted and changed through ongoing involvement and intimate interaction but the content and the details of these interactions are shaped by and embedded in culturally patterned practices. The challenge to the psychotherapist is to keep her awareness of the ontology of these familial attachments while at the same time remaining receptive to variations in patterns which may be very different from her own and of which she is only partially conscious.

This is why I often find it a useful starting point in therapy to engage with mothers and fathers and others in their role as kin and parents and I often ask questions about the rights and responsibilities of these roles in relation to the children. For example, in the case of Mrs Ullah decribed in Chapter 3, it was extremely difficult to get from her some clarity about what kind of help she would like. In Mrs Ullah's own view the troubles she and her family were facing were due to sorcery practised by her affines on her. The sessions with Mrs Ullah on her own and an interpreter often moved towards an impasse: my questions about different aspects of family life or the issues the family were facing were met with more repetition from Mrs Ullah about the sorcery and her husband's vices. In one area, however, we seemed to be able to move forward and develop a sense of mutual understanding. This was in our conversations about motherhood and our responsibilities towards our children. In this Mrs Ullah was able to be lucid and realistic about her eldest son's reluctance to study and the shyness and obsessional behaviour of her youngest son. The sequence ended with Mrs Ullah asking for help for her youngest son and this was the first time she permitted herself to be in charge in a direct way. This did not solve the difficulties Mrs Ullah, her children and the family were facing, but it did provide an immediate point for joining with Mrs Ullah and also informed some of the subsequent interventions. These were aimed at developing the youngest son's self-respect by encouraging communication between him and his father, so that the son had more opportunities to show his father respect and the father had more opportunity to show his son love and care. In this way the son was able to prove not only his allegiance to his father but also his impending manhood and Mr Ullah was able to affirm his traditional role as the head of the family and although Mrs Ullah herself still needed support, the relationship between her and her husband improved.

5

Ritual, Meaning and Therapeutic Efficacy

In the previous chapters I have examined some of the difficulties which therapists and anthropologists are likely to meet in cross-cultural encounters and I have pointed to the delusive nature of observation when we look at others without first looking at ourselves. But this also led me to recognise that some characteristics are shared by human beings anywhere whatever their cultural and social context. In Chapter 4 I concluded that all humans exist in and as a result of social relationships and consequently deep and prolonged attachment between children and their carers is, as far as humans are concerned, an ontological phenomenon. It is this human predicament which gives rise to the social constructive nature of the world as it appears to us or to what Taussig refers to as 'second nature' (1993: xiii). What then does this human predicament encompass? What are the mechanisms by which humans anywhere manage to imbue a natural quality to culture? These questions are relevant to the practice of cross-cultural therapy because the answers will give a variety of pointers to where connections between therapist and clients may be anchored.

In this chapter and the following chapter, I examine two such mechanisms. I turn first to ritual in this chapter and move on to taboo in Chapter 6. Something which may loosely be defined as ritual and taboo are found in all human societies and also appear everywhere to be deeply affected by cultural themes of meaning. Both highlight the strains and stresses which are imposed on human lives by social structures and conventions, and because they are not fixed, because changes in rituals and in taboos can be documented over time, both also encompass the processes through which people comment upon and reconstruct these conditions. This uniqueness of ritual and taboo in somehow providing nodes where social and individual predicaments connect has not been lost on systemic or family psychotherapy. Thus Bateson's original text for the application of cybernetics to social systems was a postscript to a book which was entirely devoted to the examination of one ritual, Naven, among the Iatmul (Bateson 1958 [1932]) and there has recently been an increase of interest in ritual (Imber-Black et al. 1988; Laird 1991;

Woodcock 1995; Child 1996a, 1996b) and in the connection between secrets and socially sanctioned etiquette and ideology (Hare-Mustin 1991; Jones 1991; Cooklin and Gorell Barnes 1993; Imber-Black 1993).

In systemic psychotherapy the intuition that ritual and taboo offer special opportunities for the psychotherapeutic treatment of individuals in their family contexts has mostly been put to use in intra-cultural work, that is to say in the work which white therapists have carried out with white clients. Although anthropologists and family therapists have shared a fascination with ritual and taboo it is not until recently that a curiosity about how these ideas may be applied cross-culturally have begun to emerge. Perhaps it should not surprise us that it has taken so long, for as we have seen in the case of ideas about families and kinship ideology, intra-cultural work does not necessarily uncover assumptions which may be problematic cross-culturally. In intra-cultural work it is possible, if not desirable, to play down difference, that is to say to assume consensus and understanding and also to be uncritical about the extent to which clients and therapist are alike. As a consequence an emphasis on meaning may seem relatively straightforward. In cross-cultural encounters, on the other hand, whether they take place in research, in therapy, in the street or anywhere, meaning may be much less accessible. Therefore, we have to ask ourselves the question of how responsible practice is possible. I suggest that by examining ritual we may move towards an answer.

Ritual, it may be argued, is something we all recognise when we see it. A sequence of action in which actors actively participate by carrying out similar or complementary tasks singularly or together, where the order of the sequence is prescribed and where reference may be made to some more or less obscure objects or texts which many, if not all, of the participants cannot explain, resonates with us and fascinates us. If ritual can be so intuitively understood do psychotherapists need to contemplate any further? Is it not enough to have an operational definition so that we know more or less what we are talking about? I shall argue that systemic psychotherapists and family therapists need to theorise more carefully about ritual. They need to do this not in order to isolate ritual as something special and outstanding (although ritual might be seen in this light) but in order to understand cultural phenomena and how such phenomena work on individual persons, some of whom are our clients. I draw on anthropological work to show that it is not the aspect which generally is thought to be the essence of ritual, namely the emphasis on meaning and symbols, which provides ritual with its efficacy in therapy. Instead I consider that the power of ritual is located in the very nature of ritualised action and this in turn is why thinking and talking about ritual may be useful in cross-cultural therapeutic work.

I begin by examining problems in the interpretation of ritual. I then consider different types of rituals and I discuss in detail the difficulties with an exclusive emphasis on meaning. Finally I describe an alternative view and outline its implications for psychotherapy.

THE PROBLEM WITH RITUAL

I must confess that as an anthropologist I was baffled to discover the elegance and panache with which some family therapists claimed to be designing and using rituals in treatment (Imber-Black et al. 1988). During my ethnographic work I had encountered many different kinds of rituals which were not immediately accessible to me. To some extent I had copied the actions of other people so as not to stand apart and to respect the wishes of my friends and my informants that I should participate. I had placed my forehead in front of the feet of my Nepali Thakuri classificatory sister's husband (*dhog karnu*) after he had touched my forehead applying a mixture of yogurt, tumeric and rice (*tika*) at certain festivals during the year. I had performed a similar action (without the *tika*) in the Sikh *gurdwara* in front of the *Guru Granth Saheb* (the sacred scriptures of the Gurus) and returned to my seat amongst the women knowing full well that the entire congregation had been watching my every step. I had sat around the ritual fire at the *brathbanda* (initiation) of a young Thakuri man listening to the Brahmin reciting many verses in Sanskrit which could not be translated into Nepali by any of the other people taking part in the ritual, including the Brahmin himself.

I do not, for one moment, assume that all these other people were motivated by the same need as I or that their intentions for participating in these various rituals were similar to mine. I took part because I wanted to be accepted and because I wanted to experience the ritual. But all these other people were already accepted and knew what it would be like. They would have had different reasons from mine and perhaps from each other for participating. I am fairly sure about this because I know that the rituals which I call my own are not necessarily performed with consensus or attributed the same meaning by all those who take part. Indeed it seems to be one characteristic of ritual that it may be meaningless, hollow and that nobody really has a clue what it is about, apart from the fact that it has been performed by many others before.

How then can outsiders understand ritual? In his study of the Gnau penis bleeding rituals Lewis shows how difficult this can be (Lewis 1980). The Gnau include about one thousand people who live in the Sepik area of New Guinea and they practise puberty rituals for both boys and girls. Lewis found the boys' rituals especially intriguing. The rites take one day and take place in the hamlet where the boy's maternal relatives are particularly important guests. His mother's brother, or in his place a male relative of his mother's, should perform the actual bleeding and the ritual is to be kept a deep secret from women. The men, including the father of the boy and his paternal relatives gather and chew betel. This they spit on the boy's body so that he becomes covered in red. The men then wash although the boy does not. Traditionally the mother's brother then makes a sharp awl from wallaby bone to which he ties certain scented leaves, moss and ferns to use in the penis bleeding, although sometimes nowadays a razor or a bit of broken glass may be used instead. I quote Lewis's own fieldnotes:

> Wowulden [the boy] was held in the arms of Patik [his father] [Lewis does not identify the relationship between the persons in this extract, but I have according to the information Lewis gives in other sections of his book] with his head resting right back on Patik's shoulder, Patik's arms coming around him binding Wowulden's arms bent up across his chest. Patik's legs thrust the body of Wowulden forward so that his pelvis and penis was offered to Saibuten [a mother's brother] who was to stab him. They were standing slightly downhill. There was a brief flurry as someone thought he saw two girls on the hill. They yelled at them to go; it was a false alarm. Wowulden kept his position, resting back on Patik with his head right back on Patik's shoulder and upraised. Saibuten, bent over the *kuti* [the awl], was whispering spells into it. Then he took Wowulden's penis, rolled back the foreskin and bored the *kuti*'s point into the dorsum of the penis just above the glans. It was not rapidly done and he seemed to dig it well in and hold it there. Wowulden's whole body stiffened but held the position: he gave one brief moan. Saibuten withdrew the *kuti* and there was an exclamation of approval, congratulation and satisfaction from the older men watching. Wowulden immediately crouched down and held a split length of big bamboo containing water into which blood from his penis flowed for some time. Tawo . . . and Bilki [two other men] turned to me wreathed in smiles. Tawo bobbing and thumping his foot, slightly turning as he swayed his body downwards, saying that it was something wholly good they had done, just as their fathers had done it for them . . . Wowulden was still crouched down and bleeding. Parku [a mother's brother] stood over him and, taking a splinter of razor blade, stabbed his own penis so that as he stood with Wowulden crouched between his legs, his blood fell on to Wowulden's shoulders and gradually ran, shining in the sun, down his spine. The blood on his shoulders and back was smeared, some smeared on his forehead. Parku's blood was also collected in a piece of banana leaf containing some of the cooked *wa'agep* [stew]. They took care that no blood fell on the ground. (Lewis 1980: 78)

On certain other occasions Gnau men bleed their penises in secret and away from women. One such occasion is on the puberty rites of a sister's daughter, but there are many others and whenever the bleeding takes place men bathe first and then bleed themselves and not as other people in the same geographical area (Hogbin 1970; Mead 1970 [1938, 1940]) the other way around. These other people or rather the ethnographers who have studied them have reported that penis bleeding is like menstruation, but when Lewis asked directly the Gnau clearly stated 'no, it is not like menstruation' (Lewis 1980: 2). So we have here the associations of red, bleeding from the genitals, puberty rites, secrecy, cross-gender leading to an idea that this ritual performed during the puberty rites for a boy and also regularly by men in secret should be interpreted as a kind of symbolic menstruation which also may reflect men's envy of women's reproductive power. These connections seem reasonable to our minds even though the Gnau themselves think nothing of the kind. Lewis asks,

> By what right or argument shall I maintain that it is symbolic menarche even though they disagree? That it is a 'natural symbol' and they are silent about it? Is it symbolic in itself? Only to me? Or to them also, though somehow unadmitted, hidden from their conscious minds? (1980: 106)

The difficulty lies in the idea that penis bleeding is a symbol or a metaphor. We cannot distinguish whether the Gnau disagree with the metaphor or with the classification of menstruation and penis bleeding in a category together. Whichever way, the focus is ours and they do not see it like that. We have selected certain features of the ritual which for reasons that have to do with ourselves stand out. At the same time we have neglected others, for example secrecy, taboo, blood, ritual heat and general social relationships. In his careful analysis Lewis advocates scepticism towards explanations which incorporate symbolism or expressions which are not apparent and not explicit in the minds of the actors. By widening his enquiry he is able to suggest that for the Gnau, penis bleeding rituals have more to do with men's protection of women and other dependants and the safe growth and development of youngsters than with gender politics, consciously or unconsciously expressed. In fact this interpretation is also much more in line with what the Gnau themselves said, although many people were able to say very little about it. Arriving at this conclusion, however, is no occasion for intellectual conceit, for even if Lewis's own view is now nearer to that of the Gnau, he also emphasises that the rituals (and any ritual) are more like a painting or a work of art than an annotated text.

RITUAL AND SOCIETY

We might find the idea of a ritual as a work of art attractive and we might share the opinion that it is beautiful, expressive or evocative. But to appeal to aesthetics will not absolve us of our difficulties. On the contrary it might compound them. Whole continents were robbed by colonists who considered the objects of the natives beautiful, but this was usually typical of a particular stage of the colonising process and generally did not result in indigenous people being understood on their own terms. We are still left with the question of how to access ritual.

Ritual has become one of those concepts, which has taken on a kind of special existence in anthropology. It has come to denote particular types of events often subsumed under the larger category of religion and generally assumed to be worthy of scrutiny and elegant analysis aimed at uncovering deep secrets about how societies and cultures operate and this is often irrespective of whether the people performing the rituals see it this way or not. This idea that through ritual something is revealed about society in general and that this something can be understood relatively straightforwardly by outsiders derives from the work of Emile Durkheim, whose ideas about ritual can be found in *The Elementary Forms of Religious Life* (1915).

Durkheim's argument goes something like this. In contrast to animals who are largely genetically pre-programmed, human beings think and live conceptually. This creates great potential for cooperation, cohesion and communication but only if there also is restraint. Society is based on shared moral laws or compulsions and one of the ways in which this is accomplished is through ritual: 'We cooperate because we think alike, and we think alike thanks to ritual' (Gellner 1992: 37). Ritual is thus assumed to operate directly on individuals so that they internalise the codes or structures, the categories and classifications (the collective representations) which maintain the social order. For example in the case of initiation rituals which involve the marking of the human body, the compulsion is accomplished especially effectively through the administration of pain which takes on the form of a memory inscribed on the body (Das 1995). Ritual thus has an integrating effect as well as a socialising effect. It integrates us with each other and is considered to be a pretty good thing for us and for society. There are echoes here of Radcliffe-Brown's functionalism and also of the view sometimes expressed in family therapy that as a therapeutic approach rituals have a healing effect because of the almost natural efficacy of symbols to unite and integrate.

Imber-Black reports on such an integrating ritual designed during therapy with a heterosexual couple. The intervention involved the couple each wearing T-shirts with key symbols on the front. The symbols were derived from sequences of interaction in which the partners called each other names and which ususally tended to contribute to further deterioration of their communication (Imber-Black 1988). The man's favourite accusation of his spouse was that she was 'mouthy' while the woman repeatedley used the characterisation 'evil' about him. The therapist encouraged the couple to buy T-shirts with appropriate symbols and to put them on every time an argument was looming. This they did: his T-shirt had a picture of a snake on the front and hers a picture of a pair of bright red lips. Again as in the case of the Gnau penis bleeding ritual it seems to us reasonable to accept that intuitively the associations – viper = evil; giant red lips = mouthy; T-shirt = informality – make sense and perhaps even encompass some deeper integrative meanings for the couple.

One difficulty with this assumption is that the way ritual operates on individual persons is obscure. Imber-Black does not demonstrate how the symbols facilitate a process of change. It is simply assumed that it is the efficacy of symbols presumably derived from their shared meanings which account for the success of the therapy. But actually it is difficult to discover what it was about the symbols chosen which made the intervention successful. This is a well-recognised difficulty with Durkheim's ideas. Collective representations can be seen to mould and shape the subjective states of individuals, but cannot account for the continued existence of the human potential for reconstitution, invention, change and agency. For Durkheim once human beings are compelled by the social order there seems to be nothing left for them but to conform. It is not possible to distinguish those aspects which are external to individuals from those which are internal and private or personal. The two are as one. In this way a large area of human activity and relationships cannot be explained, for Durkheim's individual would be devoid of agency and would not be able to recognise choice nor be able to change except as a result of general social changes. It therefore appears to be a distinct possibility that something else happened during the therapy with the arguing couple which led to an improvement of their relationship.

There is something of a paradox in placing great emphasis on the capacity of symbols to create meaning, to speak to us without words and to express many different meanings at the same time, as Imber-Black following Victor Turner proposes (Imber-Black 1988). As Lewis showed it is these qualities of symbols, which are troublesome when we try to explain and interpret what others do and this was indeed the source of my astonishment as a trainee family therapist as far as the design and enactment of rituals in therapy were concerned. I now consider that serious problems about how to understand and interpret rituals were being overlooked. At best something else might have been happening when the rituals seemed to bring about positive results. At worst the creation and execution of new rituals in therapy provided a platform for the therapist's omnipotence and manipulation. As a minimum require-ment therefore any sort of claim to the efficacy of rituals designed and carried out during therapy must include some account of how clients construct and develop symbols from their own points of view. To be fair Imber-Black and her colleagues seem to be aware of these dangers when, in the postcript to the book quoted above, they point out that they are becoming more interested in the 'normative and naturally occurring rituals in the lives of families' (Imber-Black et al. 1988: 403).

If there are then risks in the use of rituals when practising intra-culturally, how much more serious might these risks be in cross-cultural practice? Consider for example the use of rituals involving burying or burning either in the therapy room or as a prescription to be carried out between therapy sessions (Imber-Black et al. 1988; Imber-Black and Roberts 1992). Burial is not only associated with death but also with immersion in the womb of the Earth, with the Earth Mother (Cooper 1970: 174) and with religious conversion (Smith, personal communica-tion) and amongst some people, such as Hindus, not at all the preferred method of disposing of bodily remains. Similarly, fire may denote destruction, but is also associated with purification, transformation, the lifegiving powers of the Sun; renewal of life, impregnation, power, strength and energy (Cooper 1970: 66). We are dealing with cultural

symbols which may vary greatly in meaning between different populations. Lewis's analysis was based on extensive and careful ethnographic
work over several years, but cross-cultural work may involve working
with families from cultural backgrounds about which the therapist knows
very little. Even if the therapist has some prior cultural experience,
understanding what a ritual is all about culturally or personally to clients
may be difficult.

I met with a young Trinidadian woman, Barbara, over a period of nine
months when she was studying in England as a result of having been
selected for further training by the company she worked for in Trinidad.
Barbara was an extremely successful secretary/manager and also the
mother of two daughters. During the time she spent in England her two
daughters were being cared for by her elderly mother in Trinidad.
Barbara had had her first baby at 17 and the second, two years later and
although the relationship with the girls' father had lasted more than ten
years she had always been quite clear that she never intended to marry
this man. Her own mother had never married and Barbara's father was a
different man from the father of her four brothers and sisters. Barbara
found it very difficult being so far away from home and from her now
teenage daughters who she felt needed her protection and guidance.
Several issues came up in our conversations. Barbara was upset about
never having spoken to her biological father. She was especially angry
with her mother for not assisting her in making contact, even though she
knew that her father lived near her home in Trinidad and she frequently
met him in the street. Barbara had also been upset by the news that her
eldest daughter had started menstruating while she was away and felt that
she should be back home to advise her and teach her about womanhood.
She was preoccupied with whether or not she herself should get married.
She wondered with some urgency if she should get married in church to
her current boyfriend, who she described as a good man. This decision
felt urgent because her mother was getting old and 'she would be so
proud to see me married before she dies'. Her mother had always dreamt
of having one of her daughters married in church in a white dress and
Barbara talked about the white wedding dress she would buy and about
the dress her mother would wear.

It did not seem difficult for a white European therapist from a
Protestant background, like myself, to connect with the themes Barbara
presented. Here were the themes of fertility and virginity and a holy
union between a man and a woman in matrimony woven beautifully
together in Barbara's account. There was also marriage as a symbol of
legitimacy and the painful experience of a child who had been denied
this. In fact this way of understanding and connecting the different strands
in Barbara's account was wrong. Not completely wrong, but wrong
enough to be a misrepresentation.

Reporting on Christianity and other religious influences in Trinidad,
Littlewood observes that Trinidadian Catholicism is nominal and that

there is little interest in the Virgin, who stands neglected and in poor repair in village churches (Littlewood 1993: 141). This observation may not be relevant to the outlook Barbara presented in the therapy, but does at least suggest that one should be cautious in assuming that virginity and the white bride have the same symbolic meaning in Trinidad as they are attributed, for example, in European Catholic countries. Indeed Littlewood also reports on different conventions with respect to sexual procreative relationships. Partners may *friend* or *frequent*, that is to say have a sexual relationship without living together, or they may be *living* (cohabiting). *Living* implies an economic dependence to a certain extent and may be the framework for a stable relationship in which no one strives for a church wedding. In fact men are always expected to support the children they have fathered financially and emotionally no matter what the circumstances. Church marriage conveys *respectability* and suggests that the couple is striving for certain middle-class, white ideals and it also means that a wife could expect to be provided for financially by her husband (Littlewood 1993).

The difference between these sentiments and those more familiar to Europeans is subtle but nevertheless salient for the way Barbara presented her preoccupation with relationships and marriage and for the way she spoke about her white wedding dress. In Trinidad 'recognised paternity, but not virginity, is of importance' (Littlewood 1993: 50) and paternity is not a result of a church marriage, since other unions between men and women are also socially binding. Barbara herself confirmed this. I asked her whether the issue which caused her most shame in relation to her father was the fact that her parents had not been married or the fact that her father (and her mother) had not openly acknowledged her as their child. Barbara answered that it was the latter which she could not bear and which had left her feeling unprotected all her life. She went on to talk about how despite her anger towards her mother she knew that it had also been shameful for her and that her wish to be a white bride was in part a wish to give her mother respectability. For her own part she felt that being married in church would mean that she would finally have someone who would look after her. The therapy went on to explore how Barbara could begin to talk to her mother about these issues so that she could become clearer about how and on what basis she could make choices for herself.

Barbara's notion of the symbol of the white wedding dress and of marriage was influenced by general Trinidadian cultural themes and I could not understand the meaning Barbara was attributing to these without having some idea of how these meanings differed from those which I might attribute to the same symbols. For Barbara the white wedding dress was both a cultural and a personal symbol of *respectability* and did not connect to ideas of virginity or sexual shame. She also personally connected her own wish for a church marriage to her lifelong wish to be looked after, something she had missed out on even though

Trinidadian children generally do not miss out on this whatever the relationship between their biological parents. As far as Barbara is concerned, Durkheim was right to suppose that rituals and the symbols employed in rituals tell us something about society. But what it tells about individuals must be interpreted against the background of their personal circumstances and cannot be read off directly from social conventions. This means that meaning must be checked out, not against the background of general ideology but against the way particular persons feel and think and the way they connect a symbol to their own life situation. As far as ritual is concerned this procedure involves several difficult problems and I shall return to these below. First it is necessary to look a bit closer at what ritual is.

WHAT IS RITUAL?

What then is ritual? Recently family therapists have opted for an emphasis on symbols and have followed Turner's definition of a ritual as: 'prescribed formal behaviour for occasions not given over to technological routine, having reference to beliefs in mystical beings or powers. The symbol is the smallest unit of ritual' (1967: 19). This emphasis on symbols can be found for example in the work of Roberts (1988), Imber-Black and Roberts (1992), Papp and Imber-Black (1996), Whiting (1988) and Child (1996b). Although Turner suggested a more dynamic idea of the interaction of persons in cultures and in society than Durkheim, he also emphasised the idea of the collective. He called this *communitas* and by this he meant 'a bond uniting . . . people over and above any formal social bonds' (Turner 1974: 45) and he suggested that secular rituals were similar to religious ones, except for the reference to mystical beings or powers. But if ritual symbols can be secular how do we decide when something is symbolic and when it is not in everyday life? Surely all communication and all use of language, however concretising, involves some use of symbols. How do we as observers decide whether meaning is representational (represents something as it really is, or really seen to be) metaphorical or invocative (Taylor 1985a)? As we saw from Lewis's material this is particularly difficult in cross-cultural work, but it may also be a problem in intra-cultural work. A distinction between ritual involving multiple meanings on different levels on the one hand and ordinary tasks which do not have such meanings on the other (Roberts 1988: 8), does not stand up except for the fact that in the case of ritual those involved (including the therapist) *believe* that they are doing something different.

It is, however, equally difficult to see what is achieved if we end up with a definition of ritual which is so general that it includes virtually everything we do regularly. Thus quoting Bocock, Goody argues that if we include in our definition of ritual:

'handshaking, teeth cleaning, taking medicines, car riding, eating, entertaining guests, drinking tea, or coffee, beer, sherry, whisky etc., taking the dog for a walk, watching television, going to the cinema, listening to records, visiting relatives, routines at work, singing at work, children's street games, hunting and so on' then one can . . . go on adding activities *ad infinitum*. And what's the point? We have then a category that includes almost all action that is standardised in some way or other, and we then have to begin all over again breaking it down into some more meaningful categories. (Goody 1977: 27)

And we might include in this list having psychotherapy or giving papers at conferences. If ritual action involves prescription and repetition how is this different from other social action, since routinisation, regularisation and repeated patterns of interaction lie at the very base of social life itself (Goody 1977: 28)? Family therapists have not been particularly interested in this difference. For example, the Milan therapists, who were the first to think about and introduce ritual in their practice, in 1977 defined ritual as referring 'to an action or a series of actions, sometimes accompanied by verbal formulas or expressions, that are to be carried out by all members of the family' (Selvini Palazzoli et al. 1977: 452). The Milan team had earlier described the use of symbolic action, such as a burial of a dead child's clothes (Selvini Palazzoli et al. 1974) but in general they placed more emphasis on the formal (the action) rather than on the symbolic (the meaning) aspects of ritual. Thus a well-known ritual used by this group is their odd days/even days prescription (on even days the father is to bathe the son/on odd days the mother).

The Milan therapists made an important contribution to the creation of family therapy as an approach which deliberately set out to focus on patterns of interaction, repetition and routinisation, but this was before anyone in family therapy was seriously interested in diversity in meaning and polysemy. It is, I think, fair to say that much of the early family therapy practice, including that of the early Milan approach, assumed that everybody, regardless of gender, class, culture and so on, thought, felt and behaved on the basis of similar principles. We are no longer so sure about this. So how is the weekly clinical meeting or brushing one's teeth different from daily worship? How is ritual different from the general patterns which family therapists have been trained to spot and which can be observed, punctuated and commented upon in family therapy sessions?

First a word of warning about dichotomies. It might be tempting to keep a distinction between that which is religious and that which is secular. In anthropology such dichotomies have been responsible for much colonising theory and practice. For example in the debate about science and religion: we have science, they have religion and magic (Lloyd 1990; Tambiah 1990; Just 1991; Taussig 1993); or in the debate about rationality: we have rationality, they have irrationality (Winch 1979; Shweder 1984; Hastrup 1995). These dichotomies go back to standards set in nineteenth-century European society and in anthropology they are associated with the names of James Frazer and Edward Tylor. Human beings were seen to be inherently rational and scientific, intent on finding out about what causes what in the world and on building up rules for regulating our own behaviour and judging our own success. People in other societies where the standards were different were consequently considered to be not very good at using their brains or to be confused. This was 'primitive man', who was seen to be prone to magical and animistic thinking. Perhaps surprisingly there are echoes of these views in much more recent work. Thus O'Connor and Hoorwitz (1988) consider that ritual operates with the help of pre-scientific modes of thought and the use of contagious and imitative magic, and in this context they quote Piaget, who described prescientific modes of thought as inherently childish (Piaget 1954 [1937]; Piaget and Inhelder 1956 [1948]). According to Piaget children do not develop formal operational thinking which is characteristic of abstract and generalising thought until they reach a certain stage of maturity. Before this the logic children use is preoperational, that is to say concrete and undifferentiated, magical and animistic. Humans are thus considered to be inherently rational and scientific even if this is not evident until a certain stage of cognitive maturation is reached. Grown adults from different societies where the standard for experimentation and explanation are different from those operating in the West and who therefore do not fit the model, are consequently considered to be like children. This view is remarkably similar to those held by early anthropologists. It overlooks the non-rational, that is to say those points in a cognitive structure which are beyond standards of logic and science:

> Someone who only read the Piagetian literature would never guess that every child is immersed in a 'framed' universe made up of distinctive constitutive presuppositions, customs, traditions, expressive rituals, and arbitrary classifications, and that somehow the expressive symbols and nonrational ideas of one generation are rapidly becoming part of the emerging sense of self in the younger generation. (Shweder 1984: 53)

It also overlooks what we know, namely that the development of a consistent, integrated and generalised worldview in a child is linked to the interpersonal social interaction and communication which takes place between children and those who care for them (Trevarthen 1980, 1987; Trevarthen and Logotheti 1989; see also Chapter 4) and is not something which happens in isolation inside the child. Thus if the prevailing mode of defining and thinking about personhood is in terms of social context rather than inherent private qualities (Krause 1995) this will also affect the developmental stages which children pass through and the way these are theorised (Kurtz 1992).

One further observation about the dichotomous view should be made. The tendency in family therapy to consider rituals as beneficial (Woodcock 1995; Child 1996a, 1996b) and able to unlock stuckness in families by invoking special meaning and mystery (O'Connor and Hoorwitz 1988) may also be seen as part of this tradition except that in this case the nonscientific, that which is not normally celebrated, the mystical and the transcendental, is romanticised. This overlooks the fact that rituals can be put to different uses. Some may be aimed at healing, bringing together or performing special acts, assisting life-cycle changes or marking seasonal changes whereas others may involve the expression of oppressive anger, the use of power, physical torture, perversity, malevolence and sexual or physical abuse (Schieffelin 1976; Girard 1977 [1972]; Valeri 1985; Laird 1991; Sinason 1994). We cannot assume rituals to be benign and to have positive emotional connotations for all those who take part.

DIFFERENT KINDS OF RITUALS

The difficulty with ritual is not just the elusiveness of its definition, but also the existence of many different kinds of rituals. Even when we may intuitively feel that we can identify what it is we are talking about, the similarities may gloss over important differences. Classification of rituals may be made according to many different principles, for example according to the timing or according to location. Recently Humphrey and Laidlaw (1994) have suggested a more fundamental and encompassing distinction between liturgical rituals and performance centred rituals. Liturgical rituals are rituals in which contemporary practice is aimed at reproducing the original meanings of texts or of original forms of the ritual. Examples of these types of rituals are the sacraments in Catholicism or the daily Hindu worship (*puja*) and the correct way of performing these rituals remains, as it probably always has been, a focus for religous concern and debate, such as for example the debate which culminated in the Protestant Reformation in Europe. For the purpose of therapy I would include rituals which are deeply embedded in either cultural or family traditions and in which prescription is an important issue. Liturgical rituals may achieve an effect insofar as the very act of carrying them out leads to a change of state or to a conscious emotional experience in the participants. They may also be carried out in order to achieve certain ends, for example to prevent misfortune, to ask for forgiveness, to effect a recovery from illness or as in the case of the Gnau puberty rituals, to effect the healthy and proper maturation of young men. In this sense ritual procedures may be causally effective (Gardner 1983). Equally they could also be carried out as part of regular routines or a habit without the participants bothering too much about why they are doing what they are doing, except perhaps to refer to the notion that 'these kinds of rituals have always been done in this way' or to consider the regular participation in the rituals as preventative.

It may be tempting to use the terms 'script' or 'text' to describe the principles upon which liturgical rituals are based. But this would be misleading. The idea of script has also been used to give a description of expectations about patterns of behaviour and thought which are not ritualised and which are part of the routines of everyday life (Byng-Hall 1995) and although it is the case that many rituals involve the ritual reading of certain texts (for example the continuous and complete reading of the *Guru Granth Saheb* on certain occasions in Sikh temples or of the Mahzor on the Jewish holy day of Yom-Kippur), it is not in the ancient and/or obscure texts that the clue to the meaning of the ritual is to be found. There is a difference between ritual practice and religious commentary (Humphrey and Laidlaw 1994).

It is not, however, enough that ritual action should be performed in a prescribed sequence. It should also be apprehended by those who perform the acts and it should be given meaning, even if this meaning is that it is without meaning as is the case in the Jain *puja* described by Humphrey and Laidlaw (1994). Jains use the word 'meaningless' in a religious sense, since all external actions (including ritual) are irrelevant to an understanding of the transformation of the soul (Humphrey and Laidlaw 1994: 2). In other cases, such as when a ritual is believed to achieve or effect an aim causally, the meaning of the ritual cannot be established without reference to what the participants themselves believe. Liturgical rituals tend to be addressed to the self or to the self in relation to someone other (God or deity), and only indirectly at an audience which may or may not be present, but the fact that the meaning of a ritual is personal and private does not of course exclude the possibility that it is also shared either by several persons or by a community.

The emphasis on a set sequence in liturgical rituals stands in contrast to those rituals which clearly address audiences and therefore may be described as performance rituals. In these rituals the question is not so much 'Have we got it right?' as 'Has it worked?' (Humphrey and Laidlaw 1994: 11). Their efficacy depends on whether the performance is convincing and accepted as authentic by the audience and not, as in liturgical rituals, on whether particular actions have been carried out in a particular sequence. In performative rituals the ritual performers may draw on a repertoire of ritual acts as well as on improvisation to make the ritual successful. A famous example of a performance-centred ritual of this kind, is the account of the shaman in an essay by Lévi-Strauss entitled 'The Sorcerer and his Magic' (1963).

This is the story of Quesalid, a Kwaikutl Indian and it was obtained by Franz Boas, one of the founding fathers of American anthropology. It was first published in 1930, but is famous both in anthropology and in psychotherapy (Frank and Frank 1961). Quesalid was curious and sceptical about shamanistic practices and therefore sought the company of shamans, so that he could find out more. They eventually offered to make him a member of their group and he was taught one of the most guarded secrets of their healing practices:

> The shaman hides a little tuft of down in a corner of his mouth, and he throws it up, covered with blood, at the proper moment – after having bitten

his tongue or made his gums bleed – and solemnly presents it to his patient and the onlookers as the pathological foreign body extracted as a result of his sucking and manipulations. (Lévi-Strauss 1963: 175)

Quesalid was pretty disgusted with what he had learnt, but wanted to continue his enquiries. However, this was not so simple. Soon he was called upon to act as the healer for a family with a sick member and the treatment he administered was a resounding success. Later when he visited a neighbouring community he was amazed to discover that they used a different technique. Instead of spitting the illness out in the form of a bloody worm, these shamans merely spat a bit of saliva into their hands and presented this as the sickness. Once when this treatment had not worked Quesalid asked if he could try his own method. He was again successful, impressing the old shaman with his technique. However, this experience presented him with a dilemma. He had had few illusions about his own technique, but now he had found a technique which was more false, more mystifying and more dishonest than his own! The shaman who had failed to cure pleaded with him to reveal the secret so that he could regain his respect as well as his livelihood, but Quesalid resisted. The shaman was disgraced and soon left the community and Quesalid moved on to become a famous healer defending the technique of the bloody worm against rival schools.

Lévi-Strauss muses about the similarities between this practice and that of modern science where different paradigms also might have different validity and asks from which frame of reference we shall judge them. Since authenticity derives from the social consensus and failure is a result of this consensus breaking down rather than of the actual failures and successes of the shamans this question has no easy answers. All that can be said is that the outcome is uncertain until somehow the audience is convinced and that this is not necessarily related to whether or not the illness is controlled or cured (which we might distinguish from whether or not the patient feels better). Rather it involves social relations and the status and power of the shaman: 'Quesalid did not become a great shaman because he cured his patients; he cured his patients because he had become a great shaman' (Lévi-Strauss 1963: 180).

There are of course many rituals which combine elements of both liturgical and performance-centred rituals. Initiation rituals such as that described for the Gnau involve both a sequence of prescribed action which is believed to effect the proper growth of the initiant and an audience, and it may also achieve a change of state in the boy and in other participants. Similarly in the *bar mitzva*, the Jewish rite of passage for boys, there is some notion of a sequence, but the performative aspects both in the sense of involving an audience and in the sense of affecting a change in the states of the participants, also plays a dominant role. The social group is brought together and the ritual is constitutive of the new status of the boy expressed in his ability to read in public and behave like a responsible adult man. Davis's description of the way the *bar mitzva* was carried out in four very different Jewish families emphasises both the extent to which the liturgical and the performative aspects of a ritual may vary. Thus in an orthodox Hasidic family where ritual was a way of life the *bar mitzva* was one of many rituals carried out throughout the year and a person's lifetime. As a consequence the *bar mitzva* for the son in this family was aimed to work directly on the child's experience of himself and to effect his change of status (Davis 1988: 187–8). There was a more public ceremony afterwards which was performance centred, but the actural *bar mitzva* was considered to have been completed in the first *aliyah* (the first blessing of the Torah in the Rebbe's congregation the day after his 13th birthday).

In another family where religion and cultural identity was not so particularly emphasised the *bar mitzva* of the son was an occasion for much more improvisation. In this family it was a 'family project' planned by the family together and in this way much more performance centred. The boy demonstrated his independence and competence as a young man in the party afterwards in ways which had not been prescribed (for example he sang and danced with the sexy lead singer of the band which was entertaining) rather than during the more religious part of the ceremony.

HEALING RITUALS

As psychotherapists we may find ourselves in sympathy with Quesalid and accept that our work legitimately involves persuasion and perhaps even milder forms of trickery. The more serious issue, however, is about the connection we make with our clients and the principles which we can agree form the basis for this. This is not only important in our practice as psychotherapists or family therapists but also in training. Do we ourselves confuse liturgical and performative aspects of rituals? Do we claim to join and facilitate when in fact we direct and dominate? What are our credentials as healers? Do we have a framework?

Bateson's analysis of Naven was not motivated by the need to find solutions, but rather by a wish to understand what was going on in Iatmul society. It was ritual as an instance of social interaction and as I have noted, therapists also make use of this idea in trying to understand the way social and cultural themes are connected to or articulate individual and personal ones. Nevertheless, therapists are also to varying degrees in the business of offering solutions and therefore of trying to heal. As we have seen, in rituals, such as those performed by Quesalid, the specialist draws on a repertoire of skills and also uses a great deal of improvisation. It is the expertise of the shaman and the acknowledgement of this by the audience or the community rather than the performance of the ritual per se, which aims to achieve a cure. The western therapist uses a different culturally specific professional framework and style, but nevertheless the parallel is clear: the psychotherapist or the family therapist is a western kind of shaman. Most rituals generated and performed during western psychotherapy are performance rituals of this kind. Their authenticity is derived from an agreement between patients and therapists, and between family members, about the terms used and about the parameters of the performance. They are constitutive, in that the aim is to facilitate a new experience and a change of emotional or cognitive states in those who take part while at the same time marking such changes. They are not, as in the case of liturgical rituals, seen to derive efficacy from the carrying out of a set sequence of prescribed acts nor is it assumed that they can effect a specific cause. It is the general and collective experience that counts. Theoretically it may be possible that a ritual designed with the help of a therapist could become a kind of liturgical ritual, but for this to happen the ritual would have to be assimilated into the family tradition, incorporated into the family's beliefs about cause and effect, repeated regularly and attributed a prescribed sequence of action imbued with importance and meaning even if this could not be articulated by all those who took part. While therapists might hope that their intervention could have such a pervasive influence in the lives of their clients, I have not been able to find a convincing example of a ritual designed and performed in therapy being incorporated into family tradition.

In contrast to these performance-centred rituals which are characteristic of therapy, liturgical rituals may not be aimed directly at healing or achieving solutions. Nevertheless, healing may be an aspect of both the intention and the result of the rituals even if these are not part of the original (official) aim of the ritual. This is because the efficacy of liturgical ritual derives from a sequence of ritualised action itself and in this way operates directly on the body of the performer. Liturgical rituals are less task orientated and perhaps this is why they are popular as measures to be taken in order to achieve all sorts of other purposes. Thus a person may perform a prayer for a specific purpose, such as to achieve recovery or good health, but the same prayer may equally be made routinely, as part of something one does every day, every year or at regular intervals. The action in the ritual may take on many different meanings apart from those which might be deciphered historically by examining context, texts and records. Each person who takes part may have a different intention: to please God, to purify oneself, to effect personal discipline, to repent, to affect the lives of loved ones, to keep the routine and so on, none of which may be connected with the historical or religious explanation of ritual. As with ritual itself the healing aspect of ritual is exceedingly difficult to pin down. On the one hand performative rituals officially aimed at healing cannot avoid being directive or instructive even if they also may involve a good deal of consensus. For therapists and healers they pose Quesalid's dilemma of cause and effect, expertise, legitimacy and responsible practice. On the other hand, liturgical rituals which appeal to some vague notion of collectivity while encompassing many individual interpretations cannot be designed in therapy. This leaves two options.

The therapist may copy or take part in rituals with clients. This is probably the closest way a therapist can experience the world from the client's point of view. By taking part as a participant the therapist is exposed to aspects of ritual which cannot be observed and in this way is able to access a new angle which is not acessible through words. It is, however, worth remembering my experience from Nepal: while I gained new insight participation was not the same as understanding and there was no sudden revelation of *the* meaning of it all.

The second option is to talk about ritual in therapy. This can be therapeutic such as in the attempts reported by Woodcock (1995) to help refugee families reclaim and reawaken 'naturally occurring' life-cycle rituals or seasonal rituals, which have been temporarily lost or suppressed. These are liturgical rituals which have marked collective and personal meanings and by talking about them the rituals are to some extent recreated and cultural as well as general human themes relating to issues of time and space validated. Talking about ritual in therapy can also be a way of addressing issues of identity and social change, such as with the Ismaili Gujerati family mentioned in Chapter 4. One of the issues for the parents in this family was that their eldest daughter had decided to marry a white English man, and since the father had been an important official in their local mosque and since the mother was a devout Muslim, this had upset them both very much. They could not, however, agree on how to approach the problem and blamed each other consistently for their predicament and for the stalemate they felt they were in, in terms of solving the problem of how to carry out the wedding. Should they give in altogether and have a Church of England wedding or should they insist on certain aspects of their own traditional wedding ceremony? The tension between the parents was reduced considerably after a session was spent on the wedding ceremony. In this session we discussed the way they could best integrate their own traditional wedding ritual with that of the Church of England. We considered all their own rituals in detail as well as those normally carried out as part of an English wedding. Since a Gujerati wedding involves many different gifts from different relatives on one side to relatives on the other side, we discussed which of their traditional marriage presentations they felt they wanted to make and which they would be willing to leave out. Who did they feel should be invited? What had happened at their own wedding? Which rituals would they want to include given the great difference between the two types of weddings and given that they both wanted the new couple to start their married life auspiciously? Which English rituals did they find particularly distasteful? In this case the marriage ritual signalled the family's cultural and religious identity and therefore took on a special meaning standing apart from English marriage rituals. However, we were also able to find several parallels between the way things were done in their own community and the way English rituals conveyed the same issues.

While it is thus the case that ritual is imbued with special significance in most cultures and that conversations and explorations around 'naturally occurring rituals' therefore may be therapeutic, it is also clear that similar conversations and explorations can equally well take place around other non-ritual cultural aspects and themes. What then is so special about the 'doing' and the action in ritual? It is now time to take a closer look at the distinction between action and meaning which already has been alluded to several times.

THE POWER OF RITUALS

In family therapy few have been concerned with distinctions between different types of rituals or between different aspects of the same ritual. The result has been a variety of definitions and a lack of clarity about what exactly it is that we think makes rituals efficacious in therapy. From the outset there has been a tension between the more prescribed and action orientated approach of the early Milan group, and the approaches which have been inspired by the anthropologist Victor Turner focusing on the role of symbols. This tension is still there. In a recent journal article Shamai (1995) describes violence against a partner in a couple as a ritual, and places emphasis on action and behaviour, while Woodcock (1995) writing in the same issue places much more emphasis on meaning and on the existential issues with which families, in this case families in exile, have to contend. In a commentary on the two papers Child (1996a) notes the incongruity between the two approaches. On the one hand the unplanned, power driven, unthinking enactment of violence, on the other, the planned, prescribed and directed repetition of tradition. On both counts it is, as I have already discussed, difficult to see how ritualisation differs from more general phenomena. In the first case, the violence towards a partner is an instance of a repeated pattern of interaction which includes the routinisation and regularisation of everyday life in that family. In the second case, talking about rituals during treatment is an instance of general interaction and communication around cultural themes which all have the possibility of conveying meaning and receiving existentialist interpretations. Such interpretations could of course be therapeutic and therefore healing, but equally possibly they could help re-enact abusive, negative and destructive moments. To some extent Child himself reproduces this duality but he also includes an observation of the *process* of ritualisation, noting that this includes enactments which have a characteristic structure and mode of attention and which 'gives ritual proper its quality of "solemn observance"' (Child 1996a: 120). Here I think that Child is on the right track and I shall now explain why.

I have already noted the problems with Turner's definition of ritual which emphasises the role of symbols in ritual (Turner 1967: 19). We know that symbols are characterised by polysemy, that symbols can have many meanings. Indeed it is this characteristic which is often cited as the power of symbols to unite. However, as we have seen, it is precisely this polysemy which also is troublesome when we try to explain and understand what others do. How do we find out which meaning clients or informants hold to be important? How do we find out whether certain symbols really unite? Certainly we can talk about it, but that is often easier said than done and what of the instance where a person does not know? We cannot dismiss this as a ritual which has lost its efficacy. Performing ritual implies particular types of action, verbal and non-verbal, in which the authorship of the actor is to some extent suspended. A person may intentionally decide to perform a ritual, but once in the ritual he or she is likely (to varying degrees) to suspend all personal purpose and calculation. Nevertheless, going through the ritual is an experience which may evoke a variety of emotional and cognitive states. This is why psychoanalysts have likened rituals to dreams (Bott 1972). In rituals, as in dreams, symbolic representations disguise and transform dangerous thoughts and emotions. As we have seen similar assumptions have been made about the use of symbols in family therapy and this is partly why rituals have been considered to constitute powerful and successful interventions with families.

Another reason why the search for meaning is unproductive in trying to understand ritual is that it presumes that ritual is a form of communication. Durkheim, Turner, Geertz, Douglas and Radcliffe-Brown are all anthropologists who considered ritual in this light. Participants in rituals were seen to communicate something to each other and we as outsiders could observe this process which was then also communicating the same thing to us. I have already noted the difficulty in assuming that the meaning of symbols or ritual is something which can be observed. But there are other difficulties with the approach which considers ritual as communication. Even if it is the case that a ritual can be validly seen as evidence that people hold this or that belief, as Durkheim believed was the case, it does not follow that the purpose of performing the ritual is to communicate that belief. Humphrey and Laidlaw cite the following example in a footnote in order to clarify the idea of a communicative act:

> When you blush, this is evidence that you are embarrassed, because blushing is a natural sign of embarrassment. It does not follow that you blush in order to communicate your embarrassment. The notion of communication is tied to that of non-natural meaning. Communicative behaviour is directed towards a potential recipient, who is intended to understand the act in question in a particular way. (1994: 85)

If communicative behaviour implies intention and direction then we would expect people who participate in rituals to know that they do so in order to communicate with their fellow participants. Of course people may say this about rituals but equally often they do not and this raises the question that if people want to say something to each other, why do they not just say it? Why do they need ritual? As Lewis pointed out it has more often been the case that what the anthropologist thought a ritual was communicating was what the anthropologist had surmised and this would then be offered back to the actors as an explanation of what they mean even when they do not know it (Lewis 1980: 117–18). It is obvious that family therapists run the same risks.

RITUALISED ACTION

Let me summarise my argument so far. As therapists we need to have a theory about how ritual works on individuals. This is not only relevant to those psychotherapists who work with ritual but also of general interest because in thinking about ritual we are also thinking about how individuals connect to others and to a collective, be this a family, a group, a culture or a society. On the one hand a theory which points to the power of symbols alone cannot separate ritual from any other aspects of culture and it also has trouble addressing polysemy and understanding diversity in meaning. On the other hand, a theory which includes all patterned behaviour and interaction as ritual is so general that it does not tell us anything at all. So what do we do? I now turn to examine the idea that the most essential aspect of ritual is action, that is to say ritualised action and not symbols or meaning generally.

Rituals are, as are other events, imbued with culture and so they are not immediately accessible to outsiders. They may be more or less accessible so that therapy, where therapists and clients share a common social and cultural background, may produce fewer difficulties than cross-cultural work. Even then there are other kinds of differences such as those based on gender, class, age, sexual orientation, religious outlook, family history, and so on. Across cultures rituals do, however, share certain characteristics. For example, rituals tend to mark or highlight certain types of events, such as the passing of the life cycle, the passing of the year or the seasons and so on. This is why, I think, noting these and talking about these in cross-cultural work, anchored as they are to the human predicament, can also be a good anchor for cross-cultural communication and joining. The performance of ritual activity everywhere also calls for specific expertise, knowledge and prescribed sequences of action. Finally, rituals everywhere tend to be performed with an air of commitment or with what Humphrey and Laidlaw (1994) have called a ritual stance.

The aim of writers such as Humphrey and Laidlaw, and Lewis, as well as others is to question that ritual can be understood in terms of a linguistic model. They prefer to consider ritual, not as a special set of ideas but as a quality of action and they talk about ritualisation rather than about ritual (Humphrey and Laidlaw 1994). Lewis writes:

> It accords with experience and what people say to point first to the practical side of ritual, that people have established ways to do it. It is primarily action, a way of doing, making, creating, showing, expressing, arousing – a complex form of stimulus to which people respond. Things done in ritual also have the power to arouse or to release, to serve as substitutes, as focusses for fantasy: they meet needs and stem from motivations. (Lewis 1980: 118)

What then if we start with a more practical side of ritual, what if we start with ritual action? Apart from avoiding the assumptions and the pitfalls relating to meaning and communication (i.e. whose meaning and who is communicating with whom), there are other advantages. For one thing this might appeal to family therapists in particular, since they are generally adept at recognising patterns of interaction, repetition and routinisation. As mentioned earlier, some interesting work was done by the Milan therapists prescribing formal action and behaviour in what they called family rituals (Selvini Palazzoli et al. 1977). They defined ritual as action, but of course this was when psychotherapists and family therapists tended to assume that everybody – regardless of gender, class, culture and so on – thought, felt and behaved on the basis of similar principles. One achievement since then has been that we are no longer so sure about this. In addition, Bateson, whose interest in the mental health field began with the observation of a ritual, made some interesting, and for us still relevant, comments about ritualised action.

Bateson was influenced by Durkheim and Radcliffe-Brown, but he also had his own views on anthropology and he did not consider rituals to be straightforwardly integrative. The Naven ritual was clearly about conflict between mothers' brothers and sisters' sons and between men and women. So why did no one seem to suffer any real offence and no one came to blows? Because ritual is a kind of metacommunication similar to play (Bateson 1973: 154). Both these types of behaviour frame episodes or sequences of action with the message that within this frame something different from normal action is taking place. The action within the frame does not mean the same as the action ouside the frame. Bateson's famous example was that of two young monkeys having a playfight. The monkeys were performing the same actions as if they were fighting and yet it was evident to Bateson as well as to the monkeys themselves that this was not a fight. Something about the sequence carried the message that this was play. The same could be said for ritual. Ritual too frames an episode of action as different from that which is not ritual and there is usually no doubt about what is occurring to those taking part or those observing.

Bateson termed this metacommunication because he saw it as communication about the frame or the rules of behaviour and not necessarily as conscious or easily available to those who perform rituals or play games. Bateson was in the end more interested in the system than in the actors and it was from the point of view of the mechanics and function of ritual in the social field that he approached cybernetics (Rappaport 1971). But if we see the issue from the actors' point of view in terms of the consequences and intentions of their actions we get a somewhat different picture. Humphrey and Laidlaw (1994) quote Taylor (1985a) and his argument that from an individual point of view it is possible to speak to someone, even outside ritual and play, for reasons other than a wish to communicate:

> Let us say that you and I are strangers travelling together through some southern country. It is terribly hot, the atmosphere is stifling. I turn to you and say; 'Whew, it's hot'. This does not tell you anything you did not know; neither that it is hot, nor that I suffer from heat. Both these facts were plain to you before. Nor were they beyond your power to formulate; you probably already had formulated them. (Taylor 1985a: 259)

Taylor goes on to argue that the comment on the temperature would have created a rapport or would have struck up a conversation. It would have created a public space in which the fact of the stifling heat was placed between him and his fellow traveller. Indeed he considers that the function of symbolic communication in general is to create a public space where certain matters are placed before us and where we are reminded that knowledge is not the property of the individual.

This idea of a public space is more subtle than Durkheim's idea of the social collectivity. As I mentioned it is difficult to see how in Durkheim's model an emphasis on symbols and meaning can in fact mediate between the subjective state of individuals and social institutions. Even if we could show that there is a consensus about the meaning of certain symbols between all participants (which we cannot) how is this shared quality incorporated into the ideas, thoughts and behaviours of individual persons? Clearly we need something more detailed than a loose notion of socialisation. Individuals are not simply subjugated to the collective. Social categories also allow individual experiences to be rearticulated in new ways or else we would never have any change in society or in therapy.

A focus on action offers an opportunity to include these important aspects of social life, because action involves both the mind and the body of an actor. In order to carry out an act the reasons and the intention for acting and the procedure must be internalised. This means that at least to some extent an actor will be able to reflect on what she has done. It was her body that did it. She must have had an intention, an emotion and perhaps some expertise and practice in acting in this way. In this ritual action falls into the general category of phenomena which Bourdieu has referred to as 'habitus'. 'Habitus' is the mediating link between the individual subjective world and the cultural world into which the individual is born and which he or she shares with others (Bourdieu 1977 [1972]). 'Habitus' refers to the practical ways of doing things – the way of walking, the way of organising the house, the way of touching others and so on. These are all tasks encoded and imprinted to varying degrees through conscious and unconscious processes on to the child from birth and even before birth when the child is being expected as well as through adult lives. They become a kind of second nature and a matter of routine. Thus how to perform a ritual may, just as any technological activity, call for specific expertise, apprenticeship and prescribed sequences of action. These sequences can be learnt or copied but they also contain elements of culturally constructed routines so that learning to perform a specific ritual in a culture other than one's own may not come 'naturally'. I felt clumsy when performing *puja* among Hindu villagers in Nepal, but my clumsiness did not detract from the efficacy of the ritual in the eyes of my informants.

It seems to me that this fits well with what we know about ritual. Ritual action stands apart from normal kinds of action, including speech, and this quality appears to be recognised cross-culturally. Part of the reason for this is that in ritual, far from aiming to communicate certain common messages either to other performers, to the performers themselves or to audiences, the messages in ritual are not fixed (Bell 1992). They can have many different meanings and receive many different interpretations, but they do all establish a point of reference, a public space. This is a space where we may move between 'map' and 'territory' (Bateson 1973), where actors are and are not at the same time the authors of their action and where a kind of freedom is created for individual performers to 'choose to attend to . . . meanings and, if they wish, choose to make them their own' (Humphrey and Laidlaw 1994: 208). This is the ritual stance in which the intention to mean is more important than the meaning itself.

The freedom created in this way is considerable and special, and rituals may facilitate creativity, resolution and new solutions. But equally this very same freedom also allows for the particularly insidious consequences of destructive and abusive rituals, such as rituals involving torture or sexual violence or the repeated performance of such acts which because of their repetition and their meaninglessness appear to emulate ritualised action. The dissociation which many victims of sexual or ritual abuse may experience and which operates as a protective mechanism (Summit 1983; Sinason 1994) may in part be brought on by the nature of ritualised action itself to establish a space which is set apart from ordinary social space. This is a crucial point. Ritual is not always a good thing. It is in the nature of ritualised action and not in the existence of shared symbols that the power of rituals is embedded and this power includes the possibility both to harm and to heal.

More generally this explains many aspects of ritual which otherwise do not make sense. It explains, for example, why rituals which are lagging behind or are considered to be hollow, or to be out of step with social ideology or with the political orientation of the performers, can still be performed with satisfaction and importance. It explains why rituals which are incomprehensible can be efficacious. Thus O'Connor and Hoorwitz (1988) report on their success with children who are terminally ill or phobic, by introducing rituals in which the children punch, hug or squeeze specially selected soft toys. It also explains how rituals may be a particular and desperate way of exerting agency as in the case of compulsive and obsessive rituals (Freud 1985 [1907]). Finally the idea that the power of ritual lies in ritual action allows us to understand the search for 'total freedom' which seems to characterise the behaviour of ritualistic, satanist and repeated perpetrators of abuse (Cooklin and Gorell Barnes 1994; Mollon 1994; Sinason 1994) in a new light. And it fits with the observation which many therapists experienced in working with abuse have noted, namely that for these patients to interpret symptomatic behaviour symbolically tends to be therapeutically counterproductive (Brown 1993).

TALKING ABOUT RITUAL

There are then three reasons why ritual action is more central to ritual and also for psychotherapists a better place to start thinking about ritual than symbolism. Firstly, ritual action is a human ontological phenomenon, a kind of human 'second nature' and therefore an obvious place to anchor cross-cultural and interpersonal communication. Second, ritualised action can be accessed (through conversation, observation or copying) more easily and more reliably than can symbols and symbolisation. This is not to say that action itself cannot be symbolic, only that it is a more experience-near (Kohut 1971; Geertz 1974) place to start finding out. Most people can talk about what they do or did or what they should have done and even if they cannot, they usually have an idea of their own intentions. Third, the freedom and creativity which ritual offers can be used to both harm or to heal. Ritual is not in itself a good thing, but it is the use to which ritual is put which may be helpful or harmful.

I am not arguing that talking about meaning cannot be therapeutically efficacious or that it is a waste of time. Nor do I wish to say that ritual action cannot involve communication. The problem is that talking about meaning and symbols is something we do every time we communicate whether we are explicit about this or not. It is not possible to move from a mode where meaning does not play a role to a mode where meaning is central. Meaning, symbols and communication are not the vital ingredients of ritual, because they are aspects of all action and interaction. It is ritualisation which singles out ritual and this implies a certain type of action performed with a stance of commitment and which stands apart from other everyday types of action. Rituals can be more or less ritualised and when rituals include a substantial element of improvisation they are closer to a performance in which the success depends on the way the performance is received by the audience, including the other actors. This is not to say that performance rituals are not rituals, only to suggest that they are not very ritualised (Humphrey and Laidlaw 1994).

The point about how actors understand rituals should not escape the therapist. The Gnau considered that the penis bleeding ritual was vital to ensure the successful growth of a young man and his dependants and the efficacy derived from the fact that certain acts were performed and 'certain good things done', as one of the participants of Lewis's account exclaimed. It was a complicated and extensive investigation which led Lewis to put together a convincing account and to question the validity of the statements of other ethnographers. It might be argued that to some extent the anthropologist may be excused for focusing on the collective, because anthropology is aimed more at understanding the context which constitutes the background to the lives of their informants, rather than at understanding the informants themselves. This is not so, as I have argued in Chapter 2. But by attempting to understand symbols and shared meanings first therapists make the same mistake. It is persons, actors or agents (whatever you want to call them), who come to us for therapy, it is not the system or the culture. We cannot, therefore, as therapists begin with general and unspecific meanings. If we do this we run the risk of interpreting rituals from the therapist's own rather than the client's point of view. Thus we may see rituals as facilitating a particular freedom for individual persons as far as symbolisation is concerned and not as Durkheim suggested as a social straitjacket.

To access our clients' points of view is a complex procedure. As I have tried to show talking about ritual can be helpful in therapy. However, I do not advocate talking about ritual and symbols in a generalised way. I always check things out with individuals and start, if I can, with the personal experiences clients might have had. I aim to highlight agency and not orthodoxy, etiquette or convention as such. I ask questions about the ritualised actions performed during the course of rituals and if objects are involved I ask about these too. Only as a second stage do I ask about how different persons understand these actions, whether these have cultural or personal meanings, and whether these meanings are shared by anyone.

If someone has died I enquire about what has happened to the body and about the actions around the funeral or the cremation. Who did what? Who did what with whom? What did it mean to them? If a wedding is mentioned I may ask in the same way about the actions the couple performed to get married. What did other family members do? And so on. If one is prepared to go slowly and hear a lot of detail, this way of talking can get close to recreating the sentiments of the ritual. But it is important to remember that what for one person may carry healing connotations may for another carry connotations of unhappiness and even abuse.

For the therapist to copy or take part in a ritual may sometimes be helpful. This is probably one of the closest ways a therapist can experience the world from the clients' points of view. By taking part the therapist can achieve some insight into the ritual processes experienced by their clients. But there may not be any sudden revelation of *the* meaning of it all, for ritual is more like a work of art than a clear unambiguous statement.

I would myself be extremely hesitant about prescribing rituals, especially about choosing symbols which derive from general statements given by families and family members in therapy without first painstakingly investigating these. Like Lewis I would worry that I would find *my* meaning and attribute this to my clients even though they did not know that this is what they meant. Because of the nature of ritual, ritual in therapy is tricky ground and from the point of view of interpreting symbols I suggest that the most constructive therapeutic stance is one of caution and self-doubt.

6

Taboos and Secrets

I have suggested that it is possible to recognise a special connection between the individual actor(s) and the collectivity in ritual. This is because actors in ritual are and are not, at the same time, the authors of their actions and it is this which constitutes the ontological nature of ritual. Human beings exist in communities and they must make use of certain specific themes of meaning in order to communicate. These themes must therefore be internalised, but because it is difficult to access these collective aspects directly, I suggested that ritual is better approached through the observation and assessment of the ritualised action in which individual agents repeatedly engage. Taboo and secrets have a similar ontological status as far as human beings are concerned. Taboo and secrets are also shaped and influenced by cultural themes of meaning and social institutions and they must also to varying degrees be internalised by individual persons so that they may become part of a person's habitual way of doing things and of a shared framework for communicating about the world.

In many societies rituals involve taboos and taboos involve ritual. For example tabooed objects, names or ideas may be of special use during rituals in order to denote sacredness, as is the case in the Gnau initiation rituals, or special rituals may be needed if a particular taboo has been broken. Life cycle rituals may also involve the observation of certain taboos. For example when a man died in the Himalayan Hindu community where I worked as an anthropologist, his close patrilineal relatives were considered to be polluted for a certain amount of time and certain foods were taboo to them, while they themselves also were taboo to other people (they should not touch or eat with them). This period of pollution and taboo ended with a final ritual in which the persons affected bathed and ate a specially prepared meal. The point is that ritual and taboo may be used as vehicles for the articulation of cultural themes, but as we have seen in relation to ritual, the meaning of such cultural themes may not necessarily be understood or even be conscious to individual persons.

Does this mean that they are secret or that taboos are secrets? This is a difficult and perhaps ethnocentric question. Western style psychotherapies are aimed at the articulation of the unsaid. Sometimes the unsaid is that which is not commonly known; sometimes the unsaid is the uncanny (Freud 1955 [1919]) and sometimes it is something from which I wish to protect myself and others because of shame, honour and status. Different levels of awareness and consciousness are implied. With secrets and taboos therapists are working at the edge between that which is known and that which is not known (to themselves and others), often spilling into areas of personal, social and cultural life which are on the dark side. These areas are dangerous, not only because they are often defined as such culturally, but also because it is here therapists may be accused of being suggestive, directional and manipulative while at the same time running the risk at best of being culturally insensitive and at worst of neglecting suffering, abuse and civil rights.

This chapter is about the unsaid and about that which cannot be said. It is about the flip side of what we usually write and talk about and it is about the kinds of issues which therapists need to keep in mind when working both intra-culturally and cross-culturally with these issues. It is also about that which our cultural lenses filter out, about that which it is difficult to be aware of because we are not able to see that it exists. There are no easy prescriptions to be had here, but some observations can be made about ways of thinking about these issues which may stimulate self-reflection. In this chapter I consider taboo, secrecy and privacy in a cross-cultural perspective. I discuss some deeper and more universal themes which are embedded in secrets and taboos, such as mimesis, incest, the transmission of patterns over generations, and I end this chapter with a discussion of the more invisible cultural patterns which play a role in family life in any society.

THE POWER OF COPYING, MIMESIS AND TABOO

In the previous chapter I described Quesalid, the Kwaikutl shaman, who despite starting out as a sceptic about shamanistic healing, had found a successful technique. This technique involved producing a substance which symbolised or stood for the illness. Quesalid had hit on what Taussig has called the 'magic of mimesis' (1993: 13) in which 'the notion of the copy, in magical practice, affecting the original to such a degree that the representation shares in or acquires the properties of the rep-resented' (Taussig 1993: 47). This is Frazer's sympathetic magic, but far from being exclusively the property of so-called 'primitive minds' as Frazer held it to be, Taussig elegantly shows how this mimetic technique implicates the observer, in this case the Europeans. He gives the example of the Cuna Indians who live on the San Blas Islands off Panama. The Cuna shamans use wooden figures to cure illness. These figures take many different shapes, but at the beginning of the twentieth century they no longer looked like Indians, but were clearly identifiable as white people in that they incorporated the clothes or regalia of Europeans.

Some were even representations of well known colonial figures such as one of General Douglas MacArthur: 'Why should these figures be carved as "European types"? Why are they Other? Why are they Colonial Other?' (Taussig 1993: 7). Taussig is in no doubt about the world-shattering nature of this observation for anthropology and for cross-cultural practices in general.

> For if I take the figurines seriously, it seems that I am honour-bound to respond to the mimicry of my-self in ways other than the defensive man-oeuvre of the powerful subjecting it to scrutiny as yet another primitive artifact, grist to the analytical machinery of Euro-American anthropology. The very mimicry corrodes the alterity by which my science is nourished. For now I too am part of the object of study. The Indians have made me alter to myself. (Taussig 1993: 8)

Taussig is here concerned to show how the mimetic faculty, the capacity or perhaps even the compulsion to copy, to mime and to Other, is a fundamental aspect of our humanity and how this ability has received a new expression with the growth of audio and visual technology during modernity. Contrary to those who view human societies in terms of a discontinuity between ancient and modern, primitive and civilised, Taussig points to the contemporary role of mimesis in relationships between persons, societies, cultures and nations. Far from being the property of primitive mistaken minds, the urge to control our environment (including other people) by copying, imitating, portraying and representing is a process which is inherent in the way we look at and interact with the world, even though this may not be obvious to us or even if it seems to us that we are describing something as it really is.

Mimesis as a therapeutic technique is well known in systemic psychotherapy. For example, Minuchin describes how when the father in a family took off his coat and lit a cigarette, he, the therapist, consciously asked this man for a cigarette and also took off his coat. He then proceeded by scratching his head in a fumbling way so as to 'increase his kinship with the puzzled, fumbling patient' (Minuchin 1974: 129). This is mimesis as a more or less conscious stance, aimed at the manipulation of a connection and a relationship. The therapist seems to know what he is doing and uses mimesis as a deliberate technique. In the spirit of the modernist position the therapist is outside the system able to look in and able to be certain about what he sees and what is needed. The therapist is in control. But another example, also from Minuchin, provides a different insight and pulls Taussig's two-way view back into focus. This is the example of what happens when infants are spoonfed (Minuchin 1974). All of us who have cared for infants have experienced this: we open our own mouths as the infant we are feeding opens his or hers. Who is mimicking whom here, the mother or the infant? The mother is mimicking the infant in order to persuade him or her to eat and to eat in a particular way, but is the infant mimicking the mother's mimicry? Taussig refers to a similar example and comments

> And what then was the adult imitating in the first place – a real reality, as we might like to simplistically describe the issue, such as the child's tone of voice or behaviour? Or instead was the adult imitating the child's mimicry of the adult's mimicry? In which case we seem to be doing something quite strange, going round and round and unable to see that we are doing so, simulating and dissimulating at one and the same time for the sake of our epistemic health and the robust good cheer of realness. (Taussig 1993: 77)

In a parallel way the therapist is influenced by the same constraints and processes which influence her clients. Like the clients the therapist is also being selective, if not exactly secretive. What we select is not just a matter of what is really out there, but also a matter of what we are able to see as a result of our history and our past relationships. We impose our own view of relationships on nature and yet we manage not only to convince ourselves that this view is natural but we also, like Quesalid, employ it in order to control the world around us.

Anthropologists have long recognised that the likeness between special and potent objects or representations and the original does not have to be exact. The Cuna figure of General MacArthur was not wearing khaki nor the correct headgear and he appeared to have a German Iron Cross pinned below his left breast pocket (Taussig 1993). The figure was not a faithful copy. In fact copies may be extremely schematic representations of the original, so much so that it is difficult to believe that the likeness itself serves as the only grounds for the connection. There also seems to be something more at play. Something which we might describe as some kind of convention about the way the world is perceived in different societies and cultures and which may account for the contact or association between the original and the double. Let us look at the Gnau again since some of this material is already familiar.

FOOD AND OTHER TABOOS

During the puberty rites there are certain restrictions on the food which the initiates may eat. They must not eat salt or food cooked in salt, they must not eat coconut or meat or food roasted over the fire (Lewis 1980: 82). These foods are taboo. Taboo, although used in English, is not a European word. It originates from the Polynesian *tabu*, meaning something like forbidden and sacred, and was brought to Europe in the wake of Captain Cook's voyages (Steiner 1967). Before Captain Cook's travels in the eighteenth century there does not seem to have been an English word for this idea, but this does not of course mean that the concept itself was foreign. The Gnau also do not have a term, but they do have the idea of something being forbidden and dangerous. Different foods are forbidden at different stages of life, so that for infants up to about four

years old everything except mother's milk is forbidden, whereas for
mature persons who have achieved hunting success and who have healthy
successful families with several children, everything except for the
creatures most associated with death and killing are allowed. The theme
behind these principles is the same as the guiding theme in the penis
bleeding rituals, namely the wish to secure sound human growth and
development. Good growth depends on the condition of the blood and
different foods affect the blood in different ways (Lewis 1975). Each
person operates these themes in a personal manner according to his or her
own circumstances. We are not talking about a cast iron rule here. The
time when a man may feel that he and his wife can move on to a food,
which until then has been classified as dangerous, depends on how he
considers his own achievements in hunting and his wife's success in giving
birth and rearing children. There is a kind of association between a person
and the fauna and flora which is the source of his or her nourishment and
his or her continued life. The progress of achievements which a hunter
experiences during his life relates to the rules about eating the animals
which he hunts. For example, a man who has hunted well will – only
when he has proven his achievements – be able to eat the eagles, kites
and hawks that also hunt so well that the marsupials which live in the
high tree-tops are their prey (Lewis 1980: 157). Furthermore a man can
never, without breaking a taboo, eat anything which he himself has shot,
because 'by shooting it he has put something of himself into it' (Lewis
1980: 174). The tabooed object (in this case the animal) is thus a kind of
double or a copy in that it shares some characteristics and some identity
with the original (in this case the hunter) and because of the association
between the two. But in making the identification the hunter is also
attempting to control the basic processes which necessitate him connecting with the object in the first place. He must live, develop and
mature and he must do this according to the economic practices in Gnau
society. These processes pose danger, but by considering the food forbidden there is also an attempt to control that danger. The hunter cannot
himself eat his prey but must give it to those of his kinsmen, who do not
consider this food taboo and can freely accept it.

We see here that what appears as a relatively simple act, the forbidding
of something, is imbued with a cultural rationale and with meaning,
which may have wide-ranging implications for the life of a person or a
group of persons and for the way this is conceptualised. Taboo therefore
refers to more than 'a block on communication as well as on action'
(Cooklin and Gorell Barnes 1993: 297) for the absence of communication
or of action is like a pause, a mirror or a negative copy of the noise.
Taboo is a kind of communication and, as Taussig noted, this points to a
perspective on the original which may not be obvious from the scrutiny
of the original itself. The original itself is produced and constructed as a
result of the operation of social relationships and of the process of a string
of originals and copies relating to each other. In our efforts to punctuate,

delimit and select we inevitably distort these processes, but we may also be tempted to overlook them altogether. Taboos are therefore like other gestures equally imbued with meaning.

Taboos similar to the ones described for the Gnau often feature in cross-cultural therapy and they may baffle and worry the therapist. Should they be observed? How can therapists be sensitive to these issues without knowing the rules, when the issues themselves cannot be talked about and only be indirectly inferred? What are rules for in the first place? Are they 'natural' or are rules necessary because if they were not there people would do as they please?

In most societies where people observe food taboos, the breaking of a taboo can be made good by conducting a ritual or by some kind of fine or other payment. The breaking of other taboos such as incest or homicide may have more serious consequences, but generally speaking all societies have rules (although different rules) and in all societies people also break the rules. While the differences are interesting and may be important it is equally important that therapists realise that in these respects clients are faced with similar types of constraints and similar types of choices as are therapists themselves. Other people's culture no more serves as a dogmatic blueprint and is no less influenced by persons and their actions than is one's own (Krause 1995).

Food is an archetypal medium for nurturing and care everywhere and because of these connotations food also tends to be a marker of cultural and class distinctions (Bourdieu 1984). At the same time the choice and availability of food products are very sensitive to seasonal and economic fluctuations and food is therefore an expedient medium for signifying ethnicity, ambition, status and taste. It is therefore not surprising that the idea of food restrictions and taboos is widespread and habitual. The sort of food people eat and who they share it with and who they do not share it with, conveys important information about social relationships. As far as I know this is the case in all societies and this means that talking about food in this way can be a good way for therapists and clients to connect. The acts of giving and taking of food may not, of course, be an aspect of most family or psychotherapeutic work. I have never served food myself during a therapeutic session, but I have frequently accepted food while on home visits as part of my work as a family therapist in an NHS family clinic. In most cultures the act of accepting food conveys honour and respect on the giver and the sharing conveys joining and establishes a relationship. It is easy to see how sharing food in this way can be of help to the therapeutic process. Apart from the joining around the consumption of something it produces an opportunity for the therapist to be curious about the food, its preparation, its origin and the social relationships behind its production.

Perhaps, however, by far the most common instances of these types of taboos occurring in the therapy room relate to the relationship between men and women or between generations. Taboos on the naming of certain relatives and certain actions towards these relatives are common in many cultures. Thus for example amongst the Hindu Thakuris and Chetris in Nepal with whom I worked, a woman must at all times avoid her husband's elder brother, she must not mention this man by name or be alone in close proximity to him. She must always cover her head and face in his presence. With her husband's younger brother, however, she can be close, jovial and even flirtatious and this man would also be a good choice for a husband should her first husband die. In the same way a woman should never mention her husband's name to herself, to others or to his face. If she needs to address her husband she must do so by calling him the father of her children and she must also observe a taboo of not speaking about sexual matters in front of her husband in public at least. These taboos reflect aspects of patrilineal kinship systems and they are well known to therapists who work with families from South Asia as well as from many other societies. In therapy they need not cause problems, for the therapist may be able to find ways around the breaking of the taboo, such as separate sessions or ways of speaking which avoid directly mentioning the tabooed subject.

Sometimes, however, there is no way around breaking a taboo. I met with a Bangladeshi family, the Mahmouda family, in which the eldest son was suffering from chronic headaches so badly that he was seriously missing out in school. I had spent the whole of the first session hearing the history of the involvement of this family with many previous professionals and exploring what each of the parents and the five other children thought about the eldest son's headaches and why he had become afflicted in this way. No one had any idea and the headaches remained a puzzle. We began the second session with greetings and niceties and straight after that Mrs Mahmouda asked if she could speak. I had an idea that something was seriously wrong and in any case I would not expect a Bangladeshi woman to speak first with her husband present. So I stopped her and asked Mr Mahmouda's permission to hear what his wife had to say. He agreed and then became more and more uncomfortable as his wife for the next half hour told in detail about his sexual exploits with other women in which she had caught him, and also about his violence towards her. I acknowledged the embarrassment which Mr Mahmouda must feel and I then focused on the marital violence (Krause 1995).

Since taboos are often about keeping the status quo, they may have to be challenged in therapy in order for things to change and for new choices to be made and as I noted above people in all cultures themselves break taboos. Whether or not this is offensive depends on other aspects of the interaction. An African-American therapist colleague was asked to join a multicultural team of therapists to meet with a Muslim family from Rwanda consisting of a mother, her sister and three daughters, two of them young women. There were also several other professionals involved with this family and in a pre-session meeting my colleague attempted to shake the hand of the Muslim Swahili speaking interpreter. She was clearly disconcerted by the gesture which to my colleague was a respectful and friendly way of greeting a stranger. This did not surprise the team, a majority of whom were themselves Muslims, since any kind of physical contact between a woman and a strange man is strictly taboo in Muslim cultures. During the session the therapist sensitively and respectfully heard about the protracted problems which this family was experiencing and which were related both to traditional issues of inheritance and to tensions generated by living in a context where dominant cultural values are different from those of the family and which therefore particularly affected the relationship between the two generations of women. He spoke quietly showing great awareness of cultural differences. At the end of the meeting when saying goodbye, the mother in the family, a thoroughly traditional woman, followed by her daughters indicated that she wanted to shake the hand of my male colleague (Smith, personal communication).

By itself then breaking a taboo of this kind need not have negative effects. Indeed following rules dogmatically may cause more difficulties for the therapy than if the therapist is able to communicate his or her readiness to listen and to accept and learn about cultural differences. The therapist who shows awareness of her own cultural traditions and constructions may in this way show more awareness of culture. Conveying that differences can be tolerated may provide more points for joining than does faking similarity. It is difficult to make hard and fast rules about how this should be done, since so much depends on particular contexts, but perhaps the biggest challenge to therapists is how they can use themselves in genuinely therapeutic interaction without 'colonising' their clients.

Therapists themselves have taboos and sometimes these areas which may be no-go areas for discussion, are also areas where a certain view is strictly upheld by avoidance. Therapists' own taboos may pose more difficulties in therapy, firstly because they may not be conscious or explicit to the therapist and second, because they may be instrumental in upholding social divisions, discrimination and prejudice which may be backed by dominant social institutions. For example Cooklin and Gorell Barnes (1993) describe the case of a mixed race heterosexual couple who were having marital difficulties. They were both well educated from middle-class backgrounds, he a Hindu from India and she white English. His father had suffered great disappointment when in this country he could not pursue his academic profession and ended up in a lowly manual job. It was not until the therapist and the team found some way of naming the racial differences that the couple began to discuss these issues which they had never touched on before. As the therapist Cooklin had at first focused on the Britishness and the middle-classness of the couple and avoided speaking about the much more uncomfortable and messy subject of race which implicated both him and the wife in a different way.

The taboos which therapists and other health professionals themselves either wittingly or unwittingly uphold, may also perpetuate discrimination in more subtle ways. I met with a Somali refugee family in which the mother, Mrs Mohamed, had fled with seven children ranging in age between 16 and 3, after her own brother had been shot and killed in front of her. Her husband was still in Somalia and she had received no news from him for about a year. Mrs Mohamed had been referred because her eldest daughter, who was 15 and an epileptic, had several times presented herself at the accident and emergency department of a local hospital. At the time of our meetings Mrs Mohamed was anxiously awaiting a decision about whether or not she would be granted asylum. She was living in a bed and breakfast which was the sixth bed and breakfast she had been in during that year. The frequent upheaval of moving on had had a devastating effect on the children's attempt to settle down and build new friendships and new lives. Mrs Mohamed herself was a quiet unassuming woman who worked hard to keep her family. Nevertheless the size of the family and the difficulties which faced Mrs Mohamed in looking after the children often brought social workers to despair. In our third meeting Mrs Mohamed told me (through an interpreter) that she had not in fact given birth to two of her children. They were the children of her husband's brother, who was still in Somalia. Mrs Mohamed went on to say that she had told this to a social worker and that this person had seemed disturbed by this information, had asked many questions about the parents of these two children and had talked about the legal implications of the information and about adoption. Mrs Mohamed was now afraid that these two children would not be considered to be the same as the others and that she would not be considered to be their parent. Her worst fear, precipitated by the social worker's questions, was that they would be sent back to Somalia.

Mrs Mohamed's eldest daughter had in her help-seeking sought help for her mother rather than for herself, but once the family was scrutinised closely the clash between two kinship systems and two world views became obvious. With the popular Anglo-American emphasis on the biological relationship in the (mostly nuclear) family, deviations from this norm are suppressed. This suppression takes the form of casting deviations in terms which apply to the ideal. In the case of adoption, where the relationship between parents and children is based not on a biological, but on a social connection, this has led to secrecy about the actual adoptive relationship and to an emphasis on the symbolic, in this case biological ideal (Strathern 1992a; Hartman 1993). This is probably why the lives of so many adoptive children in England and America have been surrounded by mystery and taboo. More recent trends show that awareness of the damaging effects of such secrecy have been recognised publicly but the controversial nature of this material also suggests that this area continues to be emotionally charged.

There is plenty of evidence that Somali men and women conceptualise the issue of kinship and biological and social connections in a different way from, say, white British. Here the extended family of agnates, meaning all those who are patrilineally related, receives far more emphasis than does the nuclear unit (Lewis 1962). Agnates are the 'hard' or the 'bony' part of kinship, but these relationships, as well as other kinship relationships, are seen to be forged by social rather than biological ties and this is particularly clear for women for whom infibulation is a concrete manifestation of their social relationship to their agnates (Talle 1993). The agnatic relationship is literally stamped on their bodies during this operation. It is quite clear then that when biological aspects of kinship are de-emphasised adoption has a different meaning and does not stand out as an anomaly from social and legal points of view in the same way as is the case in English or American kinship systems. Mrs Mohamed's own children and her husband's brother's children are all agnates of the same generation sharing vital bodily substances by virtue of belonging to the same kinship group. According to this view they are all her children as well as the children of her brother-in-law and his wife and her caring for them produces no legal or social difficulty and no need for a taboo on mentioning the relationship.

Taboos are a function of the rules applied in a society or a culture. Rules are about what is allowed and what is not allowed and taboos are a kind of reflection of these, a kind of negative double. As I have tried to show with several of the examples in this section, despite appearing as a relatively straightforward rule, taboos encompass complicated issues and themes of meaning connected to the social relationships in which they operate and for a variety of reasons some of them cultural, some of them familial and some of them personal, they evoke uncomfortable or unwelcome feelings or stigma. For example, the breaking of the taboo on mentioning skin colour evoked race relations and the issue of adoption evoked a challenge to the ideal of biological based family relationships. Similar stigmas may be evoked in Euro-American societies by the issues of infertility treatment (Schaffer and Diamond 1993), conception before marriage (Mason 1993), eating disorders (Roberto 1993) and illnesses such as AIDS or severe mental illness (Black 1993; Papp 1993). For people in other societies different issues may have this power and this is at least partially dependent on the operation of established social institutions, their history and the authority embedded in them. Boyd-Franklin (1993) shows how secrets in African-American families about parentage were 'created' by the demands of the institution of slavery in which there was no regard for the family life of slaves and which also condoned the rape and sexual exploitation of African women by white male slave masters. In a society where white colour symbolised status this set up painful lines of division within the African-American communities themselves and consequently encouraged secrecy and taboos in relation to parentage even inside families.

Taboos and sex

It is clear, then, that taboos vary. What is taboo in one society may not be
so in another. What is taboo for clients is not necessarily taboo for the
therapist and vice versa. We all have taboos, however, and some taboos
are more obvious than others. Those connected with legal frameworks,
the transgression of which lead to punishment, may be more clear than
those which are aspects of the habitual ways in which we live our lives.
There is one general area in which taboos appear to be universal and
where particularly strong emotions and reactions are evoked. This is in the
area of sexual relationships. Sex appears to matter everywhere. In a broad
sense sexual relationships feature as a biological necessity. They also feature
as habitual and intimate aspects of any person's existence and they feature
in ideas about morality and in the legal frameworks pertaining to public
punishment. At all these levels sexual relationships, it seems, must be
controlled and this is why Douglas (1984 [1966]) has argued that taboo
backed up by ideas about consequent pollution if the taboo is broken,
provides an efficient and pervasive vehicle for such control. This raises all
sorts of questions about the nature of human beings. Are humans inherently promiscuous and therefore need to be controlled through social
institutions and moral themes or is control of sexual relationships and
marriage (which are not the same) a result of human evolution? These
questions have been widely debated (Fox 1983 [1980]) and I shall not
engage in that debate here. I am not concerned with the biological reasons
for and origins of human prohibitions on incest. Rather, I am concerned
with taboos in connection with sexual relationships in the context of
cultural systems and the way these evoke strong emotions and reactions.

But Douglas did not simply point to control. She also recognised the
for us by now familiar idea that a system or an image may hold in it its
own contradiction:

> When the community is attacked from outside at least the external danger
> fosters solidarity within. When it is attacked from within by wanton
> individuals, they can be punished and the structure publicly affirmed. But it is
> possible for the structure to be self-defeating. . . . Perhaps all social systems are
> built on contradiction, in some sense at war with themselves. (Douglas 1984:
> 140)

Douglas goes on to note that this 'being at war with itself' is particularly
characteristic in social systems when it comes to sexual relations and
speculates that this is perhaps because social pressures on sexuality are
more explosive than other social pressures. Douglas was writing about
patterns in social and cultural systems and not specifically about the way
these are internalised but we may read into her statement a comment
about how this may be experienced by individual persons, who after all
are the agents of contradiction. For the therapist this is a reminder that
therapists and clients are involved in the same wider context even if at

times they appear to be expressing different sides of the same contradiction. In this way in Euro-American societies, for example, both the perpetration of sexual abuse and the reactions and processes surrounding its detection are aspects of the same general dominant cultural themes relating to sexuality.

Girard's notion of the sacred conveys the idea in a different way. Because of its potency and dangerous qualities, sexuality belongs to the sacred. The sacred 'consists of all those forces whose dominance over man increases or seems to increase in proportion to man's effort to master them' (Girard 1977 [1972]: 31). The existence of taboos about sex, like other taboos, thus signify a kind of battle. It is a battle not only between what is allowed and what is not allowed in terms of social rules and cultural conventions, but also a battle between what, given these rules and conventions, a person knows and what a person does not know because it has been left out. Left out is perhaps not quite the correct way of putting it because like Taussig's copy it is more that the difference between what is known and what is not known does not come into view.

In this respect anthropological material appears to lend general support to Freud. Sexuality is a worldwide arena for the operation of taboos and therefore for the expression of overt and covert social and psychological tension. The Oedipus complex and its shortcomings have already been commented on in Chapter 4. Here I suggested that while the classic Oedipus complex does not apply cross-culturally, the need for persons to feel supported, valued and cared for is a precondition for all kinship systems. What then of Freud's specific ideas about taboo?

In *Totem and Taboo* (1953 [1913–14]) Freud was influenced by anthropologists of the day as well as by Darwin. He was fascinated by Frazer's widely publicised accounts of totemism in Australia in *The Golden Bough* (Frazer 1890). Totemism refers to the practice of ritually worshipping animals which serve as a totem or an emblem for the clan or the group and in many parts of the world, including Australia, the totem is also taboo. This means that for the members of the group there is a prohibition on killing this animal and also a prohibition on eating it. There may also be a further crucial prohibition on marriage between persons who have the same totem, or to put it another way the group of people who share the same totem is exogamous. Freud did not agree with Westermarck that prohibitions on sexual intercourse between close relatives derive from a kind of natural aversion developed between relatives who enjoy a non-sexual physical intimacy, such as for example brothers and sisters might do. He did not see the incest taboo as a sort of natural extension in society of human nature. Rather he thought that the very existence of the taboo was evidence of a contradiction. The taboo was evidence that human beings feel sexually attracted to those to whom they are close and whom they love, and that this attraction is unconscious or repressed. Instead of confidence there is ambivalence. For Freud this view was further vindicated by the central importance which another nineteenth-century anthropologist, Robertson Smith, placed on the ritual killing of the animal which is taboo and on its consumption on certain occasions. This led Freud to see a similarity between totems connected with exogamy and the Oedipus complex; a similarity between Australian Aborigines and Viennese neurotics and to a hypothesis which he himself referred to as 'fantastic' (Freud 1953). It was a fantastic thesis because it sought to explain the institution or a collection of emotional dispositions by referring to an actual event in the distant past and in this connection Freud had been impressed by Frazer's account of a king who was scapegoated and killed by people who had worshipped him (Frazer 1890). At the same time Freud had also been impressed by Darwin's ideas about early humans and their social organisation into hordes. Since it was commonplace then to assume that contemporary hunters and gatherers such as the Australian Aborigines were fairly accurate representations of 'early humans', it is not difficult to see how Freud could have attributed the totemism described for Australians to early humans and the event described by Frazer to a repetition of a 'primal event' which went as follows:

> The primal horde was dominated by a powerful male, a father figure, who kept the women to himself and who banished the younger males, including his sons, who challenged him. The young males and sons could only take so much of this and eventually took revenge. This time it was they who banished the dominant male and father and they may even have killed or devoured him. But this made them feel guilty and because he was dead he became even more powerful than when he was alive. In this way his power and his sacredness became ensconced in and represented by the totem. To honour their father from that time the young males obeyed the law which prohibited incest. They never again found permanent female partners from their own groups and families and they even abstained from following their desires as far as fleeting sexual encounters were concerned. The event was of such monumental importance for the life of individuals and for the group that somehow it was stamped onto their minds and their memories. Henceforth the Oedipus complex has operated as a muffled echo of this event.

No one, not even Freud himself, thought that a hypothesis of this kind, also sometimes referred to as a contract theory, could be proven and we may find its discriminatory overtones objectionable. It is nevertheless interesting because it is grappling with ideas which are central to the communication between persons from different cultural backgrounds and to cross-cultural therapeutic practice. Whatever else we might think of it, the hypothesis offers a view on what all humans might have in common, without immediately referring us back to, or reducing this to biology. There is a notion that the psychological or the psychic make-up of human beings is such that it leaves room for and is influenced by what has gone before; that as far as humans are concerned it is not simply a question of each individual learning everything from scratch. That there is a capacity to tune into a collective mind or to a collective memory (with varying degrees of consciousness). To this extent Freud's fantastic theory was a theory about human beings living in cultures.

But it also raised questions about the level of the collectivity, some of which I addressed in Chapter 4. To what extent is the collective memory a phylogenetic memory, that is to say a memory in which a repeatedly occurring event has activated pathways in our brains which have set up certain patterns and predispositions for patterns of emotion, cognition and behaviour, which in turn are inherited by subsequent generations? And to what extent is it a cultural memory, influenced and changed by cultural themes which may have their own coherence or contradictions? To what extent are patterns shared by individuals in all cultures and to what extent are they culturally specific? And if they are both what can be said about the interface? For the clinician to address these questions at the level of mentality or the psyche may seem highly speculative. On the other hand it is also clear that any simple biological reductionism cannot address cultural diversity in symptom presentation, patterns of behaviour or aetiology (Littlewood 1993). There is, therefore, plenty of scope for misunderstanding, misinterpretation and discrimination.

There are it seems to me two steps in the argument. The first relates to the ontology of taboo. It relates to taboo as a fundamental social and psychological aspect of human ambivalence towards rules and regulations particularly in the area of sexual relationships, conception and ensuing birth. It refers to the connection between taboo and the area which Freud named the uncanny, and explained as that which is 'secretly familiar'. By this Freud meant something (notably the genitalia of the mother and her body) which was once well known and which has undergone repression and has returned in a distorted form (Freud 1955). What appears as reality is really a distortion or 'a façade behind which spiritual doubles are active' (Taussig 1993: 125). Taboos everywhere have this characteristic: they both ensure the pretence of normality and increase the explosive and dangerous powers of transgressions.

The second step concerns the extent to which the tensions and contradictions, which appear to be part and parcel of taboos related to sexuality themselves, form a cross-cultural pattern, or whether these are culturally specific. I shall address the first step in relation to secrets in families first and return to the second step below.

SECRETS AND TABOOS

A secret is not the same as a taboo but secrets nevertheless have some of the same characteristics as taboos. For example the Gnau men have knowledge about how to ensure the growth of their families which is a secret to Gnau women and this secrecy gives value, power and potency to their knowledge. On the other hand while probably most adult Gnau would be aware that the food taboos which operate around the initiation rituals are connected with the power of this knowledge, neither men nor women may be able to explain the precise nature of these food taboos. A secret may be something which only some people know and which is aimed at keeping other people ignorant, whereas taboos may be something no one knows about even though the prohibition is observed and transgressions are punished. Secrets may subsequently become taboos and be passed down in families to subsequent generations without younger members knowing why certain subjects may not or cannot be discussed. It may also work the other way around that secrets may be secret precisely because they reflect or echo wider social and cultural taboos and the shame associated with the breaking of these.

Secrets and taboos may then be seen as two sides of the same coin. The keeping of secrets involves individuals in conscious intentions. It is within a person's control to choose to keep a secret or not, even if the pressure to do so is overwhelming and even if the reason for the secrecy is not known. The full justification for the observation of a taboo, however, is rarely clear, because to paraphrase Fortes, taboos reflect the morally binding forces of social relationships, which cannot be repudiated if one wishes to be a normal person. In this sense taboos are ordained aversions integral to personal and social identity (Fortes 1987 [1966]: 126–9) and they are maintained by powerful sanctions including the most powerful social institutions. For better or worse taboos belong to the very fabric of social life, that is to say to those basic orientations which must be internalised in order to operate. These are also the orientations which appear most natural or as 'the way it really is' to social agents and they are therefore difficult to challenge. To challenge a secret is to challenge the status quo. To challenge a taboo may be to defy morality.

This implies that while secrets can be exposed and disclosed, it is difficult to imagine any social or cultural order without taboos. The nature of taboo may vary but there will always be some kind of prohibition to uphold social classification, boundaries and order. In the terms used by systemic therapists there will always be some kind of punctuation (Bateson 1973). In a sense taboo *is* the ultimate punctuation, and if we choose to look beyond this the tabooed subject reflects, mirrors or is a double of that which can easily be discussed. Taboos are therefore not simply what is out of reach. Some taboos are beyond recognition, inherent in the cultural glasses which we wear. Other taboos can just be glimpsed through the shadow they cast on our communication about other subjects and yet other taboos take the form of clear prohibitions which are upheld by rules and punished if transgressed. Whether taboos have any of these characteristics they also always, as do secrets, contribute to communication through the silence they prescribe.

The way the keeping of secrets contributes to the status quo and draws in others without these others necessarily being aware of this process is described by Jones. One of her clients was a man who during his child-hood was physically and sexually abused by his mother as well as his father and who took on himself the role of the family's saviour, a 'Mr Fix-it'. In his own family with his wife and children he continued to play this role feeling somehow that if he did not continue to sacrifice himself in this way by always being central to decisions and trying his utmost to keep everyone happy, no one would care for him or want to be with him. When he was able to share this secret he also became able to explore different options for connecting inside his current family (Jones 1991: 65). The secret which referred to what had happened to him in the past and which drove this man to behave in this way had also over the years created a response and a particular pattern of behaviour from his family members. He had become involved in a sort of chain of doubling and mimesis which did not just involve himself but also the other members of his family.

Secrecy about sexual abuse is buttressed by social and cultural taboos on sex and incest. As we have seen it is always the case that personal taboos and secrets reflect social and cultural orientations but in the case of sexual abuse this underpinning is particularly vigorous. It may even be argued that sexual abuse in families as well as in society generally is tolerated partly as a result of the doubling effect of taboo which encourages both prohibition and transgression. Such an argument has been made for satanist abuse which may involve incest or sexual abuse or both (Sinason 1994) and the difficulties which the press, the police and the judiciary process have in understanding and adequately redressing this phenomenon have been cited as evidence for this (Tate 1994).

It is well known that issues and events which have been kept secret or have been taboo in families tend to have more noxious effects on families and family members than do aspects of openly articulated family ideology, even when this is malfunctioning or clearly disadvantages certain members (Sluzki 1988). The effect can take the form of relationship problems, somatic symptoms or behaviour dangerous to persons themselves or to others. Pincus and Dare (1978) describe an 11-year-old girl who was referred to them because of her extremely risky behaviour, which was worrying her teachers and friends of her family and eventually also her parents. She would climb high trees or jump from high banks seemingly with no fear. Otherwise she was an extremely pleasant and well-behaved girl. Pincus and Dare worked with the parents and discovered that they both came from careful, respectable middle-class families in which deviation was not tolerated and conflicts avoided. They also discovered that despite a sensuous and in many ways adventurous life-style, the parents had stopped having a sexual relationship since their daughter was born because they did not want more children and because they considered contraception too risky. Pincus and Dare argue that once the parents were able to acknowledge their needs for excitement with the therapists without fearing punishment (as in their own families of origin) or catastrophes, their daughter was able to stop taking risks for her parents.

This work was based on the assumption that secrets and taboo are features of 'normal' families and that the tensions which ensue pose a kind of developmental challenge to family life. Following Freud, Pincus and Dare consider that the secrets which exist in all families are 'about power and dependence, about love and hate, about the wish to take care of and the wish to hurt, feelings which are inevitably bound up with sex, birth and death' (1978: 16). In this view all persons and all families are faced with the challenge of resolving these contradictions and the resolution can be a source of pain and conflict but also of imagination and creativity. The two will go together. Pincus and Dare do not make it their business to consider the way general social and cultural attitudes and taboos influence the existence of contradictions and the process of resolution. It appears to be fairly straightforward to access these and the therapist is in the advantageous position of being able to see 'what is really going on'. The tabooed or secret area can be found and behaviour and communication adjusted accordingly. But what happens when the secret is even deeper and the taboo a reflection of something even more dangerous? When neither can be uncovered or broken? When there is no sudden revelation and adjustment? When conflict is not wholesome but sinister and destructive?

Most therapists, I imagine, have treated clients or families for whom there seem to be something which cannot be talked about. Many therapists have perhaps also experienced arriving at such a conclusion through intuition rather than having been told directly. In this situation the therapist finds herself in the middle of the difficult context of taboo and there may not be an obvious way to address these issues nor any clear conclusion. I met with an Irish family in which these issues seemed to have been implicated in the mental breakdown of a young woman.

This family consisted of the mother and stepfather of 22-year-old George. George was a young woman, who at the age of 19 had changed her name from Anna to George by decree. Despite having made this change, in other respects George seemed to be happy enough to be identified with womanhood. Thus it was acceptable to her that others refer to her as sister, mother and daughter and she also did not object to the pronouns 'she' or 'her'. The family also included George's younger sister, who I never met, and George's younger half-sister who was aged nine, as well as her own son, Chris, who was aged seven. George, who was then Anna, had become pregnant when she was 15 and her mother had promised that she would help Anna take care of the baby. At the time the family was referred George's mother was still fulfilling her promise and functioned in several ways as the one who carried the main responsibility for her grandchild, although everyone, including Chris, were well aware that George was his biological mother. Five months before referral George had had a breakdown and spent some time as an inpatient on a psychiatric ward. She continued to visit a day centre and there had been two crises since then. On one occasion when everyone was at home she had attempted to throw herself out of a window and on another occasion while waiting for a doctor's appointment she had cut her wrist in the toilet of the doctor's surgery. The recent breakdown had been connected by Anna's mother with an episode of sexual abuse when Anna was five. She had surprised her husband's father, Anna's paternal grandfather, with his hand under Anna's skirt. She had whisked Anna away and banned the grandfather from ever coming in the house or near Anna again. She had not discussed this with Anna. The mother had herself been abused, but in a much more ferocious manner by her own grandfather and had never really spoken to anyone about this.

As I met with this family an oppressive stillness came to characterise our meetings. It was as if no one could move. George answered questions lucidly but with long pauses. George's mother seemed to be searching for something through her relationship with her eldest daughter, and her stepfather seemed to be aloof and puzzled. I became preoccupied with a pattern which I had gleaned about the way secrets had arisen in this family and also about the way they had been handled. In one family meeting George had managed to convey that only after her breakdown did she feel that her mother was beginning to listen to her, but following that she could not say what it was that she would want her mother to hear. I felt that there were other issues which were secret or even that a vital taboo had been broken, but because of George's severe symptoms I also felt that I could not ask or address this directly. I decided to vent my curiosity about George's name change, which after all in the cultural and social context of this family had been a powerful and unusual thing to do. I had also begun to form a link in my own mind between identity issues which for any young person must be acutely gendered, George's experience of independence and the paralysing victimisation which the sexual abuse of children by adults brings to mind. I had wondered to myself and colleagues with whom I discussed this case what had been going on around the period of Anna's name change. Therefore I began to explore with George the differences between George and Anna and the different ways the two would think and deal with the present situation. George reacted with reluctance, but she did explain that Anna had been a 'bimbo' who could not do things for herself. Following this cue I suggested that changing names had been a brave attempt to grow up and I wondered whether George would be able to talk about what it had been like for Anna before.

George had answered that she could talk about these things, but after this, the third meeting, I never saw George again. Instead her mother came on her own several times and in these sessions she talked about her own abuse, about managing on her own, sometimes living on the streets with no one to teach her how to be a mother and about how she had wanted things to be much better for Anna. She had been attending parent-craft classes and had done everything by the book and Anna's pregnancy had been a shock to her. We also spent some time on how she could best help George to become independent and be a mother to her son now. At the end of our meetings she told me that George was doing many more things in the house, taking charge of Chris more and that she had just started a part-time job as a sales assistant.

I do not believe that I got to the bottom of the secret. There was always in my mind a lingering doubt about whether or not this young woman was still being abused by someone in the family. However, it was also my impression that getting to the bottom of the issue was more complicated than flushing out an abuser. Indeed I do not think it was possible to go much further at that time because the secret was a taboo which was not accessible to George or her mother. What did however become clear during the mother's sessions was that she saw the issues in terms of a pattern which she sought to break and that Anna's name change was a spectacular example of a similar wish. The pattern did not simply involve behaviour and interaction but also processes of identity and gender formation and was not confined to internal family dynamics alone. It also implicated wider cultural orientations, some of them specific to Irish Catholic populations, others more generally European and Christian and shared, if not necessarily consciously, by me as a Danish protestant.

If then, as I suggest, we must acknowledge that secrets involving incest (and possibly sex generally) always involve taboos and therefore cultural themes pertaining to rules and morality, and if we accept that this means that we cannot simply understand this in terms of internal psychic processes, we must concede that the work of the therapist is greatly complicated. If this is the case when clients and therapist share a significant amount of cultural understanding, how much more complicated does therapy become when we consider the same situation cross-culturally. In cross-cultural therapy we not only have the issue that what happens inside people in their hearts or in their minds and between people in their relationships is influenced, constituted and sometimes shaped by social and cultural processes, we also have the difficulty that we as therapists may not be aware of and much less understand the general social and cultural processes which provide the context for the personal relationships of our clients.

I met with a Sikh Punjabi family in which a 14-year-old girl, Surjit, had been seriously and viciously sexually abused by her own father and his friends over a long period of time. The sexual abuse had been preceded and accompanied by emotional and physical abuse. Surjit's mother had eventually moved into a refuge with her two children, Surjit and her 4-year-old sister. This had followed Surjit's call to the police when one day she had feared for her own life and for that of her sister while her mother was at work. She had been attacked by her father and his friends while they were drunk.

In the refuge Surjit had calmed down but she was fearful of going to school, although she did sometimes go, and she suffered from frequent and petrifying nightmares. She never spoke to her mother about the details of the things her father had done to her, although the mother knew that her daughter had suffered as she had herself suffered appalling physical abuse. Surjit's mother had no relatives in England having come to join her husband sometime after their wedding. Now facing the prospect of life as a single parent she had begun to contemplate the idea of being rehoused in a different area of London and building a new life for herself and her daughters, although she was still very unsure whether it might not be best to go back to the Punjab and join her ageing mother and married brothers there. This option would bring disgrace on the whole family.

The sessions took place in Punjabi with the help of an interpreter. Frequently, however, Surjit deliberately spoke in English so that her mother could not understand her, although while she was speaking about her suffering steady streams of tears rolled down her mother's cheeks. I (and a team of colleagues observing from behind a one-way mirror) felt an acute dilemma with this family. Surjit clearly needed her mother's attention and care and yet she made almost no demands on her mother. On the contrary she indicated that she could not speak to her mother, not because her mother would not believe her but because it would be too devastating for her mother's self- and public image, that she or her daughter were known in the community to have been the victims of abuse in this way. For this reason Surjit insisted on protecting her mother from the details of her own abuse. The dilemma of the team was this: on the one hand Surjit needed her mother. How would she eventually make sense of all that had happened to her without her mother's support and reassurance? On the other hand, her mother had no family, no relatives of her own in England and in this sense no support from the community. She had come as a daughter-in-law to her husband's family's house and she had had daughters and no sons. For all these reasons her self-esteem was likely to be low and Surjit herself had probably already internalised some of these aspects of gendered self-identity on top of having suffered the dehumanisation of extreme abusive behaviour.

After some discussion the team decided not to press for an open discussion of the abuse at this moment. While we were aware that there was no one who could take on the role of Surjit's confidante and intimate carer, we also did not feel that Surjit or her mother would be able at this point to take up and sustain these new roles with regard to each other. The roles were not culturally appropriate until some other work had been done which could strengthen Surjit's mother in a culturally appropriate way and prepare her somewhat for her new situation as a separated woman living on her own or for facing the reaction of her family should she decide to move back to India. Yet we also thought that for Surjit to continue to protect her mother so deeply was damaging for her. We imagined that at some point in the perhaps not so distant future Surjit and her mother would be able to talk, but to press for that now may turn out to be counterproductive. We therefore decided to construct a therapeutic plan which involved finding someone in the refuge who could have close and daily contact with Surjit while still being sensitive to the needs of Surjit's mother to be the parent in charge. Unfortunately soon after our last meeting Surjit's father discovered the address of the refuge and the family had to move to a new (secret) address.

Maitra (1996) has reported a similar situation in which a young Bangladeshi girl, who was known to have been sexually abused by her father, insisted on her father not being confronted and on returning home, in this way infuriating social workers and other professionals in charge of her statutory protection. Maitra describes the tension between the girl's emotional suffering and her family's, and especially her mother's concern with the honour of the family and the daughter's long-term social interests, mostly in relation to her marriageability. She argues that the girl's own attachment to her father, who in other contexts acted as a competent carer, cannot simply be considered as a pattern of disturbed behaviour characteristic of sexually abusive families, but must be considered against the background of Bangladeshi kinship and family obligations. In this area, concern with family honour and shame is paramount and it is to be expected that a young daughter of marriageable age would place the reputation of the family before her own emotional well-being. It is interesting to note that in this case the role of the mother of the girl was crucial. When she was able to share with her daughter what had happened and assure her daughter that she had not behaved unacceptably the girl became able to discuss the abuse with the therapist. There was no hint that the mother was felt to be responsible for not protecting her daughter, rather the two were brought together by a notion of shared womanhood in a patrilineal society strongly orientated towards fertility and kinship.

CULTURE AND BACKGROUND UNDERSTANDING

We have seen how the content of taboos and secrets is cultural material, that taboos and secrets are affected, influenced and even shaped by cultural themes and meanings. The two examples of the young women and their families from the Indian subcontinent just described illustrate a cultural emphasis in relationships between parents and children and in rules about interaction and communication in these relationships. For them the orientation of the mother/daughter relationship is characterised by an imbalance which is reflected in social organisation and which also receives emotional expression in the patterns of attachment between them. In Chapter 4 I discussed the Oedipal pattern which seems to fit relationships between fathers and sons in South Asia. This is a pattern which reverses the European one insofar as it is often the father who slays the son in myths rather than the other way around. After the deed the father repents (Ramanujan 1983). For a man a son is considered a continuation of himself, he longs for continuity while the son himself longs for independence. For the mother and the daughter it is the other way around. The mother longs for independence while the daughter seeks continuity. This has been described for Tamil Nadu by Trawick (1992) and much of what she observed in terms of the emotions and attachments of mothers and daughters accords with my own observations of these relationships both amongst Nepalese Hindus and Sikh Punjabis.

The relationship between a mother and her daughter is characterised by a sad love. A woman's natal home is always referred to as her 'mother's home' even though it belongs to her father and her mother was brought there from her own father's home following marriage. Similarly the place of origin of both men and women is the mother's vulva and this contrasts with the Greek formulation 'springing from a man's loins' (Trawick 1992: 165). But the closeness which a young girl may have with her mother terminates at her marriage which many of my informants likened to her death as far as her mother is concerned. When a woman marries in these patrilineal societies she tends to become a member of her husband's kin-group and it is for this group she produces offspring. If her offspring are sons this will increase her status there, if not she remains to some extent an outsider all her life (Kakar 1978; Fruzetti 1990 [1982]), but in any case from the beginning the role of a daughter-in-law contrasts starkly with that of a daughter. There are thus a number of reasons why a daughter appears to be more anxious about a break in the mother/daughter relationship than a mother. While the mother is in some ways a daughter's most reliable protector (a role which is also extended to her brother) her powers are also limited because of her structural position in a patrilineal society. The anxiety which women feel with regard to their own mothers and which they in turn pass on to their daughters was vividly demonstrated to me whenever the women I lived with in the Himalayas took part in women-only activities, such as going on outings to collect roots and ferns or during exclusion because of our monthly periods. Many of the songs which were sung on such occasions were laments and concerned with mothers and mothers' homes, often detailing a kind of longing for the mother's company and touch and a sad, frustrated love which cannot find expression. And yet on the other hand such songs also showed that women were not simply split by the structural requirements of the social and largely male world. They were also strong and resourceful with plenty of appetite for the pleasures of sex and motherhood (Raheja and Gold 1994). Above all there was a tremendous feeling of gendered divisions both in terms of economics and labour, but also in terms of emotional attachment and support.

Several aspects of these themes played a role in the relationships between the mothers and the daughters in the two cases described and in the way the interaction around the abuse unfolded. The difference between the emphases in these themes (and the patterns of attachments which they express) and those which tend to be described for western families is significant and these differences ought to raise questions for therapists about treatment and also about theoretical frameworks. The mothers and the daughters were following rules at different levels. There was, for example, for Surjit a rule of not talking about sexually explicit matters in front of her mother, a rule about which she must have been conscious and which depended on her observing a taboo. But there were other and less explicit, perhaps even unconscious, rules which resulted from the observation of repeated patterns of behaviour, such as the gender differences which Surjit must have observed and felt from infancy and early childhood. In her family these differences were distorted and abusive but even in benign non-abusive families a Punjabi child will begin to learn early about the seating of men and women, boys and girls, about correct behaviour and action towards different kin, about the order in which senior and junior men and women should be greeted and about the order in which people should be served and eat and so on.

The way such behaviour becomes 'second nature' has been examined by Toren (1990) for Fiji. On the island of Gau in central Fiji people are extremely preoccupied with etiquette, seating patterns at family and communal get-togethers and the expression of shame and shyness towards anyone senior in age or in rank. All this is epitomised by the seating pattern below or above the round bowl in which *yaqona*, a mildly intoxicating drink, is brewed and from which it is served on all ceremonial occasions. Toren's data, which was derived from children's drawings and stories, shows that children's perception is that chiefs and other high ranking people are paramount because such people sit in the area labelled 'above' or are said to be above, whereas a woman or a young man is below because he or she sits in an area labelled 'below' or is said to sit below. Adults do not see it this way. For them where the high chief sits *is* above, because the quality of being above is inherent in him, and where women and young men sit *is* below (Toren 1990: 226). The child's perception of hierarchy develops and matures as his or her perception of 'below' becomes linked to other aspects of experience such as bodily postures of deference, sitting down and being quiet and expressing shame and shyness. And all this the child assimilates and learns in interaction and communication with caretakers and other Fijians in a manner described by Trevarthen (1987) for other populations. In this way social processes enter into cognitive development and produce culturally specific constructs and expectations and cognitive activity can therefore never be seen to be unmediated.

This has important epistemological and methodological implications for cross-cultural therapy as indeed it has for anthropology. In Chapter 2 I described the development of anthropology from an 'armchair discipline' to one in which a much greater emphasis on ethnographic fieldwork, and on an attempt to see the world 'from the native's point of view', developed (Geertz 1974). In Chapter 5 some of the complexities of this tension between the 'inside' and the 'outside' view were discussed in relation to ritual. It should now be clear, I hope, that the process of getting away from a framework in which one can arrive at 'a view from the inside' by attributing to individuals the anthropologist's view from the outside (Bourdieu 1977 [1972]: 96), is crucial, but also complex. In the final section of this chapter and in the two chapters which follow I want to develop the idea that this aim cannot be achieved in any absolute way, and that it is the tension itself between the 'inside' view and the 'outside' view which is a crucial tool in cross-cultural psychotherapy. Of course this tension has always been present in intracultural therapy too – psychotherapists, psychiatrists, psychoanalysts and medical doctors have to varying degrees been required to see the predicament and the suffering of their patients from their patients' points of view. But in the name of scientific endeavour it has also been downplayed and minimised. Mitchell (1993) has suggested that the expertise of the analyst and therapist is perceived to be changing. The answer to the question of what the therapist knows is not 'how the mind works' or 'how experience is structured'. Instead:

> the analyst knows a collection of ways of thinking about how the mind works and about how experience is structured that are likely to be useful in the patient's efforts to understand himself and live with a greater sense of freedom and satisfaction in the world in which he finds himself. The state of psychoanalytic knowledge is not anchored in enduring truths or proof, but rather in its use value for making sense of life, deepening relationships with others and expanding and enriching the texture of experience. (Mitchell 1993: 64–5)

It is obvious that working cross-culturally with clients and patients who are manifestly different from oneself creates a challenge to this expertise and that for this endeavour the kind of material discussed by Toren (1990) and summarised above in relation to the families of the two young South Asian women is relevant. Bateson (1958 [1932]) called this ethos, Bourdieu (1977) has referred to it as habitus and Taylor (1993) has coined the phrase 'background understanding' but whichever term we use it refers to sequences of interaction or behaviour or to aspects of meaning which occur repeatedly and which patients, clients or informants probably do not recognise as belonging to the socially-constructed context which forms the background to their lives. This is a different way of describing taboo and, as is the case with taboo, we are concerned with the grey area between what can be talked about and what cannot be talked about, between following a rule consciously and doing or avoiding doing something as a habit without knowing why. Before closing this chapter it is to these issues I wish to turn.

The changing remit of the psychoanalyst applauded by Mitchell has been aimed at exposing some of the more untenable claims to 'objectivity' and 'science' in fields which focus on the study of human beings. In family therapy a similar process took the form of second-order cybernetics, co-construction and ecological approaches. In anthropology, as I discussed in Chapter 2, where conducting fieldwork involves a serious personal, social and epistemological shift, the 'scientific method' tended to invite an overemphasis on the observer's role and this in turn produced texts, films, photographs and so on which presented practice as more formal, more totalising and more object-like than it really is (Bourdieu 1977). Such materials then tended to become recognised as part of scientific theories in which there is a fundamental confusion. This is the confusion between the way interaction works in practice and the rules and models for practice (LiPuma 1993). What happens is that a sequence of action is observed, for example:

> When Mary and Robert are ready to go out Robert helps Mary into her coat and opens the door for her and walks out after her. Mary accepts this and walks out in front. Furthermore the same thing happens when John and Ann go out and it has also been seen to sometimes happen when Jane and Peter leave the house.

From this observation of a repeated pattern one may arrive at an idea that there is some kind of etiquette in this society which refers to gender relations (perhaps domination, perhaps elevation, but probably not equality). Often, however, this kind of observation gets transformed from being an observed regularity to being considered as a consciously respected rule, something like: men *must* behave like this when they leave the house with their female partners and they know that this is right; or an unconscious regulating social mechanism, something like: if you asked people about this pattern of behaviour nobody had thought about it and answered that they had always done it that way, but you have observed that in order to keep their positions of power men must humour their female partners in a variety of ways (this being one of them) and women seem to make the most of it.

What has happened is that we have ignored the instance when John, Peter, Mary and Ann interact in this manner and the complexity of the conscious and unconscious decisions they make then. We have moved from *a model of reality* to *the reality of the model* (Taylor 1993), or in the language of linguistics from *speech* to *language,* or in Bateson's terminology mentioned in Chapter 4 from the *territory* to the *map.* In Fijian terms we have also moved from the child's conception to the adult's explanation. Most social sciences focus on the *model* for behaviour or the *map* even though these theories are derived from observations of human beings living through actual sequences of behaviour. When social scientists think and talk like this it is as if the rules apply themselves and as if we forget that in real life the application of any rule depends on an agent with a body and on his or her intention, motivation, emotion and reinterpretation and that in reality there is always uncertainty, suspense and heterogeneity.

When the observer considers herself to be part of what she is observing, it may be less easy to overlook these uncertainties simply because one knows that they exist from personal experience. I have always thought that the most impressive thinkers and clinicians are those who are able to attribute to the action of others the complexity and nuances which they themselves experience. But this raises another problem: no one person is able to be aware and understand all the issues which are involved in the correct application of a rule. Nor can any one person be aware of all the rules and all the patterns of behaviour which impinge on him or her in any social or cultural context (Bourdieu 1977). There is always an area which remains obscure for participants and what happens in this area can therefore not be a result of participants simply following the rules. In Fiji, for example, Toren (1990) observed people involuntarily shying away from a touch of the head or people virtually unconsciously seating themselves in the correct position when in the company of others. This was also the case amongst the Thakuris with whom I worked in Nepal where people automatically avoided touching women who were considered to be polluted because of their monthly periods or when people who are senior or of high rank almost mechanically were greeted by placing one's forehead on their feet. This is what Bourdieu means by *habitus*:

> systems of durable, transposable dispositions, structured structures predisposed to function as structuring structures, that is, as principles of the generation and structuring of practices and representations which can be objectively 'regulated' and 'regular' without in any way being the product of obedience to rules, objectively adapted to their goals without presupposing a conscious aiming at ends or an express mastery. (1977: 72)

A person may perform these actions in accordance with and in order to conform with certain cultural themes (in the examples given above the theme was hierarchy) on a regular basis, but this does not mean that we can assume that this person is consciously aiming at this end. This same person may rationalise her behaviour in terms of following a rule, but this does not explain the behaviour or all the patterned behaviour which we might observe as rule-governed behaviour. Toren's work shows that adults may consider certain behaviours, such as sitting in a certain place or greeting a person in a certain way, as an *expression* of hierarchy and this enters into discourse about social organisation and the proper way to do things. What is obscure from an adult point of view and therefore from general discourse but what children intuitively learn, is that these very same behaviours are also constitutive of hierarchy. This is not only because neither Fijians nor Nepali Thakuris talk about how such behaviour is cognitively and emotionally constructed, but also because it is inscribed in body posture, in avoidance, in non-verbal communication and in taboo.

Finally it is because such behaviours are *explained* as rule-governed and become articulated in repeated patterns of interaction, in ritual and in ceremonies that their constitutive function is ensured (Connerton 1989).

CULTURAL PATTERNS

All this amounts to a theory about how cultural patterns of behaviour and of the meaning of that behaviour is passed from one generation to the next. It emphasises cognition as a developmental process and one which is mediated by cultural themes of meaning. It also highlights the doxic or 'second-nature' characteristic of some behaviours and meanings, so concealed to individual agents that they seem to be the only 'natural' way of doing things. Perhaps most importantly, this theory emphasises the social context in which this process takes place. As an answer to the second part of my question about the universality of taboo it thus confirms that not only the content of taboo but also the tensions and contradictions associated with taboo are culturally specific.

The social context is particular and involves infants and children and those who care for them as well as adults in immediate private and public relationships. It therefore first and foremost involves families. So when Byng-Hall talks about transgenerational family scripts, by which he means 'the family's shared expectations of how family roles are to be performed within various contexts' (1995: 4), he is also talking about 'blueprints for action' (1995: 137) or about rules and patterns of behaviour which the actors are following or performing, mostly unconsciously, and which acquire these characteristics precisely because they are embedded in repeated sequences of behaviour. Byng-Hall's interest is in the way families construct their own myths and how both articulated and unarticulated aspects of such myths organise family life and the emotional orientation of family members. Byng-Hall writes about the way family patterns, particularly those which give rise to dysfunctional interactions and psychological disorders, are transmitted across generations. Children might attempt to recreate the scripts by which the parents have conducted their relationship and family life (replicative scripts) or they may consciously try to steer their own procreative families in the opposite directions (corrective scripts). Either way parents do guide, steer or influence what children do and there are developmental, cognitive and emotional consequences of the interaction and the meaning of it.

Families are not cultures, but families incorporate cultural themes and social patterns of interactions and behaviour to varying degrees. The kind of cultural background understanding which I have discussed above and which we may refer to as ethos or habitus, is subtle. It refers to a kind of inarticulate familiarity, a sense of knowing what is fitting and right in a particular context without the actors or agents necessarily being aware that they have this knowledge. Because it is latent rather than obvious this cultural content in fundamental and constitutive principles about interaction poses a challenge to the systemic and the individual psychotherapist. The challenge is to acknowledge that individual persons internalise cultural patterns to such an extent that some of these become 'second nature', and in particular for the therapist to discover this process in herself.

I met with a Cantonese speaking family over a period of 18 months. This family consisted of Mr and Mrs Chan and their four children, a daughter aged 16 and three sons aged 15, 11 and 5. Mr and Mrs Chan were deeply concerned about the behaviour of their eldest son, Wing, who was being rude to his mother to such an extent that Mrs Chan felt that she could not manage him. In addition, and equally worrying, the boy was smoking excessively as well as roaming the streets of the inner city area in which the family lived with boys several years his senior. Wing was moderately learning disabled and attended a special school. Most of our sessions were conducted with Mr and Mrs Chan, Wing and Wing's youngest brother, but occasionally the other family members also attended. I was helped by a Cantonese speaking interpreter but Wing mostly spoke English to me.

Mr Chan's family originated in China. He was the eldest of several brothers and sisters and he recalled that his father treated him harshly, beating him up severely if he was disobedient or misbehaved in any other way. He left home when he was 16 and came to Hong Kong in his early twenties and it was here he met his wife at a time when her family, that is to say her parents and their two daughters, had already planned to come to England. Mrs Chan was the eldest of the two and contrary to her sister who held a well-paid professional job, she had left school early. It was to her that both her mother and her sister would turn if they needed domestic help or any other practical support. At times during the period when her own children had been growing up this had often drained Mrs Chan to the point of exhaustion, but she had never felt that she could refuse her parents' or her sister's requests. All the Chan children had been born in England and Mr Chan worked long hours in the catering trade.

Hierarchy as a cultural model for communication (Hsu 1995) quickly became clear to me in our sessions. Mr and Mrs Chan did not often speak directly to each other except when Mr Chan, who was a quiet and gentle man, in a low voice would stop his wife from talking too much or veering off the point. Both parents spoke to Wing mostly in the form of commands, such as when they would ask him to answer my questions, to sit up or stop doing something, or to explain himself. Wing never had a conversation with either his mother or his father in the therapy room despite my attempts in the beginning of the therapy to engineer this. Mr Chan sometimes did react to what his son had said but he did this by looking directly at me and making a general comment about his son or about young people. Wing was polite and fairly quiet during our sessions.

He never spoke unless he was invited by me or his father to do so, although when addressed directly he would answer enthusiastically if he felt he had something to say. This controlled and respectful style in the therapy room contrasted with what the family told me about what happened at home. At home Wing was reported to be rude to his mother, swearing at her and openly disobeying her. Mrs Chan had found that the only way she could exert some control over her son was by giving or withholding cash from him, but even this was not effective because Wing would manipulate this situation to his own advantage. He never behaved in this way towards his father, but Mr Chan was extremely unhappy and he would often call home several times a day to check how Wing was behaving. He had promised himself that he would not treat his sons as harshly as he had been treated by his father and he had never laid a hand on his eldest son.

My attempts to draw and strengthen the boundary between the parents and Wing (and the other children) and develop the support which each parent could give the other (Minuchin 1974) in this family were to no avail. It was not possible to do this in the therapy room and at home it seemed neither practical nor comprehensible to the family. Both Mr and Mrs Chan's corrective family scripts seemed to leave them without any authority over their eldest son in a cultural context and against a cultural background which placed a high value on respect towards and acquiescence with senior family members and kin. Yet in other areas such as in the way they as husband and wife communicated and the way they both communicated with Wing in public, they adhered to etiquette and predominant Chinese cultural models for such communication.

There seemed to be no way of facilitating a more egalitarian communication between Wing and his parents even though, privately, this is what I thought needed to happen. Nevertheless a change slowly developed after Mr Chan in a session reflected upon the way he had been treated as a young man by his father and upon the way that he had wanted something different for his own children. Mr Chan was quite clear about his distaste for physical punishment, but he was equally clear about the importance for children to show respect for their parents. The central theme which had emerged at this point in the therapy was how Wing could look after himself in a dangerous world where people may want to take advantage of him and how he could learn about this without putting himself at risk. I encouraged Mr Chan to think about which aspects of the old rules about how sons and fathers should behave towards each other he would like to keep and at the same time how he could coach and guide his son in how to manage in life. When the family came back for the following session Wing had again been rude to his mother, but this time Mr Chan had made Wing kneel in front of him while he had given Wing a lecture about the way a son should behave. In the sessions which followed Mr Chan reported taking the same step on a number of other occasions when Wing had been rude or seriously disobedient. Each time when I checked, it was clear that there had been no hint of violence and that the bodily gestures and the speech which Mr Chan gave on these occasions were in effect an exposition of rules for behaviour and interaction and for resolving moral dilemmas. It seemed that my image of a chummy egalitarian conversation between father and son about life had been adapted to a much more hierarchical and more fitting style by Mr Chan. To him this style was more realistic because Wing was not yet an adult and had special needs. When we talked about this in a later session Mr Chan discussed with me how he would know when Wing would be grown-up enough not to need to kneel in front of his father any more.

If the therapist can get a glimpse of a cultural ethos and in this way acquire some degree of insight into the covert cultural themes which have been a crucial dimension of the cognitive and emotional development of their clients, this must, I think, be treated with respect and incorporated as much as possible in treatment and interventions. It is one way to try to ensure that interventions are culturally isomorphic. Such an insight may, as I have indicated, be acquired through close observation of patterns of interaction in the therapy room or through asking about the way certain tasks are normally carried out. It may also be acquired through being curious about a concept, a word or an idea, which is used repeatedly. There are, however, reasons why therapists should be cautious about reading too much into symbols and meaning. In Chapter 5 I argued that understanding symbols and meaning in ritual is more difficult than it seems. This is because by definition symbols depend on polysemy. The way one person understands a symbol may be very different from the way another person understands the same symbol even if the two speak the same language and come from similar cultural backgrounds. In a similar way the meaning of the words or the language a person uses may be highly personal.

In this chapter I have aimed to show how taboo or that which is unrecognised, which can only be recognised by its absence, or which is misrecognised (Taylor 1993) is also imbued with meanings which derive from cultural themes and orientations. I have pointed out that because they involve ritual action, avoidance, repetition of bodily gestures and patterns of interaction these aspects play a significant role in cognitive development and in shaping and reproducing cultural themes. But people, that is to say all of us – therapists, anthropologists, clients and informants – do not recognise this, because the role of these aversions seems ordained by nature and in this way outside our consciousness, or at least outside our discourse. Once we begin to talk about them we can expect a certain amount of disagreement, heterogeneity and conflict about the way they can be explained and the rules which must be or could be followed. This means that the process of understanding meaning is a developmental one and that it takes place against a background understanding, which persons do not know they have. With searching and questioning, more of this background may become revealed, but at the same time the essentialising tendencies in cultural meanings are also disclosed. It is this double process which the therapist must allow herself to experience.

7

Similarities and Differences

In cross-cultural work a recurring question concerns the extent to which cultural differences can be treated as if these were the same kind of phenomena as the differences which exist between individuals; as if it is possible to consider everything together under the heading of 'difference'. There are many ways in which being aware of individual differences intra-culturally can be useful in thinking about cross-cultural differences. For example this idea is built into the notion, which is central to systemic therapy, that if the therapist is able to develop a stance of curiosity she will be able to explore the meaning which the client attributes to something, a feeling, an idea or an event and also the different meanings which different members of a family may hold about the same problem or issue (Cecchin 1987). Yet as I have shown meaning implies polysemy and therefore meaning is always problematic. This is equally the case in encounters between individual persons from more or less similar cultural and social backgrounds as it is in cross-cultural encounters. In fact, I would go as far as to say that the less acquainted therapist and client are with the background and general worldview of each other, that is to say the greater the distance between them in this respect, the more problematic polysemy becomes. The reverse also seems to follow, namely that if we can find something which is cross-culturally applicable, we may also be able to assume that we are moving nearer to the human condition and to something which we all share and which therefore may serve as an anchor for the therapist working cross-culturally. In this way cross-cultural work provides a critical leverage on all theoretical frameworks. How then can this search for similarity proceed? Paradoxically perhaps, this requires a particular, non-generalising approach to 'difference' and it is to this I now turn in this and the following chapter.

Talking about the human condition and what we all share may sound fairly straightforward. However, as the previous chapters have shown we must be careful not to fall back on the position which conflates the way we ourselves are with human nature as a whole. Part of the problem is that there is no overall agreement about the best way of approaching this. For example there is no agreement on how psychoanalytical or psychotherapeutic and anthropological frames of reference may be bridged. Both these theoretical frameworks originate in western modernism and share many ethnocentric assumptions. Anthropology set out to understand others on their own terms and even though anthropologists purposefully or not, underestimated the complexity of this task, the process, sometimes accidentally, threw up specific material which deeply challenged western worldviews. Psychoanalytic and psychotherapeutic theories, on the other hand, have generally favoured the 'broad-sweep-of-culture' approach glossing over the experience of particular groups of people. I do not wish to dismiss this tension between the particular and the universal, rather I wish to discuss it in terms of the pragmatic concerns of the systemic or individual psychotherapist working cross-culturally.

This chapter then is about differences and similarities. It pulls together the themes discussed in previous chapters and outlines the position of the psychotherapist with regard to this material. This will bring me to address briefly the topic of power which now can be seen to have special significance against the background of conscious and unconscious social and cultural patterns. I then mention two areas in which power has specifically been recognised and which are highly intertwined with cross-cultural practice: feminism and racism. These two areas have both played important roles in bringing forth the current concerns with and interest in cross-cultural therapy. I do not have the space to examine each of these in detail, but I want to suggest that the sorts of issues which I have glossed as ethos, habitus and background understanding pose particular challenges in the areas of gender inequality and discrimination based on race, culture or ethnicity. They therefore also pose particular challenges for responsible, respectful and antidisciminatory psychotherapeutic practice.

OUTSIDE AND INSIDE

The theme of this book has been culture, but not culture as something you can see or clearly separate from everything else. The issues which I have discussed such as emotions, kinship relations, ritual and taboo are more illusory because they are located on the boundary between the internal life of an individual and the external world of relationships, customs and institutions. They have an external existence while at the same time being deeply dependent on having to meet the physical, psychological and emotional demands and needs of individuals. Over time these themes are consciously or unconsciously reproduced in conformity with the previous patterns. But these patterns may not simply be repetitions. They may change and be changed. How changeable, then, is culture? And how deep does culture run? Is culture to be seen as Geertz mockingly suggested 'as the icing on the cake' or is culture a layer cake or perhaps a marble cake (Geertz 1986) or more complexly, as Ridley suggests, is it that 'culture cooks the cake' (Strawson 1996: 4)? And if we choose the more complicated view, what are the mechanisms through which culture is reproduced? To answer these questions requires some knowledge of how far into internal worlds of relationships, cognition and emotion, cultural differences can be pushed. It has been my aim in this book to provide an assessment of this from the point of view of the interface between anthropology and psychotherapy, from the point of view of the issues in which these disciplines share an interest. Let me now summarise and pull together the different arguments.

In Chapter 2 I discussed how the aim of traditional anthropology was to attempt to see persons against the background and context in which they lived. Considering this to be 'from the native's point of view' (Geertz 1974) was putting it too strongly even if some anthropologists thought that they were doing just that. Paradoxically some contemporary anthropologists have dismissed this tension between being on the outside looking in and the need to be on the inside by focusing on their own authorship and their own internal worlds. These are the literary anthropologists, who insist that accessing other meanings must be done by taking an interest first and foremost in oneself. Whichever way one looks at this problem of accessing something outside oneself, it is clear that the process implicates something crucial about the subject in the object of study and that this should not be underestimated. This process always encompasses a kind of violence which may begin or end with physical violence such as is well documented in many colonial, ethnic and racist encounters. In the midst of these methodological difficulties, anthropology, sometimes naively, has been aimed at cataloguing human differences and variation, and ethnography has been and still is the method by which this variation is accessed and documented. In this way European anthropologists, and other Europeans as well, were brought face to face with many differences which they could never have imagined. It took a while for them to begin to become aware that to access these differences they were implicating all aspects of themselves. Families and households were discovered to be structured by different kinship principles and these kinship principles were shown to have as much to do with social organisation and cultural themes of meaning as with biology. But the structures and principles which anthropologists emphasised were also a by-product of their own preoccupation with genealogy, order and inheritance. They saw difference but they did not quite see all the differences. In part this was because kinship appears to be 'natural' and because individuals, including ethnographers, anthropologists, family therapists, psychoanalysts and psychotherapists do not easily see that the general pattern of their own primary experiences with parents and carers may not be universal. In this way their ideals and expected patterns and modes of attachment came to be seen as the norm to which most people ought to gravitate, if not adhere. Yet there is plenty of cross-cultural material which suggests that as well as playing a crucial role in reproducing social organisation, emotions, expectations and patterns of intimacy also vary cross-culturally. They are imbued with cultural meaning and provide opportunities for communicating with oneself and others. But this is not in the terms of the words alone, for experience itself, rather than the words used to describe it, must be the starting point for any kind of knowledge of relationships and communication. Language is only one aspect of what goes on. These are the issues I discussed in Chapters 3 and 4.

In Chapter 5 I discussed ritual. Rituals have attracted the interest of systemic therapists because of the development of a general trend which has become preoccupied with meaning and content as opposed to behaviour and interaction. With ritual some grave difficulties in meaning-centred approaches come to light. It is not defensible to interpret a ritual in terms which have no resonance whatsoever with the persons performing it or with the cultural themes to which such persons might refer. To call on collective denial is a cop-out designed more to rescue a theory than to understand what is going on. An interpretation must therefore make some reference to the experience, emotions, behaviour and worldview of those who are doing the experiencing, even if they are not all experts. So, from where should the anthropologist, ethnographer or psychotherapist take her cue?

As we saw, defining rituals in terms of the symbols they incorporate is tricky because this does not set rituals apart from any other kind of communication. It is a difficult task for anyone, not least an outsider, to decide when something is symbolic and when it is not in everyday life. Furthermore, symbols are not essences with a life of their own, rather they are testimony to individual persons, sometimes generations of persons, investing different, although overlapping meanings in the same representations. Indeed it is this polyvalency which is often taken to be at the root of the efficacy of symbols and when it comes to rituals people carry them out for all sorts of different private and personal reasons. Should our cue therefore be what people and individual persons say? Of course it should, but by itself this is not enough for sometimes people do not know the meaning of a ritual or why they are doing it, apart perhaps from the notion that it is 'something good' or 'something they have always done'. This need not mean that a ritual has lost its efficacy or that it is hollow, but it does mean that we cannot get very far by relying exclusively on what people say. This is why I turned to the approach which focuses on ritual action. Humans everywhere perform rituals and whenever they do, this requires that prescribed sequences of actions are performed with an air of commitment to get it right. There is also always an implicit recognition that the knowledge which facilitates this is not the property of the individual, that individuals do not make it up from scratch every time. Rather, as Taylor puts it, it is a reminder that a public, shared space is created, through the action. I referred to this as a practical approach which examines and asks about what people do before enquiring into the meaning of these actions. And I noted in passing that this was also Bateson's view of ritual behaviour among the Iatmul and that the emphasis accords well with the emphasis on behaviour and patterns of behaviour in traditional family and systemic psychotherapy. I also noted that this is a more useful and responsible place for cross-cultural therapy to start than the enquiry into the meaning of symbols, because it minimises, although it does not cut out altogether, the risk of the therapist or the anthropologist attributing to clients and informants what they mean even if, as Lewis wrote, they do not know it.

Actually the problem about understanding ritual is also a general problem about understanding the life experiences of others. Just as people may not know why they are performing certain rituals or know the meaning of certain symbols, there may be aspects of ritual which involve items or ideas which, although people may know about them, must not be named or mentioned either generally or in the company of certain relatives or persons, or in certain contexts. Such secrets and taboos were the subject of Chapter 6. Here I noted that that which is not mentioned, which must not be mentioned or which cannot be mentioned because no one is aware of its existence, is as meaningful as that which may be the subject of open discussion and debate. But while secrets are usually about keeping some people ignorant, taboos tend to have wider implications. Persons are rarely able to comprehend the full justification for keeping taboos, because the keeping of taboos is tied up with classification and boundaries between categories and with the social and political order of a society. This was why Fortes referred to taboos as 'ordained aversions' and considered them to be closely implicated in personal and social identity. In this sense taboos ensure normality and by implication also the explosive nature of the events which follow when normality is transgressed.

Some taboos are learnt early in a person's life as part of a general learning about what is allowed and about the rules which a person is expected to follow. But, as Bourdieu showed, some of these rules do not seem like rules at all, or rather in these instances the actors are not aware that they are following rules and are not trying to apply the rules correctly. To them it seems that they are simply interacting in a way which is natural. I am referring here to actions and interactions which may be glossed as 'skill' (Bloch 1992; Bruner 1996), that is to say such practices as body posture, respectful behaviour, avoidance behaviour, sexual intimacy, parental and filial intimacy, arrangement in space of house and seating, planning of houses and streets, architecture and so on. Yet in any society these interactions between many different participants over time will generate certain patterns and will, tautologically, tend to be explained as an expression of these very same patterns. So that, for example, a greeting (behaviour) may be taken to express inequality (a pattern); heterosexual intimacy may be taken to express an ideology of love; the architecture of a house may be thought to express contemporary artistic trends and so on. As Toren showed for Fiji, the reality of the situation, namely that the interactions themselves are also constitutive of the patterns (that a way of greeting itself creates and reproduces hierarchy) is only intuitively understood by children under a certain age and does not tend to be immediately accessible to adults.

Bruner tells the story about how he walked in the foothills in the Italian Alps near the home of a friend. The friend, who is a woman, greeted everybody, acquaintances, men and strangers alike, who they met on the footpath by nodding and waving. As soon as they approached the village she reprimanded Bruner for carrying on this behaviour. At first she could not explain why. Finally she said:

> Well you see, of course, it must be a stranger has a different significance in the hills than in the village – like he might attack you up there so you want to be sure you express good will. . . . I'd never thought of it before' (Bruner 1996: 153)

Cultural distinctions are thus written into behaviour, practices and interactions without the participants being immediately aware of this or aware of it at all. In terms of the consciousness and life experience of individual persons, culture or parts of culture become a kind of 'second nature'. Bourdieu has referred to these types of experiences as doxic experience:

> which provides the illusion of immediate understanding, characteristic of practical experience of the familiar universe, and which at the same time excludes from that experience any inquiry as to its own conditions of possibility. (Bourdieu 1990: 20)

A great deal of the material which we observe in psychotherapy and in family therapy and which we use to inform our opinions and interventions is made up of what for our patients are such doxic experiences. But if persons do not see the consequences of their interactions, their explanations of the meaning of these interactions can also only be half the story. Or to put it differently the meaning as it appears to each person, as it appears to be implicated in their motivation, is not necessarily shared by the next person and is not necessarily exactly like that to any other person. The acquisition of meaning is a developmental process, it depends on personal differences, on cognitive development and on ongoing interaction with others. Meaning, therefore, is heterodox and partial, it is always shifting and always in the process of becoming.

However, meaning appears as if it is fixed and this appearance is persuasive. This is because the development of doxic experiences depends on a certain permanency, a certain repetition of similar interactions and patterns. Patterns of behaviour, interaction, affect, emotion and thought arise in children because adults behave and interact with them with a certain consistency, and they manage to do this because they explain their behaviour to themselves as the following of rules. It does not matter to them that this cannot be so because they do not know all the rules they follow. It is enough that they gloss the rules as 'tradition'. These patterns, which are wholly or partially unconscious, have been described as habitus, ethos or background understanding. But meaning also appears fixed because this tends to be the way others observe it. This was another point made by Bourdieu: social science, and by extension any observation of social phenomena, is an objectifying process. Thus, for example, a statement about 'we Danes do *x* because this is what we believe is the proper way' (an explanation of behaviour as being rule governed) made by a client may become 'all Danes believe *y* and do *x*' (an attribution of essence and absoluteness to persons) in the mind of the therapist.

The question for the therapist is how to access this complexity. In an inspiring and perceptive essay White, a well-known family therapist, has commented on these issues and on the challenge they pose for the psychotherapist (White 1992). White notes the importance for the therapeutic process that patients are able to perceive, identify and inquire into the circumstances and the practices (in this case meaning rules) which impinge on and govern their lives. In Bourdieu's words White encourages us to move from a process of domesticating the exotic to one in which the domestic itself is exoticised (Bourdieu 1988). For example, in the case of a young woman who had been suffering from anorexia nervosa for a long time, White first enquired into the way the anorexia was affecting the young woman's interaction with others and then about how it was affecting her attitude and interaction with herself. In this way something which the young woman had until then considered as part of herself, as part of her essence perhaps, became objectified and externalised and therefore appeared exotic enough to see and *look at* as separate. After this unmasking of the illness, the socially constructed nature of it (Selvini Palazzoli 1974; Littlewood and Lipsedge 1986) and the constitutive power embedded in it (Foucault 1980), the path was open for the client together with the therapist to work on what she wanted from her life, on the choices she wanted to make. In the therapist's (White's) vocabulary it became possible for the client to address her own agency. Rather loosely White refers to this as deconstruction in therapy and he uses his own well-known tool of externalisation (White 1989) in the way just described. White therefore agrees with Bourdieu that meaning is heterodox and therapy is therefore about exploring and exploiting the gap between personal and cultural meanings, a gap which must be bridged by a person's own actions and behaviour, thoughts and reflections, or what Bruner has called 'meaning-making' (Bruner 1990). Therapy can therefore be perceived as a kind of re-authoring, a process which White describes in the following way:

> When it is established that particular events qualify as unique outcomes [similar to Goffman's idea of outcomes which contradict expectations] in that they are judged to be both significant and preferred, the therapist can facilitate the generation of and/or resurrection of alternative stories by orienting him/herself to these unique outcomes as one might orient oneself to mysteries. *These are mysteries that only persons can unravel as they respond to the therapist's curiosity about them.* As persons take up the task of unravelling such mysteries, they immediately engage in story-telling and meaning-making. (1992: 127; my emphasis)

Despite the importance of White's approach for placing the person in the centre of the agenda for systemic theory and practice (Pare 1995) I want to suggest that when it comes to cross-cultural work there are difficulties with it. I also want to suggest that these difficulties arise from White's conceptualisation of *the person* and from his privileging of meaning and language over action and experience. As my emphasis indicates, White considers that the central process of therapy involves firstly a person or persons together unravelling something which is a mystery, that is to say something which they do not immediately understand. Second, they do this in response to some kind of direction (curiosity) from the therapist. I want to examine briefly each of these ideas in the light of some of the material discussed in the preceding chapters.

White is quite clear in his emphasis on action being prefigured on meaning-making (1992: 123) and on the stories people have about their lives determining the effects of their lives. Despite his interest in Bourdieu, White thus does not acknowledge the routine and doxic experiences and actions in which persons constantly engage throughout their lives and to which they may attribute no meaning apart from the satisfaction of adhering to tradition or the feeling of sharing a public space. As we have seen, these actions are mostly outside consciousness and they appear as natural. To subjects they appear as the only way of doing a particular thing, performing a ritual, sowing a field, building a house or engaging in a particular interaction, greeting a particular person or even mothering a baby. These actions and experiences are not necessarily open for deconstruction and externalisation in the sense used by White. Yet they contain cultural distinctions and to this extent they are changeable and malleable. Under certain circumstances and in certain contexts, some of these experiences can make their way into consciousness and become open to reflection and reassessment and in this way become 'a mystery' as described by White. This may for example be the case during rapid social change or when persons and families live in a different social and cultural context than that in which they grew up or when persons are pushed by circumstances to choose to reflect on this. As therapists we hope and aim for this to happen in therapy.

I met with a Punjabi speaking Sikh couple over a period of some months. They had been living in England for 20 years or so, but they had no family nearby and no friends whom they counted as close. Over the years they had developed a conflictual relationship. The woman worked by far the hardest both in the home and outside while the man often was unemployed. They both expected the man to make the decisions and to be in charge of taking the family out, buying new things for the house and deciding how much money should be spent on various larger household items. He also appeared to make the decisions about when and how intimacy and sexual contact could occur. The woman in particular complained that if only they were back in the Punjab it would be so much easier for her, because there her kin and family would support and comfort her and her husband would likewise have a network of brothers and cousins on whom he could rely. Yet neither wanted to go back just now because of the education of their children. I applauded their decision to be good and conscientious parents and commiserated with the feelings of displacement and isolation which they were both suffering. I also enquired about what according to the *Guru Granth Saheb* (the sacred book of the Sikhs) and Punjabi ideas about kinship ought to be the role and responsibility of husband and wife with regard to each other. The husband stated very clearly that it was the responsibility of a husband to act in his wife's interests. After some time it became possible to discuss how, since their traditional network was not available, they could help and support each other in a new and different, although still to them acceptable, way. The husband indicated that he would like to hear his wife's point of view and for her to talk to him more. The wife said that she found her daily routines exhausting and needed more support. Initially she found it very difficult to talk like this, but slowly she became able to be more forward and in her own terms less respectful to her husband. She began to speak directly to him in the therapy room and their eye contact as well as their body language indicated an intimacy, which if not new, had at least found expression in a new setting. He did not give up his dominant position but her opinions and wishes began to influence his decisions.

For this couple some aspects of the actions and the experiences which were normally explained as expressions of Punjabi kinship, of gender roles and of inequality became available for reflection during therapy and therefore also open to change according to what the couple felt they needed and how they wanted to continue their lives together. The push for change had been initiated by their own experiences of a dysfunctional pattern. Some aspects of their doxic experiences, which were instrumental in generating and maintaining inequality and a gender hierarchy, however, remained the same and unavailable for reflection. For example, during the therapy neither husband nor wife ever spoke in a western manner about their own needs and there was never any question that the husband should not go out of the door first followed some steps behind by his wife or that the children, when present in the session, should not speak directly to their father but could address their mother in this way.

It would be unthinkable that all such doxic and background experiences should be available for reflection and choice, for that would make continuous communication difficult if not impossible. Indeed this is my first difficulty with White's notion of therapy as the unravelling of a mystery: some mysteries will always be there, because for persons they are taboo or simply do not exist. This, it might be argued does not matter much, for therapy is aimed at increasing awareness about oneself and the social and relationship contexts which provide the background for one's life. Therapy is about unmasking more and more mysteries with the help of a therapist, but there can be no absolute number, no absolute aim apart from the judgement made by the person in therapy or by the therapist and client in some agreement.

And this is where my second difficulty with White's view of therapy comes in. For White does not appear to see that the same types of processes which implicate the person and the body of his clients also implicate his own person and his own body. In other words the therapist, him- or herself, also has doxic experiences. Some of these are unconscious, others may be partially conscious and again others may have become meaningful and open for reflection as a result of the therapist's training or years of experience doing this particular work. Heterodoxy applies equally to client and therapist and accessing the meaning of others cross-culturally is complex. It is not simply a matter of the anthropologist or the psychotherapist seeing what others, namely their informants or their clients or patients, cannot see. Questions therefore arise about the extent to which the therapist is the director of the search for new meaning and new practices and, given that there are processes which are not open for reflection to the therapist herself, whether the therapist is able and equipped to direct such a search.

In a sense all communication is co-construction and talking to clients and with them generating or constructing a view of themselves and the therapy is clearly one aspect of the therapeutic process. But how do you co-construct cross-culturally when it is clear that people are not aware of all that they are doing and when what they are doing seems to them the 'natural way' and beyond questioning and conscious awareness? Or when these matters of routine, emotional orientation and background understanding are manifestly arenas for the acquisition of meanings which come to be understood as fixed and reified by culture and tradition? We seemed to have reached the limits of co-construction at least in the sense of therapist and client doing something together on equal terms. As with the 'native's point of view' we appear to have hit upon a misnomer (Obeyesekere 1990) which underestimates the directional, or even the manipulative force, of the therapist's task. If this is not recognised talk about co-construction (White 1992) or collaboration (Hoffman 1993) is in danger of becoming a label for another form of covert control.

Cecchin (1992) writes about the importance of the viability of any selection which the therapist might make in his comments and interventions, and considers that an interpretation or action is viable if it is granted coherence within a significant interactive context. Cecchin's illustration set against my own experience with a Bangladeshi family will illustrate the complexity of this idea of viability in cross-cultural work. The following is Cecchin's illustration:

Suppose a therapist closes a session with the following comment, 'I cannot avoid thinking that many problems in your family stem from the fact that your behaviour seems to be ruled by a patriarchal pattern that tends to oppress women. Some of the stories you told me succeeded in convincing me of this interpretation. Therefore, I will give you some instructions in the hope of breaking this pattern. Some of my colleagues behind the mirror, however, warned me that it is not proper to interfere with how families are organised, no matter how inappropriate we might think the organisation is. I had a long argument with them and we came to the conclusion that I will follow my conviction, but only for five therapeutic sessions. I cannot avoid trying to do what I think is right as a therapist – even if my colleagues disagree'. (1992: 92–3)

Cecchin is taking a stand and then immediately placing this stand in the context of his team in a manner which allows himself and others to reflect on it. This is not unlike White's idea of co-authoring in which the therapist, although recognising his own expertise, consciously works with the client to deconstruct this knowledge. A little more than meets the eye, however, is implicated in this stance 'that the therapist is an expert on therapeutic conversations' (Reichelt and Sveaass 1994). Consider the following example from my own practice which I have also discussed elsewhere (Krause 1995).

The Mahmouda family was a Bangladeshi Muslim family with six children between the ages of 1 and 11, who were referred because of their eldest son's severe headaches. He had missed a lot of school and his condition had been investigated by paediatricians, psychologists, a *hakim* (Ayurvedic practitioner) and a *pir* (holy man). They were referred on the advice of a child psychiatrist and I met with the family together with a Sylheti-speaking interpreter. In the first session I heard about the family background and about the treatment the son had received. I explored first with Mr Mahmouda, then with Mrs Mahmouda and then with each of the bigger children what might be wrong. I talked to Mrs Mahmouda about her son's diet. Was there something wrong with what he ate, with the way he lived or with his habits? Was he perhaps unhappy about something? Was there something wrong with his head? I asked the father and each of the older siblings the same questions and I also asked whether someone else in the family was unhappy? No one could think of anything which could be the cause of the severe pain.

The second session began with Mrs Mahmouda asking to speak and proceeding to tell me about her unhappiness and her husband's affair. She told me that sometimes her husband hits her, but most of all she conveyed her upset at losing her husband and her sexual partner. Tears rolled down her cheeks while she described in detail specific events which had happened, always referring to the day of the week, to what had been happening in the family, where the children were, what she had done, what he had done, what had happened next, who had telephoned often quoting verbatim what was said. Mrs Mahmouda spoke for a long time while her husband and the children listened in deep silence. Apart from interrupting at the beginning to check with Mr Mahmouda whether it was all right with him that his wife spoke, I let Mrs Mahmouda speak.

She said 'if God is willing we should try to live together, otherwise we should have a divorce'. I chose this point to comment and to direct the session in the following way.

Turning to Mrs Mahmouda I said 'you are very unhappy and it is important that you bring your unhappiness here and talk about it'. Turning to the children I said; 'Did all you children know that mummy was so unhappy?' They all said, 'yes' except the eldest son. I asked him directly whether he knew and he nodded. To the whole family I said that I thought there was a lot of unhappiness in this family, that both dad and mum were very unhappy and that I would not forget about this but that I wanted to go back to the headaches for a little while, because this was what we had been discussing last time they came. I asked Mr Mahmouda whether it was all right to talk to his eldest son now and I then began to track with the boy in detail the life of his headache in its physical and social context (White 1989). When does it come? When was it there last? What happened on that day? When did the headache start? What did he do? Where was he? What happened? Where were mum and dad and his brothers and sisters? What did they do? What did he have to eat? Who prepared it? How much did he eat? What kind of curry? Did he eat meat? Did he eat rice? Did he have any fresh air? Did he sleep? Mr Mahmouda contributed several times to this by adding a comment or by helping his son remember, and when this happened I checked with Mrs Mahmouda whether she agreed with her husband. As in the first session I specifically addressed Mrs Mahmouda when talking about the preparation of food and her son's diet. I also asked the boy whether seeing his mother unhappy made the headache worse. He said it was the same. I said that there were clearly two problems in this family but I could not be sure whether they were connected, but I thought that the headache would have a good chance of surviving in this unhappy situation. I ended the session by noting that since Mrs Mahmouda had said many things which might make her husband feel angry, she might not be safe from his violence. She said she did not think that she would be safe and in answer to the same question Mr Mahmouda said 'If God will it'. I made it clear that I could not concentrate on the headaches if there was more violence and if this happened we could not go on meeting like this. I also advised Mrs Mahmouda to contact the police if Mr Mahmouda was violent again.

The next sessions followed this pattern of a twofold emphasis. First I heard more about the marital relationship from both Mr and Mrs Mahmouda. Mrs Mahmouda did not report further physical violence, although both she and her husband reported much verbal abuse. I explored with them how such conflict would be dealt with in Bangladesh. How would they cope apart here? What would other members of the community think? What would their families think? The couple often argued and were verbally extremely abusive to each other. Then I tracked the headaches in the same way I had done before. During these sessions the headaches were getting better and by the seventh session the boy had not missed any school for a month and we were able to concentrate on the marital relationship, which eventually ended in separation.

Cecchin's comment that the root of the trouble his imaginary couple was suffering related to the nature of patriarchy and the oppression of women inherent in this ideology is applicable to the Mahmouda family, at least from my own point of view. However, I have no doubt that there would have been little value in pointing this out as both Mr and Mrs Mahmouda considered patrilineal kinship and the type of marital relationship this implied as the 'right' or perhaps even the 'natural' way (Gardner 1995). If I had challenged this directly I think this would have been understood to be irrelevant to why they had come. I therefore opted for showing respect for the ideal to which they were trying to adhere and this is why I asked Mr Mahmouda for permission to hear his wife and why I, a woman, did not encourage him directly and immediately to tell his side of the story which involved sexual matters. Instead I chose to engage Mr Mahmouda through his eldest son's symptoms. Similarly I do not think that Mr and Mrs Mahmouda would have been impressed had I relayed to them my own or any of my colleagues' doubt about their kinship system. The way I might or might not assess their kinship system would, I venture to guess, be irrelevant to them and their immediate predicament, which when expressed through their son's severe headaches, was something they could not ignore.

Many of my questions did of course invite them to comment on their own kinship ideology and on the way they perceived themselves in the world. But my questions addressed some of the doxic processes and some of the background understanding involved in the way I understand that a Bangladeshi person connects to his or her physical surroundings and to other persons; they did not address the theory or the model which they might be conscious of using. For example Mrs Mahmouda's context-rich style is not only well known from the great Hindu and Muslim epics, it is also the way contemporary arguments are conducted in many Indian communities (Shweder 1991). It also fits well with a context-dependent view of personhood, but this was not noteworthy or unusual to her. I had become familiar with this style during my ethnographic fieldwork, both with Nepalese Hindus in Nepal and with Sikh Punjabis in Britain and had I not recognised it I might have been impatient to move the conversation on into a style more commonly adopted in family therapy.

I also used two other lines of questioning which addressed doxic experiences. In every session the time was divided between discussing the eldest son's physical health and the family's psychological health. Neither aspect was given priority. In this way I was aiming at reflecting the absence of mind–body dualism in the Unani tradition (Good 1977; Bhattacharyya 1986; Good and Good 1992). I needed to avoid the suggestion that either physical or psychological/social aspects of persons exist independently and in this I was following a strategy used by Ayurvedic and Unani practitioners (Nichter 1981; Kakar 1982). My second line of questioning was in accordance with White's ideas about the externalisation of the symptom (White 1989), which accords well with ideas about the person found in Unani and Ayurvedic traditions, since in these traditions the emphasis is on an ecological relationship between a person and his or her physical and social environment. It was the humoral idea of ecology which informed my focus on themes which maintain and reproduce the physical body as well as the person such as diet, sleep, exercise and family relationships.

In these ways I tried to be sensitive to and curious about the implicit (doxic, background) themes which influenced and informed the experiences which the members of this family (in particular the parents and their eldest son) had of themselves in their relationships. I think that my questions were viable, but they were not initially informed by what happened in the therapy, for the events and processes about which I enquired did not enter the conversation except through my questioning. Indeed, they referred to the kind of material which seemed natural and not significant to the family. I was informed by a view from the outside, derived from my previous experience and from what I had read, while their view was from the inside. However, in our encounter we managed, I think, to find some common ground. This common ground did not, as it happens, include agreement about ideas of how persons perceive themselves in the world. In this respect their view was different from my own and from the view of the reflexive Cecchinian therapist and it remained this way. Instead the common ground consisted in finding a way of talking about the ideas which were salient to their view of themselves. The notion of the therapist as an expert in conducting therapeutic conversations is thus an overstatement, for there can be no universal 'therapeutic conversation', no universal expertise in this respect. What persons do and think, whether they are aware of this or not, must always be understood against the background of the social and cultural contexts in which they live their lives. The responsibility for gaining access to these different influences on personal lives is the therapist's, and for that she needs to position herself both on the outside and on the inside while at the same time being or becoming aware of the limitations of either view.

THE ROLE OF POWER

In the therapy room the therapist and the clients are thus not equals. The client(s) have experiences which somehow have led them to therapy, but they cannot be aware, or at least are unlikely to be aware, of all the rules and circumstances which impinge on their lives and their negative or unhappy experiences of it. The therapist may be able to detect some of these but she too is only partially aware of the circumstances and influences on her own experiences and ideas. Furthermore, she may not be aware of the extent to which her observation of others, particularly others who are very different from herself, fashions their lives into a totalising and objectifying image into which she can project her own desire for order and regularity. The whole thing seems to be a kind of 'hit or miss' endeavour and involves the same kinds of risks and uncertainties which characterise many other kinds of social relationships. Of course this is not incorrect, for to some extent therapy is like ethnographic fieldwork, simply another kind of social relationship involving human communication, and some of the same rules which apply to these other social processes also apply to therapy or fieldwork (Jenkins 1994). In this sense therapists and clients, ethnographers and informants co-construct because they communicate with each other.

However, precisely because therapy is a kind of social relationship and because the social processes which influence general social relationships also influence therapeutic relationships, therapy also tends to be an arena for the implementation and operation of general political and power relationships. This observation is not new, for the claim that psychotherapy and psychoanalysis have tended to be discriminatory against women and racist has been made often enough before both by psychotherapists and by family therapists (Walters et al. 1988; Perelberg and Miller 1990; Waldegrave 1990; Goldner 1991; Kareem 1992; Thomas 1992; Mitchell 1993). The point is that if therapists simply leave things as they are, if they do not think about this, if they do not do something different, the prevailing power and political relationships, which generally and often subtly create and reinforce discrimination based on gender, race and ethnicity (and other attributes) will also operate inside the therapy room or inside the therapeutic process wherever this takes place. This is surely anathema to responsible cross-cultural practice, so what can the therapist do about it?

The first thing to realise, I think, is that in Euro-American countries power lies with the white therapist and, to a lesser extent, also with the black therapist trained in the disciplines and theories dominated by white professionals and Euro-American philosophy. This follows directly from the therapist's responsibility of attempting to gain access not only to the client's experiences but also to the background against which these experiences have come about. Since meaning is heterodox and partial and always in the process of becoming and since it is difficult to establish whether any two individuals mean the same thing, there is always a possibility of conflict in communication. There is therefore also always the possibility that the most powerful will persuade, command or even terrorise the less powerful. And in cross-cultural communication this process always involves a kind of violence (Hastrup 1995). The therapist must therefore realise her own potential for this kind of violence which Cecchin following Maturana (1980) defines as 'the therapist's attempt to instruct the family in his or her own pattern' (Cecchin 1987: 411). But it is not enough that the therapist is aware of this inherent difficulty in the therapeutic encounter, for as we have seen in cross-cultural work the full extent of the difficulties is rarely obvious. It is also necessary that the therapist examines her own position within a field of producers of knowledge (Bourdieu 1983) and in particular becomes aware of the social, historical and professional origins of her own assumptions about issues which generally from her point of view seem natural and beyond questioning and which yet are crucial to her professional project (Surland and Stæhr Nielsen 1997). For the systemic psychotherapist and the individual psychotherapist practising cross-culturally these are issues such as kinship relations, attachment and emotions, regular and routine patterns of behaviour and interaction, ritual and taboo. It is therefore necessary that the therapist be curious in a disciplined way about herself, not just about her personal self and about her inner conflicts as is required for functioning within the processes of transference and countertransference in psychoanalysis, but more specifically about her social personhood, about the social relationships, the institutions, the professional theories, the professional organisations and the history of the society or societies which have provided the background and context for her own personal and professional life and experiences. In this sense cross-cultural therapy ought to begin by therapists looking critically at all aspects of themselves.

FEMINISM AND GENDER

Another difficulty is our tendency to objectify what we observe; to treat the lives, meanings, behaviours and thoughts of others as if they are more homogeneous than they really are and than they possibly can be. It is this tendency which in part has been responsible for seeing women in general terms, as powerless; as one side of a dichotomy between man on the one hand and woman on the other (Ortner 1974; Burck and Daniel 1995a) or as playing particular roles in society (Burck and Daniel 1995b; Inhorn 1996) and in this way proceeding as if in these respects all women are the same.

The attention to women, which 'the anthropology of women' and feminism in psychotherapy firmly placed on the agenda, was important not just to the politics of equal opportunities but also to the advancement of general social theory. It henceforth became impossible to neglect the realisation that what was observed depended at least in part on who was doing the observing. However, in the process of bringing this forth a certain stereotyping and reductionism also occurred: women were considered as a universal category and the main features of this category were, when all was said and done, derived from the physical and biological characteristics which all women share. Yet at the same time it was clear from the work which women anthropologists carried out with women informants that the behaviour, images and attributes associated with women are culturally constructed and historically specific (MacCormack and Strathern 1980; Ortner and Whitehead 1981). Women cannot therefore be a universal sociological category and we will not get far as therapists if we think of our female clients in this way. Instead we need to understand how different spheres of social life intersect for individual women. We need to understand how economic organisation, political ideology, the organisation of the state and kinship, households and families impinge on the lives of our women clients. In particular, therapists need to recognise that women tend to find themselves at the boundary between kinship relations and state structures and that kinship ideologies play a central role in the reproduction of the state, a process which is not simply unidirectional from the 'state' to the 'family' but also mutually determining. Since women are involved in these spheres and processes in a way which men are not, kinship is inherently gendered (Howell and Melhuus 1993) and it is through an emphasis on kinship rather than an emphasis on families and households alone that the full implications of these processes for women's lives can be understood (Moore 1988). Persons – women, men or children – thus do not enact biological, physiological or cognitive scenarios unmediated, and as we have seen in previous chapters, they also do not simply reproduce collective dogma or dominant ideologies mechanically. To be sure persons do not always know the full implications of what they are doing and they are not always conscious of the full meaning of what they say, but even the most ritualised and routine practices involve 'the orchestrated improvisation of common dispositions' (Bourdieu 1977 [1972]: 17) and therefore produce variation. While such variations may be the result of accident, circumstance or deliberate choice, practices, interactions and patterns of behaviour in which persons choose their own participations and which therefore are more conscious, or in the process of becoming more conscious, are also more open to choice and to the expression of agency (Giddens 1979, 1984).

What, then, makes women comply or resist dominant ideologies or indeed what makes women choose dominant symbols and discourses in their resistance? Why, for example, do some women veil themselves as protection, others as compliance with tradition and yet others as a sign of class status or political protest (El-Solh and Mabro 1994)? Such questions have steered feminist scholarship and therapists onto new paths with more attention being placed on gender and the social construction of it (Moore 1988, 1994; del Valle 1993; Burck and Daniel 1995a; Burck and Speed 1995). This move has resulted in a further breaking down of womanhood as a unified essence. It is not only a matter of appreciating the differences in the ways women think of themselves and conduct their daily lives in different societies and cultures, the differences between different notions of womanhood within the same society and the same culture often operating for the same women in different contexts and the differences between different constructions of masculinity must also be accessed and understood. This is a focus on how gender identity is acquired, how different gender identities may contradict each other and how these are implicated in types of agency and as forms of subjectivity.

This more promising direction poses difficult challenges both for anthropology and for systemic psychotherapy. I noted in Chapter 2 that there has been a tradition in social anthropology for dismissing psychology as being of little theoretical interest. Social anthropology has therefore not developed a theory of the subject (Moore 1994: 41) and as a result gender acquisition along with other constructs and skills, which children have to learn and internalise, was considered to be a pretty straightforward case of socialisation. As with the Durkheimian view of ritual, this material was considered to somehow become absorbed without it being necessary for the anthropologist to have a theory about the details of this process or the involvement of the individual in it. A full analysis of why women in some circumstances take up a particular gender identity rather than another which is equally available and of why certain identities may be adhered to rather than chosen and the conscious and unconscious aspects of these processes is an extremely complex matter. It involves not only an understanding of ethos, but also an understanding of childhood development, cognition, history, social institutions and cultural themes, language and concepts, significant emotional relationships, social relationships and some sort of organisational analysis of the way different institutions impinge on the lives of persons. It is therefore not surprising that there are relatively few such cross-cultural analyses available.

However, while social anthropology has undertheorised the subject and the notion of subjectivity, the same cannot be said for psychotherapy. The problem here has been that the subject which has been theorised has been the Euro-American subject and that the theoretical discourses in this way have reflected Euro-American popular local ideologies and discourses. In these gender has tended to be considered to be the essence of and at the core of personal identity. This conflation of the theoretical with a local European view is exemplified in Lacan's sexed subject position (Moore 1994) and in Freud's work on the Oedipus complex (Chodorow 1978). Women have tended to be seen as the objects of men who are subjects and this has had significant consequences for the development of feminine identity insofar as women's relationships and search for identity did not require them to differentiate themselves from their mothers and consequently also not from others in the way boys needed to (Gilligan 1982).

These dominant discourses and practices often appear in therapy expressed as the source of unhappy and unfulfilled lives. The relational outlook of women may be in accordance with ideal family forms, but it is a disadvantage in the more competitive and publicly defined areas of social life. It is in these publicly defined spheres that the dominant ideology of the person prevails and the notions of a person as a defined identity, as the essence of an individual, take priority over social relationships and practices. Many Euro-American women do not do well in this sphere because at best their socially constructed outlook may involve them in the experiencing of multiple realities and subjectivities, and at worst may trap them into extremes of objectification and fragmentation (Burck and Daniel 1995a). Recent court cases in England relating to the development of the new reproductive technologies reflect this dual influence on women. Although functioning overtly in the public sphere of civil rights, these technologies also have deep and pervasive influences on intimate relationships and private bodies and lives (Strathern 1992a).

In therapy Burck and Daniel advocate redressing this imbalance by interventions which question the application but not the basic principles of the dominant ideology:

> For men, this involves moving from a centrality of self to a more self-reflexive and multi-perspective position; for women, it means moving from a decentred position to one that includes more definitions of self. (Burck and Daniel 1995a: 37)

Their emphasis on the balance rather than on questioning the underlying principle is understandable for it is implicit that the therapy which they have in mind involves therapists and clients from more or less similar cultural backgrounds and that therefore the discourses and practices in question can be assumed to be more or less accessible and more or less implicitly understood. It is not difficult to agree that subjectivity is 'dynamic and multiple, always positioned in relation to particular discourses and practices and produced by these' (Henriques et al. 1984: 3) and that intimate recursive social interaction plays a central role in this process. It is more difficult to agree that the kind of bounded embodied self which is held up as the Euro-American ideal also has this sway in the rest of the world. Indeed there is much anthropological evidence to suggest that this is not so and that the self-reflexive questions which may be viable for a European client may have to be rephrased or even reconceptualised for clients from other societies and cultural backgrounds. For example, it is clear that not everywhere are persons conceptualised as separate from other persons even though they may still be thought of as individuals (Fortes 1973) and there is much ethnographic data, mainly from the Indian subcontinent, which demonstrates the existence of the idea of persons as divisible, partible and unbounded (Marriott 1976; Östör et al. 1982; Daniel 1984). In this way the Euro-American idea of the body as the locus of identity and the inner self as the locus of agency cannot be upheld as universal. Of course these ideas come closer to the shifting multiple view of subjectivity and the self proposed by postmodern critiques than to the dominant ideology which this view aims to deconstruct. But what happens when this multiple view *is* the dominant ideology? There will still be people who suffer and families with problems, but the therapist may need to cast her interventions in different idioms and refer directly or indirectly to different principles and themes of meaning. In such a case in order to be viable, reflexive questions must acknowledge local notions of self, body and person and none of these may connote bounded discrete entities. Furthermore, since this is plainly doxic knowledge, finding a way of talking about these very issues may be a challenge.

Let me try to illustrate what I am getting at. With two Bangladeshi colleagues, one a co-therapist and the other an interpreter, I met with a young woman of 16, Arina, and various members of her family. Arina had arrived in England when she was 15 in order to join her father, her brothers, her stepmother and her half-sisters. She had begun to go to college to learn English, when one evening she started to bite herself and to scream and shout uncontrollably and use extremely abusive language to anyone who came near her. She continued to behave like this for several days and nights and she was eventually admitted to a local psychiatric ward where she was tentatively diagnosed as schizophrenic and prescribed chlorpromazine. After some weeks she was referred with her family for family therapy.

When we met with Arina she came into the therapy room led by her father and her half-sister, walking slowly and with tears rolling continuously down her face. She said very little apart from 'yes' and 'no' during this first meeting, but from her father and her sister we heard that Arina had already suffered a breakdown while she had been in Bangladesh a few months before she arrived. She had left her mother and a much older brother in Bangladesh and had wanted very much to join her father and her other mother, her father's second wife, who she also called *amma*, in England. Arina's father had married a second wife a few months after she was born. Her paternal grandmother had been ill and so had her own mother and her father could not manage to look after these two women, his baby daughter and his other children and this was why, he said, he had married again. He also said that he wanted his first wife to come to England but she had not wanted to come, although she had agreed that Arina could come.

In a second session our questions about a possible split in the family along the lines of the two wives were met with denial by Arina, her half-sister and her father. Arina said that her two *ammas* had looked after her for as long as she could remember and that she used to ask either of them equally for help or comfort (see Chapter 4). She and her half-sister also both agreed that they had always been together. No one, however had any explanation or any idea about the cause of Arina's suffering. She herself complained that something would suddenly press on her head and her body and her hands and feet would feel cold and she would become frightened. We said that we wondered whether Arina was possessed but her father dismissed this possibility.

For several weeks nothing changed for Arina. She spoke very quietly and not very much and our enquiry into whether Arina had been startled, whether something had happened to her when she was a child, whether she would like to go to school, what she would like to do in the future, whether her mother knew about her condition, what she and others thought was the meaning of her suffering, whether she thought anyone in the family could help her, what they could do, produced no particular response and seemed to lead nowhere.

The fourth session was a home visit and we met family members, most of them women, whom we had not spoken to before: Arina's *amma* ((step)mother), her *phuphu* (father's sister), her *bhabi* (brother's wife) and two of her younger sisters (*bhan*), and her father was also present. In this session we asked all the women what they thought was wrong with Arina and what she should do. Neither women from the parental generation (mother and father's sister) could give any answers to this. The two younger sisters also did not know but they both responded by moving to sit near Arina and hold her hand. Talking directly to the *bhabi* (brother's wife) in this setting was more difficult. A daughter-in-law/sister-in-law, especially if she has recently married into the family and has not yet given birth to children, does not have much status and her respect for her in-laws as well as her shame (Gardner 1995) ought to prevent her from asserting herself in their company. We therefore asked Arina's father's permission to speak to Arina's *bhabi* before we proceeded with our conversation with her in front of Arina. We learnt that in fact Arina and her *bhabi* had been childhood friends, they had gone to school together in Bangladesh and although they were not kin they had also played a great deal with each other. Through the interpreter I commented that before Arina and her *bhabi* had been the same, namely little girls together, but now it was different because *bhabi* was a married woman and could not play anymore, whereas Arina was still a girl. At this point Arina's father interrupted the conversation by saying that he had heard that perhaps a cure for the kind of condition from which Arina was suffering might be marriage. Taking this up, I turned to Arina and asked her whether she thought that her father should prepare for her to marry or not. For the first time in our meetings Arina sat up and answered a loud and clear 'no'.

When we saw Arina next she had improved a little. She was talking about wanting to go to school again and wanting to learn English. Our conversation focused on how she could manage to go to school when she found it difficult to get up before 10 o'clock most days. After a bit of talking back and forth about this we asked Arina's *bhan* (her half-sister), who was almost exactly the same age as Arina and who accompanied her on most trips outside the house, what she thought that Arina should do. After some pressing she finally said that she thought that Arina should fight against the illness and then she would be able to go to school like herself. For the rest of the session and for the following sessions we used this frame of externalising (White 1989). Arina has improved further and we have continued to work with her very slowly, marking and detailing and inviting comments from her relatives about any little change she can manage.

As with the Mahmouda family we listened patiently to detailed and contextual descriptions of Arina's illness and we also persistently enquired about the symptoms in detail while also enquiring about diet, humoral influences and the general regime for Arina's daily routines. However, we think that the crucial point for Arina came when she was able to access and think about her own identity through the comments of two young women, both connected to her through kinship links, who each exemplified different roles and different identities possible for Bangladeshi girls in England in the 1990s. The connection which these young women had to Arina was in terms of kinship and therefore bodily substance (Fruzetti 1990 [1982]; Gardner 1995) and it is this which was a crucial aspect of their comments for Arina's own view of herself. Either of their roles and identities were open to Arina. But as an adolescent girl of marriageable age her predicament was complex and arriving in a strange country and having to adapt to new routines and new rules for social interaction increased this complexity. Her development into an adult role was confounded by the task of finding a way to be a young woman in a new context, a task which confronted her in the form of her suffering. In accordance with a view of selfhood and personhood, which can generally be described as socio-centric (Shweder 1991), and divisible or unbounded (Östör et al. 1982; Fruzetti 1990) it was not possible for Arina to respond while she was addressed in terms of her 'self'. For although the suffering became external to her it was also out of bounds as far as her own agency was concerned. It was when different possibilities for the development of her own gendered subjectivity came into view through her peers that she was able to make a move. Gender undoubtedly plays a role in the definition of the self and the person in most societies and cultures. It follows that, whether therapists define themselves as feminists or as critics of prevailing gender practices and ideologies or not, the issue about the connection between gender and identity and the social relationships which express and reproduce these, must be explored in therapy. However, it is not sufficient that the therapist is aware of her own attitudes and actions in relation to gender discourses and relations of dominance (Jones 1995) for as we have seen in cross-cultural therapy the issue is likely to be a wider one. Differences in kinship ideology and practice and differences in the way bodies and selves are considered in relation to the physical, spiritual and general social environment are also salient in this respect. To access these, therapists like anthropologists must not only address material about which their clients may not be aware but they must also be curious about details, some of which they may not be able to imagine.

A NOTE ON RACE AND ETHNICITY

Race, ethnicity and feminism are often talked about in the same breath. Along different lines they each show up relations of difference, whether this be focused on physical attributes, on the relations between the powerful and the powerless or on the relationship between dominant and marginalised discourses. These terms themselves have variously been employed to justify inequality or to question it, but it is clear that whether or not the terms are used, these are not the only contexts in which differences come to notice and therefore potentially come to be used as political tools. As with feminism, race and ethnicity do not simply reflect biological or physical facts, even though the terms and the discourses in which they are employed on the surface suggest this. They too are cultural constructions and as with feminism we need to be wary of essentialism.

Much has been written about the term 'race' which in Anglo-American terminology is a colonial and postmodern product. For physical anthropologists of the nineteenth century race was a biological marker referring to phenotypical features such as skin colour, hair colour and texture, eyes, stature and so on. These were then and have also subsequently been employed to denote hierarchy and to consistently place non-white populations in the lowest positions. In this way racism was and is a political relationship, in which politics did not only refer to public and institutional processes but also seeped into persons, their fantasies, their minds and the ethos of their cultural context and their patterns of interacting (Fanon 1967). The inequality did not always depend on colour. Numerous other differences such as language, religion, cuisine, dress and social practice could be used to legitimate domination, discrimination and segregation. These have been known as 'cultural racism', or 'differentialist racism' (Balibar 1991) and the choice of marker mostly depends on the history and the inclinations of the dominant groups. Thus, although race denotes a political relationship, colour and physical characteristics have no necessary political belonging (Rattansi 1994).

The task of anti-racism generally and anti-racism in therapy must therefore be to subvert the essentialising discourse of racism. To be sure we must hear the political voice of our clients and these are always in some way generated by personal experiences. But it is also necessary to be aware of our own roles in the history, institutions and social processes of the inequality, which frequently confront us in cross-cultural work. Beyond this for our part we must avoid essentialising and totalising our clients as 'black subjects' (Hall 1992) and search for ways in which we may help them discover a range of representations of themselves and in this way encourage a critical dialogue around personal politics.

It is much the same with ethnicity. Ethnicity refers to identity at the level of a group or a collection of people and involves processes which are internal and external to the group or collectivity. Inside the group people signal a self-definition of their identity to each other by sharing something. This something may be language, certain rituals, a belief, ancestral origins or something else. Outside the group people define those inside it with reference to such a trait or traits, which may be the same or different from those emphasised within the group. In everyday life this distinction between the inside and the outside of a collection of people cannot be easily made, because mostly how people see themselves bears some relation to the way others see them. In this way ethnicity has to do with the way some people define themselves in relation to other people, with the way they and others perceive their differences. It is not so much about the actual traits which groups of individuals may use to identify themselves and others, but much more about the boundaries between the group and others and between different groups (Barth 1969) and about how these boundaries can be crossed. And as with colour, none of the markers used to signify ethnicity and ethnic differences necessarily have any political belonging. They do, however, tend to become vehicles for the expression of political differences. They are socially constructed and the way this happens is related to the ideology and culture of dominant institutions, the assertion of state power and the way these are maintained through recursive and sometimes overtly oppressive interaction and communication.

Ethnicity and ethnic groups are therefore shifting and not static. They appear static because the gaze of the nation-state and the gaze of observers make them so. Take, for example, the 1991 British Census which included questions on ethnic identity. The choice of boxes to tick for ethnicity did not reflect the complexity of ethnic processes nor the number of ethnic groups and therefore implicitly assumed that ethnic categories are fixed and permanent. A similar example can be found in the National Health Service in Britain where although clients are asked how they define themselves, the categories available are limited and given. These are just two examples of how ethnic processes are always in interplay with national processes and how the latter are dominant. The nation may tolerate and even become enlivened by colourful differences in music, food, clothes, literature and so on, but the aesthetic and economic criteria for preferring one type of music over another is assigned by national 'high culture' (Banks 1996) and national politics.

And here we come back to the tendency to totalise and essentialise and to be infatuated with those who are different to the point of assuming an orderliness about them which does not apply to oneself. This process is in itself racist, or at least it can be. But anti-racism groups have also tended to overlook these issues. The categories 'race' and 'ethnic' have themselves, both by racists and anti-racists, been based on an oversimplification and on the 'misleading assumption that it is possible to produce a singular, uncontestable, objective and accurate representation of reality' (Rattansi 1992: 34) and therefore the mechanisms by which different voices are given a representation have been ignored. This latter project cannot be facilitated unless we realise that there are no general watertight or universal definitions. To access what is going on we must examine how ethnic categories and racist processes are operating in relation to specific social contexts and events (Rattansi 1994). This has special significance for the psychotherapist, for again it means attention to detail and the detail which we need to attend to must be grasped not only from our client's point of view, but also from that of the specific, local and historical background against which they live their lives. So, far from their identities being unified, inherited or passed down automatically through generations, they are in fact constructed and reconstructed. Hall puts this succinctly:

> I use 'identity' to refer to the meeting point of *suture*, between on the one hand the discourses and practices which attempt to 'interpellate', speak to us or hail us into place as the social subjects of particular discourses, and on the other hand, the processes which produce subjectivities, which construct us as subjects which can be 'spoken'. (1996: 5–6)

Whether we talk about gender, or cultural heritage or some other facet of our identity or humanity, every one of us more or less consciously chooses to act or to speak or to feel. We are aware of this. But we also engage in other activities which are far less reflected upon and which are more, perhaps wholly, unconscious. Both of these types of activities take place in the context of social relationships, a particular history, social and political structures and processes and themes of meaning and are also shaped or mediated by these. And what goes for our clients, of course, also goes for us as therapists. In the previous pages I have pointed to the complexity of these issues and I have also indicated that if the therapist does not aim to access this, her practice, and in particular her cross-cultural practice, is likely to be ethnocentric and discriminatory. It is now time to consider what the therapist herself can do with this myriad of intersecting influences.

8

Connecting across Culture

THE HUMAN PREDICAMENT

It has been my argument that the issues and facets of culture discussed in the previous chapters are present overtly or covertly in any therapeutic encounter and that in cross-cultural therapy they are especially acute. But therapy is also a context in which two or more bodies meet, a context in which two or more persons each with subjectively held beliefs and conventions more or less successfully manage to achieve intersubjectivity and establish shared conventions for communicating with each other about the world and the context which surrounds them. As with ethnography, cross-cultural therapy with, or when linguistically feasible, without, interpreters, is not an impossibility. In view of the complexity outlined in the previous chapters how then can something so simple be possible at all? In this final chapter I offer an outline for what the therapist can do to avoid ethnocentrism and for how she can bring the need to be aware of her own assumptions into play during the therapeutic process.

A colleague has supplied a description of a cross-cultural encounter which he experienced and which serves as an illustration for my present concern. The encounter was not in the context of therapy, although both parties were in the therapy business. My colleague, a South African, had returned to South Africa for a visit after the release of Nelson Mandela and the ban had been lifted on the ANC. Nine years earlier he had visited a Xhosa Sangoma woman (a diviner) and was interested in finding out more about the practice of this kind of therapy. As a result of a series of fortuitous meetings he did eventually meet with a Sangoma woman:

> Eventually, after quite an eventful morning, I found myself sitting before a Sangoma who spoke no English nor Afrikaans and I remember the deep regret that I could not speak Xhosa and that my knowledge of Zulu, which would have been quite intelligible to any Xhosa speaker, was equally pathetic. Fortunately, we had met a kind man named Stanford who, not only had guided us to the place but had also offered to wait a very long time and translate for us. The Sangoma woman asked me what I wanted. 'I have met and talked with Sangomas and Innyangas [diagnostician, oracle] of the Ndebele, Shangaan, Venda, Sotho and Zulu peoples and I wish to understand

too the way that the AmaXhosa people heal and help those who are in distress', was my reply.

This was duly translated and she looked at me with a puzzled expression verging on pity and repeated her question.

I had another go stating the same as before only adding, 'In Britain I work with many people who have problems in their lives and meet with them to talk and find ways to be useful so that we can find solutions to the difficulties in their lives and in their relationships. I am interested in how you work in your practice as a Sangoma'.

She drew herself up to her full regal height and addressed me in tones that I am sure Stanford did not fully translate. The message, however, was very clear: 'What do *you* want for yourself?' (Faris 1996)

The personal contact between clients and therapist is a crucial dimension to therapy and I have argued that the way relationships are forged, perpetuated and conceptualised may vary from one society to another, that there may be different nuances of familiarity, intimacy and distance and that all this to some extent depends on the existence and operations of other social institutions and processes. But western theories, or certainly Anglo-American theories, tend to adopt the observer's stance and this tends to objectify and totalise what is observed. While this may be justified in terms of natural science, although even here there are plenty of theories which question the position of the detached observer, it surely cannot be justified in the human sciences or in psychotherapy. The Sangoma woman knew that my colleague's general and rather impersonal request could not be anything but a ploy and that it could not yield any real and therefore worthwhile cross-cultural understanding.

Humans share certain predicaments wherever they are. All humans experience some form of suffering, live in webs of connectedness and social relations with other humans, experience some form of agency, in whatever terms and practices this may be cast, and communicate with each other through language. These are essential aspects of being human and there may be others. But only when we are talking about something human as opposed to something non-human can these characteristics be generalised. This is because such generalisations overlook the experiential dimension and it is largely, although not exclusively, with this we work in psychotherapy. To some extent then psychotherapy and the collecting of ethnographic data are only specific instances of a much more general process, namely the recursive self-interpretative processes in which all persons engage when they communicate with each other. We are always interpreting each other whether we are anthropologists or informants, therapists or clients, or just talking to each other in the course of our daily lives.

Recognising the importance of this fairly straightforward observation, has far reaching implications for the way we may think about meaning (Taylor 1985a). It is difficult to get away from the notion that meaning has to do with representation. If we know something we have a representation of it and to understand language is to understand the way we represent things and ideas in language. This is a representational theory of meaning and it is what Bateson (1973) struggled with when he noted that 'the map is not the territory'. In this way representation refers to something which describes the way something else is, or the way this something else is believed to be, and there can be many competing or complementary representations, just as this theory has no trouble with the notions that one word or one symbol may have many meanings.

Yet there are, as we have seen in the previous chapters, different conceptions of meaning possible and I have pointed to two instances. In Chapter 5 I quoted Taylor's example of the use of language as an expressive exclamation referring to two people experiencing an unbearable heat. What was said did not, strictly speaking, serve any purpose as far as communication was concerned, because each of the persons knew it was hot and were experiencing this heat directly on their own bodies. Instead their statements facilitated the creation of a public space and in this way reminded the participants that they were doing something together. Humphrey and Laidlaw took this up and applied this to ritual action, which may not involve speech. Taylor refers to this as the expressive dimension of language and includes here not only the striking up of a rapport, but also the way I talk, my tone of voice, my choice of words, the way I sit and so on (Taylor 1985a: 265). These are all aspects of communication well known to systemic psychotherapists as analogic (Bateson 1973; Selvini Palazzoli et al. 1977).

In Chapter 6 I summarised Toren's work with Fijian children in which she showed the words 'above' and 'below' to play a constitutive role in the shaping of the meaning of these terms for children around the ages of 8–10 (Toren 1990). This constitutive dimension of language demonstrates that the language we use enters into our social relationships, our emotions, our feelings, our goals and our behaviour and practices. I touched on this as far as emotions and intimate family relationships were concerned in Chapter 4.

The expressive and the constitutive dimensions of meaning point to a different aspect of language than the representative one. Indeed I want to go as far as to claim that these dimensions point to a more fundamental quality of language, for to understand what terms represent *depends* on an understanding of these very terms in their expressive and constitutive functions (Taylor 1985a: 277). The expressive and constitutive functions bear witness to language as an activity, to *parole* rather than *langue* (Saussure 1959) and to the contextual nature of speech acts:

> You cannot understand how words relate to things until you have identified the nature of the activity in which they get related to things. (Taylor's summary of Frege, 1985a: 291)

This means that in order to understand speaking as an activity, in order to understand the speech acts of others, one must understand their social practices, their social relations and social conditions. To understand these aspects of other people's lives is a challenge in any kind of psychotherapy, but in cross-cultural psychotherapy it is particularly so. Here a note on culture is in order.

The expressive and constitutive dimensions of meaning also further confirm what I have already observed: namely that culture is a complex illusion. Meaning is never permanent and always has to be established and re-established in the lives of individuals according to the social contexts and expectations in which they find themselves and according to what, against this background, they choose to do. This is what we mean by agency. The passing of practices and ideas between persons and between generations always involves different formulations and potential or actual conflict. Knowledge therefore, and culture is a form of knowledge, is a product of divergent understandings and must be discovered and established by each person for him- or herself as he or she grows and develops (Robertson 1996). This is why the idea of 'culture out there', as a defined whole, as a reification, as something which can be delineated is an illusion. But what then of its complexity? Why do we have the illusion in the first place?

We have the idea because variations in ways of doing things and ways of thinking about this go deeper than we are aware, than we can possibly be aware, and because some of these variations become more or less unconscious patterns of interaction which enter into meaning and language just as meaning and language in turn enter into social practices. These are the processes to which I have frequently referred in different ways throughout the previous chapters and for my purpose here there is not much point in asking whether thought and meaning or action and behaviour comes first. It is enough to acknowledge that these processes are universally human. There is, however, another reason why those of us who live in Euro-American societies, or industrial societies or are privileged citizens of nation-states, reify 'culture' along with other categories such as 'race' and 'ethnicity'. And this reason is political. As Baumann (1996) shows in his analysis of Southall, a multi-ethnic community on the outskirts of London, there is plenty of evidence that the different communities there – Hindus, Sikhs, Muslims, Afro-Caribbeans, white English and Irish – are involved in processes which contest and renegotiate 'culture' and 'community'. Their notion of culture is close to the view just described. Yet members of these communities also talk about belonging to a culture in a reified, totalising sense and in relation to social policy or in interaction and communication with local and national government about resources and rights, this is always the preferred discourse. Baumann makes a clear case that these processes and local definitions cannot be analysed without taking due note of the hegemony of the dominant (state) discourse, which equates culture with community and ethnic communities with religious ones. This ought to be food for thought for the white psychotherapist, whose personal and professional contexts are the dominant sections of society and who knowingly or unknowingly through this particular discourse may extend this particular kind of hegemony.

CURIOSITY

If initially we should show more interest in speech as an activity and less in language as meaning, this also implies that we should not, as has been fashionable in more recent family and systemic therapy, concentrate on meaning to the exclusion of our earlier preoccupation with behaviour and interaction. But this does not mean that we are going back to an earlier era, because for one thing we can now reject the dichotomy and see that we are surrounded by meaning, that there never has been and never will be any human activity which is devoid of meaning, and also that this can never be fixed or homogeneous except by a 'trick' of classification, designation or labelling. For another thing, we can never again see ourselves as detached observers. We must now accept ourselves as active participants, as agents in the therapeutic contexts we create. The emphasis on action and on language as activity simply means that action and interaction is a better place to begin our enquiry particularly when parameters for what can be meaningfully shared and what cannot be shared between therapist and clients have not been established. How then can the psychotherapist access the prevailing modes of social practice and social relationships of their clients, whose social and cultural backgrounds are very different from their own?

Social practices have featured in the preceding pages in two ways. First, they have featured as patterns described in the ethnographic material to which I have referred you, the reader. In this material observations made by the anthropologist/ethnographer have been condensed into general patterns, which have then been described, and these descriptions have in a general way informed me about the persons and the people who participated in the practices, which have been so described. I, and I hope you also, have been able to arrive at some notion of difference between them and me or them and you. Of course this assumes that the reporter or ethnographer can be trusted and although the question of the validity of ethnographic description is an important one, I have relied on your accepting my judgement in this respect. Second, social practices have also featured in therapeutic sessions which I have described either from my own work or from the work of others. Therapists experience and are participants in social practices in sessions both directly in the interaction between therapist and client(s) and indirectly in the interaction between the clients themselves in family or group sessions. As I noted above these experiences are similar to the experiences which therapists have in cross-cultural interactions anywhere. I do not want to suggest that psychotherapists who work cross-culturally should become anthropologists or even ethnographers. I do, however, want to suggest that cross-cultural psychotherapeutic work can benefit from therapists becoming familiar with ethnography as a mode of enquiry. Therapists have access to crucial material relating both to unconscious and conscious cultural patterns and it is, at least to some extent, a matter of how they access this and use it. Ethnographic enquiry can, when used sensitively and responsibly, be a mechanism through which therapists may take responsibility for the interpersonal and intersubjective processes which take place in the therapeutic encounters in which they are participants. This requires an explanation.

Hastrup (1992) has written about the role of astonishment (*forbløffelse*) in ethnography. She describes this as the experience of the ethnographer when she personally encounters 'another world' in the form of a meeting with a person from this 'other' perspective and she notes that this contains a paradox between moving away from exoticism towards a human connection on the one hand, and retaining a notion of differences as meaningful on the other. In broad outline this is the anthropological project. What the ethnographer does with her astonishment is of course connected to her as a person, to the context of her personal life, to the context of her profession and to the assumptions which participation in these contexts leads her to make. In addition what particularly characterises modern anthropology is the assumption that all reality *is* real, that certain concepts, behaviours and thoughts cannot a priori be privileged while others are relegated to categories such as irrationality or superstition. It is the ethnographer's and the anthropologist's task to aim to make sense of all realities, and aspects thereof, including those which are different from her own, both in personal and in professional terms.

This could equally well be read as a blueprint for the cross-culturally practising psychotherapist, and systemic therapists will recognise in the notion of astonishment a similarity with their own notion of curiosity. The systemic concept of curiosity was highlighted by the Milan group and incorporates a respectful interest in the clients, their lives and the issues which clients see as relevant to themselves. To be curious in this way is not to be inquisitive, but a way of encouraging multiplicity and polyphony (Cecchin 1987). Now the asking of questions aims, as does any other manner of communication between humans, to make sense and in terms of making sense we may make two assumptions. The first is the notion which philosophers refer to as 'the principle of charity' (Davidson 1990), namely that all humans make sense in more or less similar ways. The second is that in communicating with each other persons probably experience contrasts and contradictions first in the form of encounters with patterns which are routine, that is to say in the form of encounters with and observations of background understanding and doxic information. These experiences will trigger in persons a need for explication (Rudie 1994), but explication is usually not straightforward because these patterns are precisely those which persons least realise that they engage in.

Further, in these experiences of difference we are not dealing with fact even though for individual persons this may be how it seems. This is because in the human sciences it is virtually impossible to separate value from fact. Every difference perceived embodies a normative value judgement and facts cannot be disentangled: 'Evaluation is part of fact just as sugar is part of the taste of fruit' (Lenclud 1996: 11).

When I am faced with the differences between myself and a Punjabi woman of similar age, married with three children, who works as a professional and so on, our similarities and our talking about them are enough to create a 'shared space', but it is through the process of our communication that I might access the way the expressive and constitutive aspects of meaning operate for her and the differences between her and me in this respect. It is also through our process of communicating that I have an opportunity to learn about her analogic communication and doxic knowledge first hand, and this is a beginning, even if a small one, of a process of understanding the social practices and social relationships which constitute the background to her world. It is only when I can understand some of this that I might be able to access what it is like for her to participate in her own social practices as well as in our meeting. Taylor describes this process as a way of finding a language of perspicuous contrast:

> In trying to understand them we have to develop a language which is not simply our language of self-understanding, and certainly not theirs; but one in which the differences between us can be perspicuously stated without distortion of either one. To the extent that we fail in this, we end up judging them anachronistically, as inferior attempts at what we have attained, or equally wrong, as inhabitants of a golden age which we have lost. (Taylor 1985a: 281)

We are not talking about physical facts here, for participation is crucial and it is impossible to say a priori which positive or negative sentiments will be the basis for this. Nevertheless, the question of what it is like to be a participant, an agent, a member of this or that society, this or that social group or this or that family comes before the question of what a particular culture or society is like. This ought to be so for both anthropologists and psychotherapists. However, the psychotherapist is almost exclusively dependent on the questions she asks, since she, unlike the ethnographer, is likely to spend time with her clients in only one context, namely the therapeutic session in the therapy room or more rarely on a home visit. Her observations of doxic and background information are limited to this space and yet it is her professional responsibility to aim to understand what it is like for clients to be participants not only in this context, but also in other, wider ones. How does the therapist begin to achieve this? How can the therapist direct her curiosity so that she may be astonished?

There is nothing new in arguing, as I have done, that the therapist must begin by seeing her own position in the system (Cecchin 1987; Jones 1995; Hardham 1996) and that this is one of the first conditions for responsible and sensitive practice. But where cross-cultural work is concerned neither systemic nor individual psychotherapists push this far enough. Of course human differences must always in some way be understood and conceptualised in relation to oneself and systemic therapy is probably the therapy in which difference has been most clearly theorised (Bateson 1973, 1979). Whether or not this is overtly acknowledged and receives recognition in the form of a disciplined search into one's own assumptions is, however, an important matter. In much cross-cultural systemic practice therapists are content with pursuing curiosity until this establishes obvious differences between clients themselves. When such differences in the system are revealed therapists tend to stop enquiring about detail (Burnham and Harris 1996). But this assumes that the therapist working with clients from different cultural backgrounds than her own has no problems with basic premises and as I have shown in the preceding chapters this cannot be the case.

In cross-cultural therapy something more is therefore necessary. And this something more must focus on the therapist herself. The therapist must be curious about the differences not just between her clients but also between herself and her clients in order that she can understand their agency. This does not mean that the therapist must show that the actions of her clients make sense, for clients just like therapists themselves may be confused, deluded, badly informed or of contradictory dispositions. It means that the therapist must acquire some appreciation of why clients come to do what they do, of how they are participants in their own contexts and of how they understand themselves (Taylor 1985b). All this she must consider in relation to how she herself performs these actions. In this way the therapist's experience of astonishment in cross-cultural work and her ability to handle contrast responsibly depends on her own self-understanding. The ethnographer or the therapist in the ethnographic mode is thus like a detective for whom the little things are infinitely the most important (Hirsch et al. 1997) and who uses her own humanity to dissolve the mystery. This is not quite empathy, but empathy may be part of it.

The ability to be curious about herself depends on how much the therapist knows about herself with respect to how the social practices and social relationships in which she lives her life influence her choice of action or lead her to understand her own participation. Because of these circumstances her curiosity can never be unlimited. There will always be a possibility that she will be caught out in an untherapeutic analogic communication (Hardham, quoting Boscolo, 1996) or that she will relay some bit of doxic information to her clients of which she is not aware and which is not therapeutically useful. The question is not so much whether the therapist can avoid such incidents. I believe that in cross-cultural therapy she cannot, and maybe she cannot in any sort of therapy. The question is rather how she can make use of such incidents and how through them she can increase rather than restrict her manoeuvrability. In this it is not only a matter of what to ask but also of how to ask.

LEARNING HOW TO ASK

Briggs has written a useful book in which he draws the attention of social science researchers to the cultural influences on communicative norms (Briggs 1986). He was concerned with the validity of the questions which researchers ask in cross-cultural research, and not just with the validity of the content, but also with the meaning of the event itself to the participants. In order to ask questions, he argued, researchers must acquire a basic understanding not just of what to ask but also of how to ask. It is by now obvious that the same issues face the cross-culturally practising psychotherapist. In therapy no less than in research it is a matter of understanding (in the sense outlined above) what the client(s) say(s). Indeed, one might argue that the issues of metacommunication are more important for therapists than for researchers because the therapeutic process centres upon the personal relationship between therapist and client(s). It is therefore not only a question of whether theories in individual and systemic psychotherapy are cross-culturally valid but also a question of how therapists communicate with their clients, of whether it is possible to find a shared space or whether the premise for communication remains that of the therapist. If the therapist sets the agenda in this respect inequality or an overt imbalance of power can still ensure that questions receive an answer, but paradoxically in these answers the therapist may learn more about her own preconceptions and communicative norms than about those of her clients.

In psychotherapy there is always a tension between the need for the therapist to understand clients as much as possible from the inside and the need for the therapist to be receptive to the aspects of the client's life and self-perceptions which the client herself does not see. One could say that creative psychotherapy takes place from within this tension between the inside and outside. This may not present significant problems when the social and cultural background of therapist and clients are more or less similar. However, when the gap between therapist and clients is wide, whether it is for reasons of culture, class, age, gender, religion or experience the therapist may not be able to strike the right balance and observations from the outside may be presented as if they derive from the inside, while inside experiences may be totalised and stereotyped.

An emphasis on communication and metacommunication is not of course new in psychotherapy. In family therapy an emphasis on the process of communication between clients is part of the attention which the family therapist pays to processes which are going on in front of her very eyes in the room. Similarly, in individual psychotherapy and psycho-analysis the therapist uses the way she finds herself feeling and reacting in response to the material brought by the client to access aspects of which the client may not be conscious. The two approaches may be combined, as has happened recently as family therapists have become more interested in the self-perception of the therapist (Flaskas and Perlesz 1996) and as psychotherapists have become more respectful of the patient's point of view even if this does not fit comfortably with theory (Mitchell 1993). However, the challenge which cross-cultural material presents for both the individual and the systemic psychotherapist remains twofold. First, to be able to appreciate that clients live their lives embedded in relational frameworks and that the ethos, outlook and norms of these frameworks may vary. These variations are articulated both in behaviour and inter-actions which can be observed, and in emotion, classification and thought which are less obvious. Second and following from this, to be aware that therapists themselves are subjects embedded in similar processes and that this is why therapists tend to imbue these with their own meanings so that what they observe is not only other persons but also, and sometimes solely, themselves. Neither beliefs, ideas nor theory are exempt from the workings of these influences. Indeed theory might particularly obscure them, because theory can become so ideologically ensconced that it seems natural. The therapist needs to turn this upside down so that all ideas and behaviours which seem 'natural' are considered to be theories and as such objects for curiosity.

This implies that therapists are able to make a distinction between what is 'natural' and what is not, about and for themselves, in the first place and that in this respect they are perhaps different from other people. I do not think this is the case. Indeed as I have indicated such omnipotence is dangerous. A distinction between that which we take for granted and that which we consider curious cannot be achieved absolutely. However, it is possible to develop an awareness and in this respect individual and systemic psychotherapists could do better. Anthropological and sociological studies are rarely regarded as training material for psychotherapists. Very few, if any, trainings offer courses in kinship, either Anglo-American, or Euro-pean or kinship from other societies in the world. Training may touch or even elaborate on the topic of family and household organisation but never refer to variation in cultural principles for intimate connections and family relationships. Consequently, trainees neither learn about the variation possible nor about the socially constructed aspects of their own intimate relationships. And exactly the same point can be made with respect to personhood, ritual, classification and taboo, economic and political organ-isation. The result is that trainees, if they contemplate cross-cultural matters at all, are likely to have an 'icing on the cake' view of culture and no framework at all for understanding and accessing how cultural themes are reconstituted and changed through ordinary and ongoing social interaction.

Reading ethnographies is not of course the only way for therapists to expose themselves to cultural differences. There are many others such as engaging in cross-cultural personal relationships, social relationships and professional relationships, reading literature and travelling. Indeed, these personal encounters outside the therapy context are crucial because through cross-cultural interaction persons expose themselves to a direct experience of doxic information, background understanding and analogic communication. No one can have such first-hand knowledge about all cultures, but one or a few personal encounters with cultural difference may help to highlight one's own assumptions and direct one's curiosity so that one may allow oneself to be astonished. The professionally and politically responsible therapist may then endeavour to turn this astonishment into appreciation of perspicuous contrast, that is to say an appreciation of difference which minimises projection.

But much as the ethnographers and therapists feel justified in generalising from their own experiences, they also cannot apply these experiences directly to contexts from which they have not been derived. Or rather they do so at the risk of stereotyping, totalising and essentialising – or as Bourdieu put it, of arriving at a view from the inside by attributing to individuals the observer's view from the outside. This is because meaning is never unattached, but must always be articulated by persons embedded in particular relationships in particular spaces and at particular times. It is the therapist's job to understand this detail. And this in turn implies that meaning like culture is heterodox, always changing and shifting and in the process of being created.

In practice this means that the therapist must be cautious. She may decide on a period in the beginning of the therapy, in which understanding and how to understand is the main issue, a sort of ethnographic mode. This means going slowly, enquiring and eliciting descriptions of relevant aspects of clients' lives. It means noting analogic communication and doxic information and finding a way of being respectfully curious with clients about this. It means asking about action, both action observed in the therapy room and action described. It also means reading and making herself familiar with some of the salient themes from the clients' social and cultural backgrounds and checking these out with clients themselves. It means checking out whether understanding is shared. And it means being curious about misunderstandings and about the times when the negotiation of a public space between client and therapist has broken down. Such a period in the beginning of the therapy can help the therapist develop a way of asking ethnographic questions, that is to say questions about specific circumstances, about local context and about detail.

I have then come full circle. The therapist may be an ethnographer or at least operate within an ethnographic mode if she can make the most of being there. To do this she must take on board the most difficult methodological conundrum, namely that ethnographic questions are not unfettered. Like other questions and communications, they are anchored in the personal and the professional context of the one who asks and the assumptions she makes about how those, to whom the questions are addressed, can hear them. It is the therapist's responsibility to make these assumptions explicit to herself because self-description and reflexivity are the best tools she has available to access and understand cultural difference. To understand the participation of her clients in social relationships and cultural themes the therapist must understand how she herself participates. To understand her client's notion of kinship, she must understand the idea of kinship and be aware of her own. To understand her client's notion of taboo and classification she must understand the idea of classification and, as much as is possible within the limits of her awareness, be curious about the classifications which operate in her own social and professional contexts, about what these include and about what these leave out. And so on. This self-reflection will help the therapist to locate difference as a result of recursive interaction in particular spaces and over particular periods of time. It will help her to apprehend that what appears to be and what is portrayed in popular ideology as the inherent and essential qualities of culture, is an illusion. With this experience of participation, similarity and the possibility of connecting responsibly across culture can come into view and may become the starting point for addressing conformity, resistance and agency cross-culturally.

And this, too, will be an ongoing process.

Bibliography

Andersen, T. (1991) *The Reflecting Team: Dialogues and Dialogues about the Dialogues*. New York: W.W. Norton & Co.

Andersen, T. (1992) Reflections on Reflecting with Families. In S. McNamee and K.S. Gergen (eds), *Therapy as Social Construction*. London: Sage Publications.

Anderson, H. and Goolishan, H.A. (1988) Human Systems as Linguistic Systems: Preliminary and Evolving Ideas about the Implications for Clinical Theory. *Family Process* 27 (4), 371–93.

Anderson, H. and Goolishan, H.A. (1992) The Client is the Expert: a Not-Knowing Approach to Therapy. In S. McNamee and K. Gergen (eds), *Therapy as Social Construction*. London: Sage Publications.

Anderson, H., Goolishan, H.A. and Windermand, L. (1986) Problem Determined Systems: Towards Transformation in Family Therapy. *Journal of Strategic and Systemic Therapies* 5, 1–13.

Balibar, E. (1991) Is there a Neo-racism? In E. Balibar and I. Wallerstein (eds), *Nation and Class*. London: Verso.

Banks, M. (1996) *Ethnicity: Anthropological Constructions*. New York and London: Routledge.

Barnes, J.A. (1967) Agnation among the Enga: a Review Article. *Oceania* 37, 33–43.

Barth, F. (ed.) (1969) *Ethnic Goups and Boundaries: The Social Organisation of Culture Difference*. Bergen/London: Universitets Forlaget/George Allen and Unwin.

Basso, K. (1970) To Give Up on Words: Silence in Western Apache Culture. *South Western Journal of Anthropology* 26, 213–30.

Bateson, G. (1958 [1935]) *Naven*. London: Wildwood House Ltd.

Bateson, G. (1973) *Steps to an Ecology of Mind*. St Albans: Paladin.

Bateson, G. (1978) Comments to John Weakland. In M.M. Berger, (ed.), *Beyond the Double Bind*. New York: Bruner/Mazel.

Bateson, G. (1979) *Mind and Nature. A Necessary Unity*. London: Fontana Paperbacks.

Bateson, G. and Bateson, M.C. (1987) *Angels Fear: An Investigation into the Nature and Meaning of the Sacred*. London: Rider.

Baumann, G. (1996) *Contesting Culture. Discourses of Identity in Multi-Ethnic London*. Cambridge: Cambridge University Press.

Bell, C. (1992) *Ritual Theory, Ritual Practice*. Oxford: Oxford University Press.

Benedict, B. (1968) Family Firms and Economic Development. *Southwestern Journal of Anthropology* 24, 1–19.

Benedict, R. (1934) *Patterns of Culture*. Boston and New York: Houghton Mifflin Company.

Bennett, P. (1990) In Nanda Baba's House: The Devotional Experience in Pushti Marg Temples. In O.M. Lynch (ed.), *Divine Passions: The Social Construction of Emotion in India*. Berkeley: University of California Press.

Berger, M.M. (1978) *Beyond the Double Bind*. New York: Bruner/Mazel.

Bhattacharyya, D.P. (1986) *Pagalami: Ethnographic Knowledge in Bengal*. Syracuse: Syracuse University Press.

Black, L.W. (1993) AIDS and Secrets. In E. Imber-Black (ed.), *Secrets in Families and Family Therapy*. New York and London: W.W. Norton & Co.

Bloch, M. (1992) What Goes Without Saying: the Conceptualisation of Zafimaniry Society. In A. Kuper (ed.), *Conceptualising Society*. London: Routledge.

Bock, P.K. (1988) *Rethinking Psychological Anthropology: Continuity and Change in the Study of Human Action*. New York: W.H. Freeman & Co.

Bott, E. (1972) Psychoanalysis and Ceremony. In J. LaFontaine (ed.), *The Interpretation of Ritual*. Cambridge: Cambridge University Press.

Bouquet, M. (1993) *Reclaiming English Kinship: Portuguese Refractions of British Kinship Theory*. Manchester: Manchester University Press.

Bourdieu, P. (1977 [1972]) *Outline of a Theory of Practice*. Cambridge: Cambridge University Press.

Bourdieu, P. (1983) The Field of Cultural Production, or the Economic World Reversed. *Poetics* 12 (Nov), 311–56.

Bourdieu, P. (1984) *Distinction. A Social Critique of the Judgement of Taste*. London: Routledge & Kegan Paul.

Bourdieu, P. (1988) *Homo Academicus*. Cambridge: Polity.

Bourdieu, P. (1990) *The Logic of Practice*. Cambridge: Polity.

Bowen, M. (1978) *Family Therapy in Clinical Practice*. New York: Jason Aronson.

Boyd-Franklin, N. (1993) Racism, Secret-Keeping and African-American Families. In E. Imber-Black, J. Roberts and R. Whiting (eds), *Secrets in Families and Family Therapy*. New York and London: W.W. Norton & Co.

Briggs, C.L. (1986) *Learning How to Ask. A Sociolinguistic Appraisal of the Role of the Interview in Social Science Research*. Cambridge: Cambridge University Press.

Brown, G.N. (1993) Borderline States: Incest and Adolescence. *The Journal of Analytical Psychology* 38, 23–36.

Bruner, J. (1990) *Acts of Meaning*. Cambridge, MA: Harvard University Press.

Bruner, J. (1996) *The Culture of Education*. Cambridge, MA: Harvard University Press.

Burck, C. and Daniel, G. (1995a) *Gender and Family Therapy*. London: Karnac Books.

Burck, C. and Daniel, G. (1995b) Moving On: Gender Beliefs in Divorce and Stepfamily Process. In C. Burck and B. Speed (eds), *Gender, Power and Relationships*. London: Routledge.

Burck, C. and Speed, B. (eds) (1995) *Gender, Power and Relationships*. London and New York: Routledge.

Burnham, J. and Harris, Q. (1996) Emerging Ethnicity: A Tale of Three Cultures. In K.N. Dwivedi and V.P. Varma (eds), *Meeting the Needs of Ethnic Minority Children*. London and Bristol: Jessica Kingsley Publishers.

Byng-Hall, J. (1995) *Rewriting Family Scripts. Improvisation and Systems Change*. New York and London: The Guilford Press.

Byrne, N.O'R. and McCarthy, I.C. (1988) Moving Statutes: Re-Questing Ambivalence through Ambiguous Discourse. In V. Kenny (ed.), *Radical Constructivism. Autopoiesis and Psychotherapy. Irish Journal of Psychology* 9, 173–82.

Campbell, D. and Draper, R. (1985) *Applications of Milan Systemic Family Therapy: The Milan Approach*. London: Grune and Stratton.

Campbell, D., Draper, R. and Huffington, C. (1991) *Second Thoughts on the Theory and Practice of the Milan Approach to Family Therapy*. London: Karnac Books.

Carrithers, M. (1989) Sociality, not Agression, is the Key Human Trait. In S. Howell and R. Willis (eds), *Society at Peace: Anthropological Perspectives*. London and New York: Routledge.

Carrithers, M. (1992) *Why Humans Have Cultures: Explaining Anthroplogy and Human Diversity*. Oxford: Oxford University Press.

Cecchin, G. (1987) Hypothesizing, Circularity and Neutrality Revisited: An Invitation to Curiosity. *Family Process* 26, 405–13.

Cecchin, G. (1992) Constructing Therapeutic Possibilities. In S. McNamee and K.S. Gergen (eds), *Therapy as Social Construction*. London: Sage Publications.

Child, N. (1996a) Letter to the Editors. *Journal of Family Therapy* 18, 119–21.

Child, N. (1996b) Possessing the Key: Enchanting Work. *Context* 29, 14–19.

Chodorow, N. (1978) *The Reproduction of Mothering: Psychoanalysis and the Sociology of Gender.* Berkeley: University of California Press.

Clifford, J. (1988) *The Predicament of Culture: 20th Century Ethnography Literature and Art.* Cambridge, MA: Harvard University Press.

Clifford, J. and Marcus, G.E. (eds) (1986) *Writing Culture: The Poetics and the Politics of Ethnography.* Berkeley: University of California Press.

Connerton, P. (1989) *How Societies Remember.* Cambridge: Cambridge University Press.

Cooklin, A. and Gorell Barnes, G. (1993) Taboos and Social Order: New Encounters for Family and Therapist. In E. Imber-Black (ed.), *Secrets in Families and Family Therapy.* New York and London: W.W. Norton & Co.

Cooklin, A. and Gorell Barnes. G. (1994) The Shattered Picture of the Family: Encountering New Dimensions of Human Relations, of the Family and of Therapy. In V. Sinason (ed.), *Treating Survivors of Satanist Abuse.* New York and London: Routledge.

Cooper, J.C. (1970) *An Illustrated Encyclopaedia of Traditional Symbols.* London: Thames & Hudson.

Crapanzano, V. (1980) *Tuhami – Portrait of a Moroccan.* Chicago and London: The University of Chicago Press.

Cronen, V. and Pearce, W. (1985) Toward an Explanation of how the Milan Method Works: An Invitation to Systemic Epistemology and the Evolution of Family Systems. In D. Campbell and R. Draper (eds), *Applications of Systemic Family Therapy: The Milan Approach.* London: Grune & Stratton.

Csordas, T.J. (1994) *Embodiment and Experience: The Existential Ground of Culture and Self.* Cambridge: Cambridge University Press.

D'Andrade, R.G. (1990) Culture and Personality a False Dichotomy. In D.K. Jordan and M.J. Swartz (eds), *Personality and the Cultural Construction of Society.* Tuscaloosa and London: University of Alabama Press.

D'Andrade, R.G. (1992) Schema and Motivation. In R. D'Andrade and C. Strauss (eds), *Human Motives and Cultural Models.* Cambridge: Cambridge University Press.

Daniel, E.V. (1984) *Fluid Signs. Being a Person the Tamil Way.* Berkeley: University of California Press.

Das, V. (1990) Our Work to Cry: Your Work to Listen. In V. Das (ed.), *Mirrors of Violence.* Oxford: India Paperbacks.

Das, V. (1995) *Critical Events. An Anthropological Perspective on Contemporary India.* Delhi: Oxford University Press.

Davidson, D. (1990) *Inquiries into Truth and Interpretation.* Oxford: The Clarendon Press.

Davis, J. (1988) Mazel Tov: the Bar Mitzvah as a Multigenerational Ritual of Change and Continuity. In E. Imber-Black, J. Roberts and R. Whiting (eds), *Rituals in Families and Family Therapy.* New York and London: W.W. Norton & Co.

Dell, P.F. (1989) Violence and the Systemic View: the Problem of Power. *Family Process* 28, 1–14.

del Valle, T. (ed.) (1993) *Gendered Anthropology.* New York and London: Routledge.

de Shazer, S. (1991) *Putting Difference to Work.* New York and London: W.W. Norton & Co.

Diamond, R. (1993) Infertility: Private Pain and Secret Stigma. In E. Imber-Black (ed.), *Secrets in Families and Family Therapy.* New York and London: W.W. Norton & Co.

DiNicola, V.F. (1993) The Postmodern Language of Therapy: At the Nexus of Culture and Family. *Journal of Systemic Therapies* 12, 49–62.

Douglas, M. (1984 [1966]) *Purity and Danger. An Analysis of the Concepts of Pollution and Taboo.* London and New York: Ark Paperbacks.

Dumont, L. (1982) *On Value.* London: Oxford University Press/British Academy.

Durkheim, E. (1915) *The Elementary Forms of Religious Life.* London: Allen & Unwin.

Efran, J.S. and Clarfield, L.E. (1992) Constructivist Therapy: Sense and Unsense. In S.

McNamee and K.J. Gergen (eds), *Therapy as Social Construction.* London: Sage Publications.

El-Solh, C.F. and Mabro, J. (1994) Introduction: Islam and Muslim Women. In C.F. El-Solh and J. Mabro (eds), *Muslim Women's Choices. Religious Belief and Social Reality.* Oxford: Berg Publishers.

Engels, F. (1972 [1884]) *The Origins of the Family: Private Property and the State.* New York: International Publishers.

Epston, D. (1989) *Collected Papers.* Adelaide, South Australia: Dulwich Centre Publications.

Epston, D. and White, M. (1992) Experience, Contradiction, Narrative and Imagination. In D. Epston and M. White (eds), *Selected Papers 1989–1991.* Dulwich: Dulwich Centre Publications.

Evans-Pritchard, E.E. (1940) *The Nuer. A Description of the Modes of Livelihood and Political Institution of a Nilotic People.* Oxford: Clarendon Press.

Evans-Pritchard, E.E. (1951) *Social Anthropology.* London: Cohen & West Ltd.

Fanon, F. (1967) *Black Skin, White Masks.* New York: Grove Press.

Faris, G. (1996) Conference Address. AFT 21st Annual Conference, Bolton, Engand.

Feld, S. (1982) *Sound and Sentiment. Birds, Weeping, Poetics and Song in Kaluli Expression.* Philadelphia: University of Pennsylvania Press.

Firth, R. (1936) *We, the Tikopia. A Sociological Study of Kinship in Primitive Polynesia.* Allen & Unwin.

Firth, R., Hubert, J. and Forge, A. (1969) *Families and their Relatives.* London: Routledge and Kegan Paul.

Fisek, G.O. (1991) A Cross Cultural Examination of Proximity and Hierarchy as Dimensions of Family Structure. *Family Process* 30, 121–33.

Flaskas, C. (1996) Understanding the Therapeutic Relationship: Using Psychoanalytic Ideas in the Systemic Context. In C. Flaskas and A. Perlesz (eds), *The Therapeutic Relationship in Systemic Therapy.* London: Karnac.

Flaskas, C. (1997) Reclaiming the Idea of Truth: Some Thoughts on Theory in Response to Practice. *Journal of Family Therapy* 19 (1), 1–20.

Flaskas, C. and Perlesz, A. (eds) (1996) *The Therapeutic Relationship in Systemic Therapy.* London: Karnac.

Forde, C.D. (1950) Double Descent Among the Yakö. In A.R. Radcliffe-Brown and C.D. Forde (eds), *African Systems of Kinship and Marriage.* London: Oxford University Press.

Fortes, M. (1949) *The Web of Kinship Among the Tallensi.* London: Oxford University Press.

Fortes, M. (1973) On the Concept of the Person among the Tallensi. In *La Notion de Personne en Afrique Noire.* No. 544. Paris: Colloques Internationaux du Centre National de la Recherche Scientifique.

Fortes, M. (1987 [1966]) Totem and Taboo. In J. Goody (ed.), *Religion, Morality and the Person. Essays on Tallensi Religion.* Cambridge: Cambridge University Press.

Foucault, M. (1980) *Power/Knowledge: Selected Interviews and Other Writings.* New York: Pantheon Books.

Fox, R. (1983 [1980]) *The Red Lamp of Incest: An Enquiry into the Origins of Minds and Society.* Indiana: University of Notre Dame Press.

Frank, J.D. and Frank, J.B. (1961) *Persuasion and Healing. A Comparative Study of Psychotherapy.* Baltimore and London: The Johns Hopkins University Press.

Frazer, J.G. (1890) *The Golden Bough: A Study in Magic and Religion.* London: Macmillan.

Freud, S. (1953 [1913–14]) *Totem and Taboo.* SE Vol. 13. London: The Hogarth Press.

Freud, S. (1955 [1919]) *The Uncanny.* SE Vol 17. London: The Hogarth Press.

Freud, S. (1985 [1907]) Obsessive Actions and Religious Practices reproduced In *The Origins of Religion,* Pelican Freud Library, 13. Hammondsworth: Penguin Books.

Frosh, S., Burck, C., Strickland-Clark, L. and Morgan, K. (1996) Engaging with Change: A Process Study of Family Therapy. *Journal of Family Therapy* 18 (2), 141–62.

Fruzetti, L.M. (1990 [1982]) *The Gift of a Virgin. Women, Marriage and Ritual in Bengali Society.* Delhi: Oxford University Press.

Gardner, D.S. (1983) Performativity in Ritual: The Mianmin Case. *Man (N.S.)* 18, 346–60.

Gardner, K. (1991) *Songs at the Rivers Edge. Stories From a Bangladeshi Village.* London: Virago.

Gardner, K. (1995) *Global Migrants, Local Lives. Travel and Transformation in Rural Bangladesh.* Oxford: The Clarendon Press.

Geertz, C. (1974) From the Native's Point of View. *Bulletin of the American Academy of Arts and Sciences* 28, no. 1.

Geertz, C. (1986) Anti-anti-Relativism. *American Anthropologist* 86, 263–78.

Geertz, C. (1988) *Works and Lives: The Anthropologist as Author.* Cambridge: Polity.

Geertz, C. (1993 [1973]) Thick Description: Toward an Interpretive Theory of Culture. In C. Geertz (ed.), *The Interpretation of Cultures.* London: Fontana Press.

Gellner, E. (1985) *Relativism and the Social Sciences.* Cambridge: Cambridge University Press.

Gellner, E. (1992) *Reason and Culture. The Historic Role of Rationality and Rationalism.* Oxford: Blackwell.

Gergen, K.J. (1990) Social Understanding and the Inscription of Self. In J.W. Stigler, R.A. Shweder and G. Herdt (eds), *Cultural Psychology. Essays on Comparative Human Development.* Cambridge: Cambridge University Press.

Gergen, K.J. and Davis, K.E. (1985) *The Social Construction of the Person.* New York: Springer-Verlag.

Gergen, K.J. and Kaye, J. (1992) Beyond Narrative in the Negotiation of Therapeutic Meaning. In S. McNamee and K.J. Gergen (eds), *Therapy as Social Construction.* London: Sage.

Giddens, A. (1976) *New Rules of Sociological Method.* New York: Basic Books.

Giddens, A. (1979) *Central Problems in Social Theory.* London: Macmillan.

Giddens, A. (1984) *The Constitution of Society.* Cambridge: Polity.

Giddens, A. (1991) *Modernity and Self Identity.* Cambridge: Polity.

Gilligan, C. (1982) *In a Different Voice. Psychological Theory and Women's Development.* Cambridge, MA: Harvard University Press.

Girard, R. (1977 [1972]) *Violence and the Sacred.* Baltimore and London: The Johns Hopkins University Press.

Goldner, V. (1985) Feminism and Family Therapy. *Family Process* 24, 31–47.

Goldner, V. (1991) Sex, Power and Gender: A Feminist Systemic Analysis of the Politics of Passion. In T.J. Goodrich (ed.), *Women and Power: Prospectives for Family Therapy.* New York: W.W. Norton & Co.

Goldner, V., Penn, P., Sheinberg, M. and Walker, G. (1990) Love and Violence: Gender Paradoxes in Volatile Attachments. *Family Process* 29, 343–64.

Good, B. (1977) The Heart of What's the Matter: the Semantics of Illness in Iran. *Culture, Medicine & Psychiatry* 1, 25–58.

Good, B. and Good, M.J.D. (1992) The Comparative Study of Greco-Islamic Medicine: the Integration of Medical Knowledge into Local Symbolic Contexts. In C. Leslie and A. Young (eds), *Paths to Asian Medical Knowledge.* Berkeley: University of California Press.

Goody, J. (1977) Against 'Ritual': Loosely Structured Thoughts on a Loosely Defined Topic. In S.F. Moore and B.G. Myerhoff (eds), *Secular Ritual.* Assen/Amsterdam: Van Gorcum.

Gorell Barnes, G., Thompson, P., Daniel, G. and Burchardt, N. (1997) *Growing Up in Stepfamilies. Life Story Interviews.* Oxford: The Clarendon Press.

Haley, J. (1976) Development of a Theory: A History of a Research Project. In C.E. Sluzki and D.C. Ranson (eds), *Double Bind: The Foundation of the Communicational Approach to the Family.* New York: Grune and Stratton.

Haley, J. (1978) Ideas which Handicap Therapists. In M.M. Berger (ed.), *Beyond the Double Bind*. New York: Bruner/Mazel.

Haley, J. (1980) *Leaving Home: The Therapy of Disturbed Young People*. McGraw-Hill Book Company.

Hall, S. (1992) New Ethnicities. In J. Donald and A. Rattansi (eds), *Race, Culture & Difference*. London: Sage Publications.

Hall, S. (1996) Introduction. Who Needs 'Identity'? In S. Hall and P. du Gay (eds), *Questions of Cultural Identity*. London: Sage Publications.

Hardham, V. (1996) Embedded and Embodied in the Therapeutic Relationship: Understanding the Therapist's Use of Self Systemically. In C. Flaskas and A. Perlesz (eds), *The Therapeutic Relationship in Systemic Therapy*. London: Karnac Books.

Hare-Mustin, R.T. (1991) Sex, Lies and Headaches: The Problem is Power. In T.J. Godrich (ed.), *Women and Power. Perspectives for Family Therapy*. New York and London: W.W. Norton & Co.

Hartman, A. (1993) Secrecy in Adoption. In E. Imber-Black (ed.), *Secrets in Families and Family Therapy*. New York and London: W.W. Norton & Co.

Hastrup, K. (1992) *Det antropologiske Projekt. Om Forbløffelse*. Copenhagen: Gyldendal.

Hastrup, K. (1993) Hunger and the Hardness of Facts. *Man* 28, 727–39.

Hastrup, K. (1995) *A Passage to Anthropology. Between Experience and Theory*. London and New York: Routledge.

Hastrup, K. and Hervik, P. (1994) Introduction. In K. Hastrup and P. Hervik (eds), *Social Experience and Anthropological Knowledge*. London: Routledge.

Heald, S. and Deluz, A. (1994) *Anthropology and Psychoanalysis. An Encounter Through Culture*. London: Routledge.

Henriques, J., Hollway, W., Urwin, C., Venn, C. and Walkerdine, V. (eds) (1984) *Changing the Subject. Psychology, Social Regulation and Subjectivity*. London: Methuen.

Herzfeld, M. (1987) *Anthropology Through the Looking Glass. Critical Ethnography in the Margins of Europe*. Cambridge: Cambridge University Press.

Hirsch, E., Kuchler, S. and Pinney, C. (1997) Obituary of Alfred Gell. *Anthropology Today* 13, 2, 21–3.

Hoffman, L. (1985) Beyond Power and Control: Toward a 'Second Order' Family Systems Therapy. *Family Systems Medicine* 3 (4), 381–96.

Hoffman, L. (1988) A Constructivist Position for Family Therapy. *The Irish Journal of Psychology* 9, 110–29.

Hoffman, L. (1993) *Exchanging Voices: A Collaborative Approach to Family Therapy*. London: Karnac Books.

Hogbin, I. (1970) *The Island of Menstruating Men*. Scanton, PA: Chandler.

Holland, D. (1992) How Cultural Systems Become Desire: a Case Study of American Romance. In R. D'Andrade and C. Strauss (eds), *Human Motives and Cultural Models*. Cambridge: Cambridge University Press.

Howe, L.E.A. (1984) Comments on P. Shankman: The Thick and the Thin: on the Interpretive Theoretical Program of Clifford Geertz. *Current Anthropology* 25 (1), 274–75.

Howell, S. and Melhuus, M. (1993) The Study of Kinship; the Study of Person; a Study of Gender? In T. Del Valle (ed.), *Gendered Anthropology*. London and New York: Routledge.

Hsu, J. (1995) Family Therapy for the Chinese. Problems and Strategies. In T.-Y. Lin, W.-S. Tseng and E.-K. Eng (eds), *Chinese Society and Mental Health*. Hong-Kong: Oxford University Press.

Humphrey, C. and Laidlaw, J. (1994) *The Archetypal Actions of Ritual. A Theory of Ritual Illustrated by the Jain Rite of Worship*. Oxford: Clarendon Press.

Imber-Black. E. (1988) Normative and Therapeutic Rituals in Couples Therapy. In E. Imber-Black, J. Roberts and R. Whiting (eds), *Rituals in Families and Family Therapy*. New York and London: W.W. Norton & Co.

Imber-Black, E. (1993) Secrets in Families and Family Therapy: An Overview. In E.

Imber-Black (ed.), *Secrets in Families and Family Therapy*. New York: W.W. Norton & Co.

Imber-Black, E. and Roberts, J. (1992) *Rituals for our Times*. New York: Harper Collins.

Imber-Black, E., Roberts, J. and Whiting, R. (1988) *Rituals in Families and Family Therapy*. New York and London: W.W. Norton & Co.

Ingold, T. (1986) *Evolution and Social Life*. Cambridge: Cambridge University Press.

Ingold, T. (1992) Language is the Essence of Culture. *Group for Debates in Anthropological Theory*. A debate held in Manchester.

Inhorn, M.C. (1996) *Infertility and Patriarchy. The Cultural Politics of Gender and Family Life in Egypt*. Philadelphia: University of Pennsylvania Press.

Jadhav, S. (1996) The Cultural Origin of Western Depression. *The International Journal of Social Psychiatry* 42 (4), 269–86.

Jenkins, T. (1994) Fieldwork and the Perceptions of Everyday Life. *Man* 29 (2), 433–56.

Jones, E. (1964 [1924]) Mother-Right and Sexual Ignorance of Savages. *Essays in Applied Psychoanalysis* 2, 145–73.

Jones, E. (1991) *Working with Adult Survivors of Sexual Abuse*. London: Karnac Books.

Jones, E. (1993) *Family Systems Therapy. Developments in the Milan-Systemic Therapies*. Chichester: John Wiley & Sons.

Jones, E. (1995) The Construction of Gender in Family Therapy. In C. Burck and B. Speed (eds), *Gender, Power and Relationships*. London and New York: Routledge.

Just, R. (1991) Thinking along Different Lines. *Times Literary Supplement*, 29 November, 27.

Kakar, S. (1978) *The Inner World. A Psycho-Analytic Study of Childhood and Society in India*. Delhi: Oxford University Press.

Kakar, S. (1982) *Shamans, Mystics and Doctors*. London: Unwin Paperbacks.

Kareem, J. (1992) The Nafsiyat Intercultural Therapy Centre: Ideas and Experience in Intercultural Therapy. In J. Kareem and R. Littlewood (eds), *Intercultural Therapy. Themes, Interpretations and Practice*. Oxford: Blackwell.

Keeney, B. (1983) *Aesthetics of Change*. New York: Guilford Press.

Kleinman, A. (1987) Anthropology and Psychiatry: The Role of Culture in Cross-cultural Research on Illness. *British Journal of Psychiatry* 151, 447–54.

Kohut. H. (1971) *The Analysis of the Self*. New York: International Universities Press.

Krause, I.-B. (1980) Kinship, Hierarchy and Equality in North Western Nepal. *Contributions to Indian Sociology (new series)* 14, 169–94.

Krause, I.-B. (1982) *Kinship and Economics in North West Nepal*. Unpublished PhD Thesis. University of London.

Krause, I.-B. (1988) Caste and Agrarian Relations in North-Western Nepal. *Ethnos*, 1–2, 5–36.

Krause, I.-B. (1993) Anthropology and Family Therapy: a Case for Emotions. *Journal of Family Therapy* 15 (1): 35–56.

Krause, I.-B. (1995) Personhood, Culture and Family Therapy. *Journal of Family Therapy* 17, 363–82.

Krause, I.-B., Rosser, R., Khiani, M.L. and Lotay, N.S. (1990) Morbidity among Punjabi Medical Patients in England Measured by GHQ. *Psychological Medicine* 20, 711–19.

Kuper, A. (1982) Lineage Theory: A Critical Retrospect. *Annual Review of Anthropology* 11, 71–95.

Kuper, A. (1988) *The Invention of Primitive Society. Transformations of an Illusion*. London: Routledge.

Kurtz, S. (1992) *All the Mothers are One. Hindu India and the Cultural Reshaping of Psychoanalysis*. New York: Columbia Univesity Press.

Laird, J. (1991) Enactments of Power through Ritual. In T.J. Goodrich (ed.), *Women and Power*. New York: W.W. Norton & Co.

Lax, W.D. (1992) Postmodern Thinking in a Clinical Practice. In S. McNamee and K.S. Gergen (eds), *Therapy as Social Construction*. London: Sage.

Leach, E. (1982) *Social Anthropology*. Glasgow: Fontana Paperbacks.

Lenclud, G. (1996) The Factual and the Normative in Ethnography. *Anthropology Today* 12 (1), 7–11.

Leupnitz, D.A. (1988) *The Family Interpreted: Feminist Theory on Clinical Practice.* New York: Basic Books.

Lévi-Strauss, C. (1963) *Structural Anthropology.* Harmondsworth: Penguin Books.

Lewis, G. (1975) *Knowledge of Illness in a Sepik Society.* London: The Athlone Press.

Lewis, G. (1980) *Day of Shining Red. An Essay on Understanding Ritual.* Cambridge: Cambridge University Press.

Lewis, I. (1962) *A Pastoral Democracy: A Study of Pastoralism and Politics among the Northern Somali of the Horn of Africa.* London: International African Institute/Oxford University Press.

Lewis, I.M. (1976) *Social Anthropology in Perspective.* Penguin Books.

Lindquist, G. (1995) Travelling to the Other's Cognitive Maps or Going Native and Coming Back. *Ethnos* 60 (1–2), 5–40.

LiPuma, E. (1993) Culture and the Concept of Culture in a Theory of Practice. In C. Calhoun, E. LiPuma and M. Postone (eds), *Bourdieu. Critical Perspective.* Cambridge: Polity.

Littlewood, R. (1993) *Pathology and Identity. The Work of Mother Earth in Trinidad.* Cambridge: Cambridge University Press.

Littlewood, R. (1996a) Reason and Necessity in the Specification of the Multiple Self. *Occasional Paper* 43. London: Royal Anthropological Institute.

Littlewood, R. (1996b) Psychiatry's Culture. *International Journal of Social Psychiatry* 42, 245–68.

Littlewood, R. and Lipsedge, M. (1986) The Butterfly and the Serpent: Culture, Psychopathology and Medicine. *Culture, Medicine & Psychiatry* 11, 43–89.

Lloyd, G.E.R. (1990) *Demystifying Mentalities.* Cambridge: Cambridge University Press.

McCarthy, I.C. and Byrne, N.O'R. (1988) Mistaken Love: Conversations on the Problem of Incest in an Irish Context. *Family Process* 27, 181–99.

MacCormack, C. and Strathern, M. (eds) (1980) *Nature, Culture and Gender.* Cambridge: Cambridge University Press.

McGoldrick, M. and Gerson, R. (1989) Genograms and the Family Life Cycle. In B. Carter and M. McGoldrick (eds), *The Changing Family Life Cycle (2nd Edition).* Boston: Allyn & Bacon.

McNamee, S. and Gergen, K.J. (eds) (1992) *Therapy as Social Construction.* London: Sage.

Maitra, B. (1996) Child Abuse: a Universal 'Diagnostic' Category? The Implication of Culture in Definition and Assessment. *International Journal of Social Psychiatry,* 42, 287–304.

Malik, R. (1997) *'Depression Kills More Than a Self': Concepts of Mental Distress Amongst Pakistanis.* Unpublished PhD thesis, University of London.

Malinowski, B. (1929) *The Sexual Life of Savages in North Western Melanesia.* London: Routledge & Kegan Paul.

Malinowski, B. (1961 [1922]) *Argonauts of the Western Pacific.* New York: E.P. Dutton & Co.

Maranhao, T. (1984) Family Therapy and Anthropology. *Culture Medicine and Psychiatry* 8, 255–79.

Marcus, G.E. and Fischer, M.J. (1986) *Anthropology as Cultural Critique: An Experimental Moment in the Human Sciences.* Chicago: University of Chicago Press.

Marriott, M. (1976) Hindu Transactions: Diversity without Dualism. In B. Kapferer (ed.), *Transactions and Meaning: Directions in the Anthropology of Exchange and Symbolic Behavior.* Philadelphia: Institute for the Study of Human Issues.

Mason, M.J. (1993) Shame: Reservoir for Family Secrets. In E. Imber-Black (ed.), *Secrets in Families and Family Therapy.* New York and London: W.W. Norton & Co.

Maturana, M.R. (1980) Man and Society. In F. Benseler, D.M. Hejl and W.K. Kôck (eds), *Autopoiesis, Communication and Society.* Frankfurt and New York: Campus Verlag.

Maturana, M.R. (1988) Reality: The Search for Objectivity on the Quest for a Compelling Argument. *The Irish Journal of Psychology* 9, 25–82.

Maturana, H.R. and Varela, F.J. (1980) *Autopoiesis and Cognition: The Realization of Living.* Boston: D. Reidel.

Mead, M. (1970, [1938, 1940]) *The Mountain Arapesh, vol II: Arts and Supernaturalism.* New York: Natural History Press.

Minuchin, S. (1974) *Families and Family Therapy.* London: Tavistock Publications.

Minuchin, S., Montalvo, B., Guerney, B.G., Rosman, B.L. and Schumer, F. (1967) *Families of the Slums: An Exploration of Their Structure and Treatment.* New York: Basic Books.

Mitchell, S.A. (1993) *Hope and Dread in Psychoanalysis.* New York: Basic Books.

Mollon, P. (1994) The Impact of Evil. In V. Sinason (ed.), *Treating Survivors of Satanist Abuse.* London and New York: Routledge.

Moore, H.L. (1988) *Feminism and Anthropology.* Cambridge: Polity.

Moore, H.L. (1994) *A Passion for Difference: Essays in Anthropology and Gender.* Cambridge: Polity.

Morris, H.S. (1968) *The Indians in Uganda.* London: Weidenfeld and Nicolson.

Nadel, L., Cooper, P., Culicover, P. and Harnish, R. (1989) *Neural Connections, Mental Computations.* Cambridge, MA: MIT Press.

Nichter, M. (1981) Negotiation of Illness Experience: Ayurvedic Therapy and the Psychosocial Dimension of Illness. *Culture, Medicine & Psychiatry* 5, 5–24.

Nuckolls, C.W. (1995) The Misplaced Legacy of Gregory Bateson: Toward a Cultural Dialectic of Knowledge and Desire. *Cultural Anthropology* 10 (3), 367–94.

Obeyesekere, G. (1990) *The Work of Culture: Symbolic Transformation in Psychoanalysis and Anthropology.* Chicago: University of Chicago Press.

O'Connor, J. and Hoorwitz, A. (1988) Imitative and Contagious Magic in the Therapeutic Use of Rituals with Children. In E. Imber-Black, J. Roberts and R. Whiting (eds), *Rituals in Families and Family Therapy.* New York and London: W.W. Norton & Co.

Ortner, S. (1974) Is Female to Male as Nature is to Culture? In M. Rosaldo and L. Lamphere (eds), *Women, Culture and Society.* Stanford, CA: Stanford University Press.

Ortner, S. and Whitehead, H. (1981) *Sexual Meanings. The Cultural Construction of Gender and Sexuality.* Cambridge: Cambridge University Press.

Östör, Á., Fruzetti, L. and Barnett, S. (1982) *Concepts of Person. Kinship, Caste and Marriage in India.* Delhi: Oxford University Press.

Papp, P. (1993) The Worm in the Bud: Secrets between Parents and Children. In E. Imber-Black, J. Roberts and R. Whiting (eds), *Secrets in Families and Family Therapy.* New York and London: W.W. Norton & Co.

Papp, P. and Imber-Black, E. (1996) Family Themes: Transmission and Transformation. *Family Process* 35, 5–20.

Pare, D.A. (1995) Families and Other Cultures: The Shifting Paradigm of Family Therapy. *Family Process* 34, 1–19.

Parsons, A. (1969) *Belief, Magic and Anomie: Essays in Psychological Anthropology.* New York: The Free Press.

Penn, P. (1985) Feed Forward: Future Questions, Future Maps. *Family Process* 24 (3), 299–310.

Penn, P. and Sheinberg, M. (1991) Stories and Conversations. *Journal of Strategic and Systemic Therapies* 10 (3/4), 30–7.

Perelberg, R.J and Miller, A. (1990) *Gender and Power in Families.* London: Routledge/ Tavistock.

Piaget, J. (1954 [1937]) *The Construction of Reality in the Child.* New York: Basic Books.

Piaget, J. and Inhelder, B. (1956 [1948]) *The Child's Conception of Space.* London: Routledge & Kegan Paul.

Pincus, L. and Dare, C. (1978) *Secrets in the Family. A Psychodynamic Approach to the*

Unconscious Beliefs, Longings and Incestuous Fantasies that Shape Family Relationships. New York: Pantheon Books.

Powell, H.A. (1960) Competitive Leadership in Trobriand Political Organisation. *Journal of the Royal Anthropological Institute* 90, 118–45.

Radcliffe-Brown, A.R. (1922) *The Andaman Islanders.* Cambridge: Cambridge University Press.

Radcliffe-Brown, A.R. (1924) The Mother's Brother in South Africa. *South African Journal of Science* 21, 542–55.

Radcliffe-Brown, A.R. (1940) *Structure and Function in Primitive Societies.* London: Cohen & West.

Radcliffe-Brown, A.R. (1950) Introduction. In A.R. Radcliffe-Brown and C.D. Forde (eds), *African Systems of Kinship and Marriage.* London: Oxford University Press.

Radcliffe-Brown, A.R. and Forde, C.D. (eds) (1950) *African Systems of Kinship and Marriage.* London: Oxford University Press.

Raheja, G.G. and Gold, A.G. (1994) *Listen to the Heron's Words. Reimagining Gender and Kinship in North India.* Berkeley: University of California Press.

Ramanujan, A.K. (1983) The Indian Oedipus. In E. Lowell and A. Dundes (eds), *Oedipus. A Folklore Casebook.* New York and London: Garland Publishing Company.

Rappaport, R.A. (1971) Ritual, Sanctity and Cybernetics. *American Anthropologist* 73, 59–76.

Rattansi, A. (1992) Changing the Subject? Racism, Culture and Education. In J. Donald and A. Rattansi (eds), *Race, Culture & Difference.* London: Sage Publications.

Rattansi, A. (1994) 'Western' Racisms, Ethnicities and Identities in a 'Postmodern' Frame. In A. Rattansi and S. Westwood (eds), *Racism, Modernity and Identity. On the Western Front.* Cambridge: Polity.

Real, T. (1990) The Therapeutic Use of Self in Constructivist/Systemic Therapy. *Family Process* 29, 255–72.

Reichelt, S. and Sveaass, N. (1994) Therapy With Refugee Families. What is a 'Good' Conversation? *Family Process* 33, 247–62.

Rivers, W.H.R. (1968 [1910]) The Genealogical Method of Anthropological Inquiry. In *Kinship and Social Organisation, LSE Monographs in Social Anthropology* No. 34. London: The Athlone Press.

Roberto, L.G. (1993) Eating Disorders as Family Secrets. In E. Imber-Black (ed.), *Secrets in Families and Family Therapy.* New York and London: W.W. Norton & Co.

Roberts, J. (1988) Setting the Frame: Definition, Function and Typology of Rituals. In E. Imber-Black, J. Roberts and R. Whiting (eds), *Rituals in Families and Family Therapy.* New York and London: W.W. Norton & Co.

Robertson, A.F. (1996) The Development of Meaning: Ontogeny and Culture. *Journal of the Royal Anthropological Institute* 2 (4), 591–610.

Roland, A. (1988) *In Search of Self in India and Japan: Toward a Cross-cultural Psychology.* Princeton: Princeton University Press.

Rosaldo, M.Z. (1980) *Knowledge and Passion: Ilongot Notions of Self and Social Life.* Cambridge: Cambridge University Press.

Rosaldo, R. (1984) Grief and the Headhunter's Rage. In E.M. Bruner (ed.), *Text, Play and Story.* Washington DC: American Anthropological Association.

Rudie, I. (1994) Making Sense of New Experience. In K. Hastrup and P. Hervik (eds), *Social Experience and Anthropological Knowledge.* London: Routledge.

Sartre, J.-P. (1964) *Saint Genet: Actor and Martyr.* Translated by Bernard Frechtman. New York: Mentor.

Satir, V. (1964) *Conjoint Family Therapy.* Palo Alto: Science and Behavior.

Saussure, F. de (1959) *Course in General Linguistics.* New York: Philosophical Library.

Schaffer, J.A. and Diamond, R. (1993) Infertility: Private Pain and Secret Stigma. In E. Imber-Black (ed.), *Secrets in Families and Family Therapy.* New York and London: W.W. Norton & Co.

Scheffler, H.W. (1985) Filiation and Affiliation. *Man* (N.5) 20, 1–21.

Schieffelin, E.L. (1976) *The Sorrow of the Lonely and the Burning of the Dancers*. New York: St. Martins Press.

Schieffelin, E.L. (1985) Anger, Grief and Shame. Toward a Kalul: Ethnopsychology. In G.M. White and J. Kirkpatrick (eds), *Person, Self and Experience. Exploring Pacific Ethnopsychologies*. Berkeley: University of California Press.

Selvini Palazzoli, M. (1974) *Self Starvation: From the Intrapsychic to the Transpersonal Approach to Anorexia Nervosa*. London: Chaucer Publications.

Selvini Palazzoli, M., Boscolo, L., Cecchin, G. and Prata, G., (1974) The Treatment of Children Through Brief Therapy of their Parents. *Family Process* 13, 429–42.

Selvini Palazzoli, M., Boscolo, L., Cecchin, G. and Prata, G. (1977) Family Rituals. A Powerful Tool in Family Therapy. *Family Process* 16, 445–54.

Selvini Palazzoli, M., Boscolo, L., Cecchin, G. and Prata, G. (1978) *Paradox and Counter Paradox. A New Model in the Therapy of the Family in Schizophrenic Transaction*. New York: Jason Aronson.

Selvini Palazzoli, M., Boscolo, L., Cecchin, G. and Prata, G. (1980) Hypothesizing – Circularity – Neutrality: Three Questions for the Conductor of the Session. *Family Process* 19 (1), 3–12.

Shackle, C. and Moir, Z. (1992) *Ismaili Hymns from South Asia. An Introduction to the Ginans*. London: School of Oriental and African Studies.

Shamai, M. (1995) Using Rituals in Couple Therapy in Cases of Wife Battering. *Journal of Family Therapy*, 17, 383–96.

Shore, B. (1982) *Sala'ilua. A Samoan Mystery*. New York: Columbia University Press.

Shweder, R.A. (1973) The Between and Within of Cross-Cultural Research. *Ethos* 1, 531–43.

Shweder, R.A. (1984) Anthropology's Romantic Rebellion against the Enlightenment, or There's More to Thinking than Reason and Evidence. In R.A. Shweder and R.A. LeVine (eds), *Culture Theory. Essays on Mind, Self, and Emotion*. Cambridge: Cambridge University Press.

Shweder, R.A. (1991) *Thinking Through Culture. Expeditions in Cultural Psychology*. Cambridge, MA: Harvard University Press.

Simpson, B. (1994) Bringing the 'Nuclear' Family into Focus: Divorce and Remarriage in Contemporary Britain. *Man. The Journal of the Royal Anthropological Institute* 29 (4), 831–52.

Sinason, V. (ed.) (1994) *Treating Survivors of Satanist Abuse*. London and New York: Routledge.

Sluzki, C. (1988) *Jealousy*. Conference Address. The International Conference on Family Therapy. Rome, Italy, 28 September–1 October.

Sluzki, C.E. and Ranson, D.C. (eds) (1976) *Double Bind: The Foundation of the Communicational Approach to the Family*. New York: Grune and Stratton.

Speed, B. (1991) Reality Exists O.K? An Argument Against Constructivism and Social Constructionism. *Journal of Family Therapy* 13, 395–409.

Spiro, M.E. (1982) *Oedipus in the Trobriand*. Chicago: University of Chicago Press.

Spiro, M.E. (1987) In B. Kilborne and L.L. Langueni (eds), *Culture and Human Nature: Theoretical Papers of M.E. Spiro*. Chicago: University of Chicago Press.

Stancombe, J. and White, S. (1997) Notes on the Tenacity of Presuppositions in Process Research: Examining the Artfulness of Blamings in Family Therapy. *Journal of Family Therapy* 19 (1), 21–42.

Steiner, F. (1967) *Taboo*. Harmondsworth: Penguin.

Strathern, M. (1984) The Social Meaning of Localism. In T. Bradley and P. Lowe (eds), *Locality and Rurality. Economy and Society in Rural Regions*. Norwich: Geo Books.

Strathern, M. (1992a) *After Nature. English Kinship in the Late 20th Century*. Cambridge: Cambridge University Press.

Strathern, M. (1992b) Parts and Wholes: Refiguring Relationships in a Post-Plural World. In A. Kuper (ed.), *Conceptualizing Society*. London: Routledge.

Strawson, M. (1996) In Deepest Sympathy. Towards a Natural History of Virtue. Review of M. Ridley, The Origins of Virtue *Times Literary Supplement*, 29 Nov., 3–4.

Summit, R.C. (1983) The Child Sexual Abuse Accommodation Syndrome. *Child Abuse and Neglect* 7, 177–93.

Surland, S. and Stæhr Nielsen (1997) De Måske Egnede. *Psykolog Nyt* 8, 8–11.

Symington, N. (1986) The Analytic Experience. Lectures from the Tavistock. London: Free Association Books.

Talle, A. (1993) Transforming Women into 'Pure' Agnates: Aspects of Female Infibulation in Somalia. In V. Broch-Due, I. Rudie and T. Bleie (eds), *Carved Flesh/Cast Selves. Gendered Symbols and Social Practices*. Oxford: Berg Publishers.

Tambiah, S.T. (1990) *Magic, Science, Religion, and the Scope of Rationality*. Cambridge: Cambridge University Press.

Tate, T. (1994) Press, Politics and Paedophilia: a Practitioner's Guide to the Media. In V. Sinason (ed.), *Treating Survivors of Satanist Abuse*. London and New York: Routledge.

Taussig, M. (1993) *Mimesis and Alterity. A Particular History of the Senses*. New York: Routledge.

Taylor, C. (1985a) *Human Agency and Language. Philosophical Papers I*. Cambridge: Cambridge University Press.

Taylor, C. (1985b) *Philosophy and the Human Sciences. Philosophical Papers II*. Cambridge: Cambridge University Press.

Taylor, C. (1993) To Follow a Rule. In C. Calhoun, E. LiPuma and M. Postone (eds), *Bourdieu. Critical Perspective*. Cambridge: Polity.

Thomas, L. (1992) Racism and Psychotherapy: Working with Racism in the Consulting Room – An Analytic View. In J. Kareem and R. Littlewood (eds), *Intercultural Therapy. Themes, Interpretations and Practice*. Oxford: Blackwell.

Tomm, K. (1988) Interventive Interviewing: Part III. Intending to Ask Lineal, Circular, Strategic and Reflexive Questions. *Family Process* 27, 1–15.

Toren, C. (1990) *Making Sense of Hierarchy. Cognition as Social Process in Fiji*. London: The Athlone Press.

Toren, C. (1993) Making History: The Significance of Childhood Cognition for a Comparative Anthropology of Mind, *Man* (N.5) 28, 461–78.

Trawick, M. (1992) *Notes on Love in a Tamil Family*. Berkeley: University of California Press.

Trevarthen, C. (1980) The Foundation of Intersubjectivity. Development of Interpersonal and Cooperative Understanding in Infants. In D.R. Olson (ed.), *The Social Foundation of Language and Thought: Essays in Honour of Jerome Bruner*. New York and London: W.W. Norton & Co.

Trevarthen, C. (1987) Universal Cooperative Motives: How Infants Begin to Know the Language and Culture of their Parents. In G. Jahoda and I.M. Lewis (eds), *Acquiring Culture: Cross-Cultural Studies in Child Development*. London: Croom Helm.

Trevarthen, C. and Logotheti, K. (1989) Child in Society and Society in Children: the Nature of Basic Trust. In S. Howell and R. Willis (eds), *Societies at Peace. Anthropological Perspectives*. London and New York: Routledge.

Turner, V. (1967) *The Forest of Symbols: Aspects of Ndemba Ritual*. Ithaca, NY: Cornell University Press.

Turner, V. (1974) *Dramas, Fields and Metaphors: Symbolic Action in Human Society*. Ithaca, NY and London: Cornell University Press.

Tyler, S. (1978) *The Said and the Unsaid. Mind, Meaning and Culture*. New York and London: Academic Press.

Valeri, V. (1985) *Kingship and Sacrifice: Ritual and Society in Ancient Hawaii*. Chicago: University of Chicago Press.

Varela, F.J. (1979) *Principles of Biological Autonomy*. New York: North Holland.

von Glaserfeld (1987) The Concepts of Adaptation and Viability in a Radical Constructivist Theory of Knowledge. In von Glaserfeld (ed.), *The Construction of Knowledge*. Seaside, CA: Intersystems Publications.

Waldegrave, C. (1990) Just Therapy. *Dulwich Centre Newsletter* 1, 5–46.

Walters, M., Papp, B. and Silverstein, O. (1988) *The Invisible Web: Gender Patterns in Family Relationships*. New York: The Guilford Press.

Weiner, A. (1976) *Women of Value, Men of Renown*. Austin: University of Texas Press.

Whitaker, C. (1989) *Midnight Musings of a Family Therapist* (ed. M.O. Ryan). New York: W.W. Norton & Co.

White, M. (1989) *Selected Papers*. Adelaide, Australia: Dulwich Centre Publications.

White, M. (1992) Deconstruction and Therapy. In *Experience, Contradiction, Narrative and Imagination. Selected Papers of David Epston and Michael White*. Adelaide, Australia: Dulwich Centre Publications.

White, M. and Epston, D. (1990) *Narrative Means to Therapeutic Ends*. New York and London: W.W. Norton & Co.

Whiting, R.A. (1988) Guidelines to Designing Therapeutic Rituals. In E. Imber-Black, J. Roberts and R. Whiting (eds), *Rituals in Families and Family Therapy*. New York and London: W.W. Norton & Co.

Winch, P. (1979) Understanding a Primitive Society. In B.R. Wilson (ed.), *Rationality*. Oxford: Basil Blackwell.

Woodcock, J. (1995) Healing Rituals with Families in Exile. *Journal of Family Therapy* 17, 397–410.

Young, A. (1995) *The Harmony of Illusion. Inventing Post-Traumatic Stress Disorder*. Princeton, NJ: Princeton University Press.

Index